WRONG NUMBER

WRONG NUMBER

HOW TO EXTRACT TRUTH FROM A BLIZZARD OF QUANTITATIVE DISINFORMATION

AARON BROWN

WILEY

Copyright © 2026 by John Wiley & Sons, Inc., All rights reserved, including rights for text and data mining and training of artificial intelligence technologies or similar technologies.

Published by John Wiley & Sons, Inc., Hoboken, New Jersey.

No part of this publication may be reproduced, stored in a retrieval system, or transmitted in any form or by any means, electronic, mechanical, photocopying, recording, scanning, or otherwise, except as permitted under Section 107 or 108 of the 1976 United States Copyright Act, without either the prior written permission of the Publisher, or authorization through payment of the appropriate per-copy fee to the Copyright Clearance Center, Inc., 222 Rosewood Drive, Danvers, MA 01923, (978) 750-8400, fax (978) 750-4470, or on the web at www.copyright.com. Requests to the Publisher for permission should be addressed to the Permissions Department, John Wiley & Sons, Inc., 111 River Street, Hoboken, NJ 07030, (201) 748-6011, fax (201) 748-6008, or online at http://www.wiley.com/go/permission.

The manufacturer's authorized representative according to the EU General Product Safety Regulation is Wiley-VCH GmbH, Boschstr. 12, 69469 Weinheim, Germany, e-mail: Product_Safety@wiley.com.

Trademarks: Wiley and the Wiley logo are trademarks or registered trademarks of John Wiley & Sons, Inc. and/or its affiliates in the United States and other countries and may not be used without written permission. All other trademarks are the property of their respective owners. John Wiley & Sons, Inc. is not associated with any product or vendor mentioned in this book.

Limit of Liability/Disclaimer of Warranty: While the publisher and the authors have used their best efforts in preparing this work, including a review of the content of the work, neither the publisher nor the authors make any representations or warranties with respect to the accuracy or completeness of the contents of this work and specifically disclaim all warranties, including without limitation any implied warranties of merchantability or fitness for a particular purpose. No warranty may be created or extended by sales representatives, written sales materials or promotional statements for this work. The fact that an organization, website, or product is referred to in this work as a citation and/or potential source of further information does not mean that the publisher and authors endorse the information or services the organization, website, or product may provide or recommendations it may make. This work is sold with the understanding that the publisher is not engaged in rendering professional services. The advice and strategies contained herein may not be suitable for your situation. You should consult with a specialist where appropriate. Further, readers should be aware that websites listed in this work may have changed or disappeared between when this work was written and when it is read. Neither the publisher nor authors shall be liable for any loss of profit or any other commercial damages, including but not limited to special, incidental, consequential, or other damages.

For general information on our other products and services or for technical support, please contact our Customer Care Department within the United States at (800) 762-2974, outside the United States at (317) 572-3993 or fax (317) 572-4002.

Wiley also publishes its books in a variety of electronic formats. Some content that appears in print may not be available in electronic formats. For more information about Wiley products, visit our web site at www.wiley.com.

Library of Congress Cataloging-in-Publication Data has been applied for:

Print ISBN: 9781394379781
ePub ISBN: 9781394379798
ePdf ISBN: 9781394379804

Cover Design: Wiley
Cover Images: Public Telephone with man walking in rain: © Shutterstock/Generated with AI,
Digital binary code overlay: © Oleksii Lishchyshyn/Shutterstock,
Additional Telephone images: © lutherhill/Getty Images
Author Photo: Courtesy of the Author
Printed and bound by CPI Group (UK) Ltd, Croydon, CR0 4YY

C9781394379781_120326

CONTENTS

ACKNOWLEDGMENTS ... XVII

CHAPTER 1
    THE STORY OF *WRONG NUMBER* ... 1
    Last Century ... 1
    Never Let a Crisis Go to Waste ... 2
    I Get Involved ... 3
    It Gets Worse ... 5
    Corruption and Incompetence ... 6
    Bricks ... 7
    The Move to Video ... 8
    A Brief Word About Selection ... 9

CHAPTER 2
    DID USAID REALLY SAVE 90 MILLION LIVES?
    NOT UNLESS IT RAISED THE DEAD ... 13
    Lifesavers: The Candy with a Hole—or the Study with a Hole ... 14
    U Said, I Said ... 15
    Drill, Baby, Drill! ... 17
    What Did They Know, and When Did They Know It? ... 19
    False Perspective ... 20
    Middle-school Science-fair Projects, and Not Winners ... 20

CONTENTS

Confound It!	22
Unit of Analysis	23
Pick 133 Numbers from 1 to 4	24
Getting Technical	25
Excluding Inconvenient Truth	26
Isaac Asimov	27
A Financial Analogy	29
Two Last Digs	30
Good News!	32

CHAPTER 3
SHOULD MEDIAN WORKER PAY BE $102,000? GULLIBLE REPORTERS THINK SO — 33

Right Number, Wrong Headline	33
Precisely!	34
Back to the Future	35
Rosie the Riveter	36
Reality Bites	38
Back to Poverty, Disease, and Death	39

CHAPTER 4
COULD MORE COVID EVICTION MORATORIUMS HAVE CUT US COVID DEATH RATES BY 41%? NO — 41

Abandon Hope, All Ye Who Enter	42
Duke of Earl	43
Census to the Rescue	44
Centers for Disease Control and Prevention	45
Do It Yourself	46
Confound It, Again	47
But That's Not My Point	48
Duke: The Wrong Number School	50
The Greatest Public-health Discovery of All Time	51
High Times and Heart Attacks	52

CHAPTER 5

IS MARIJUANA BAD FOR YOUR HEART? THE HEAD SAYS "NO" — 53

He's Baaack — 53
Panel Studies and a Magic Number 3 — 54
No Substitute for Experience — 56
Answer the Phone — 57
Who Can You Trust? — 59
Confound It Again! — 60
Logistic Torture — 60
Variable Explosion — 63
The Researcher's Friend — 65
Unleash the Censors — 66
There's More — 68
It Gets Worse — 68

CHAPTER 6

NO DATA? NO PROBLEM — 69

Studies in Fiction — 69
The Ecology of Voter Participation — 70
She Is Not Alone — 73
Imputing Green — 73
Killer Filings — 75
Synthetic Connecticut — 77
Going to War — 79
Why Is There Progress? — 82

CHAPTER 7

A WOVEN WEB OF GUESSES — 83

Six Degrees of Separation — 84
Grim Test — 85
Statcheck — 86
Carlisle Deviations — 87
Benford's Law — 89

CONTENTS

Candidate Genes	91
33,266 Gun Control Papers Can't Be Wrong, or Could They?	92
Taking Stock	93
Why Don't We Know More?	95
Garbage in, Garbage Out	98
Smoking Gun	99
Race to the Bottom	100
The Wisdom of Crowds	101
No Pain, No Gain	103

CHAPTER 8

THE WAR TO MAKE THE WORLD SAFE FOR PAIN	105
Deaths of Despair	105
The VHA Study	107
The Cohort Study	108
Strong Words Based on Weak Studies	109
Smile and the World Smiles with You	111

CHAPTER 9

SMILES MAKE YOU LIVE LONGER?	113
How to Succeed in Academia Without Really Trying	113
Science Versus Business	114
p-Values in Fact	115
p-Values as Taught and the Four Ps	116
Everybody Knows	119
A Smile a Day Keeps the Doctor Away	120
The Value of Surprise and the Spiral of Power	121
Losing Power	123
This Is Your Study on Drugs	124
Big-box Versus Mom-and-pop	126
Your Mileage May Differ	128
A Winning Script	129
You Can't Handle the Truth	131

CHAPTER 10

TO TRUTH AND HONESTY, MAY THEY NEVER MEET — 133

Dishonesty Versus Limited Honesty — 133

Gino and Mendel: Fudging Data Points — 135

Balancing Usefulness and Honesty — 136

Vaccines — 137

Andrew Wakefield — 139

What's Worse? — 142

A Note on Covid Vaccines — 144

Climate Change and Other Matters — 149

Should Science Be a Contact Sport? — 150

Restart the Babbage Engine — 152

Parting Thoughts — 154

CHAPTER 11

CONFIDENCE INTERVALS IN WARTIME — 155

Confidence Game — 155

Mortality in Palestine — 157

Other Information — 158

Other Countries — 159

Three Strikes and You're Out — 160

Layers of Reliability — 162

Capture–Recapture Analysis — 163

Twice the Capture–Recapture — 165

Combining Estimates — 167

Bringing It All Together — 169

Misdirection — 171

We'll All Go Together When We Go — 172

CHAPTER 12

REPENT! THE END IS NEAR — 173

Evergreen Numbers — 174

New Yorkers Can Throw Out Their Barbeque Grills — 175

CONTENTS

Whodunit?	176
Small Change	177
Writing by Committee	178
Nobel Dreams	179

CHAPTER 13
WHO STOLE MY NOBEL PRIZE?	181
A Bandwagon	181
The Bell Curve Strikes Again	182
Paternal Head Starts	183
Redirection	184
Errors in Variables	185
Bad Is Good!	186
My Story	187
Professors Versus Wise Guys	190

CHAPTER 14
WHY ARE THERE POOR QUANTS?	191
You Ought to Have Done a Better Experiment	191
Controlling People, Not Seeking Truth	193
The Reno Conference	195
"Then Why Are You Poor?"	196
"Then Why Aren't You Rich?"	198
An NFL Adventure	200
I Built My System in a Couple of Hours One Afternoon	200
I Set a Reasonable Goal, and Achieved It	201
I Didn't Start or Stop with Publication	202
I Started with Causal Effects, and Only Claimed Prediction	203
Ending the Debate	203
Track Record	205
Binary Factor Models	207
Model Design	208
It's Not Just for Sports Betting	210
Threefold Way	211

Maintenance and Validation	213
The Hard Part	215
The Situation Today	217
Replacing the Mask	218

CHAPTER 15
STATE-ISTICS

STATE-ISTICS	219
The Three Faces of Statistics	219
Black and Quine	221
Not Wrong Numbers	222
Running on Empty	224
The Russians Are Coming	225
Bigger Problems	226
Fred	228
Greednomics	229
Measuring Greed	229
Prices and Profits	231
More Inflation	232

CHAPTER 16
DID MEDICAID EXPANSION SAVE 100,000 LIVES?

DID MEDICAID EXPANSION SAVE 100,000 LIVES?	233
Can You Trust the Expert?	233
Equal-opportunity Misrepresentation	235
Uncertainty	236
Turn the Other Cheek	237
The Oregon Trail	238
Why Do Good Studies Lead to Bad Reporting?	239
Love Story	240

CHAPTER 17
A GUN CONTROL LOVE STORY

A GUN CONTROL LOVE STORY	241
The Odd Couple	241
In the Eye of the Beholder	242
The Explosive Study	243

CONTENTS

Pick and Choose — 244
Drill Down — 247
Scare Tactics — 248
Be Wary of Public Health — 249
Call the Police — 250

CHAPTER 18
DO YOU FEEL LUCKY? WELL, DO YA PUNK? — 251
Not So Fast! — 252
Pilots Versus Stewardesses — 253
Fatal Police Shootings — 255
The Study — 256
What Should Have Happened — 258
Put Me in Coach, I'm Ready to Play, Centerfield — 260

CHAPTER 19
SEVENTH-INNING STRETCH — 261
Exploratory Data Analysis — 261
Take Me Out to the Ball Game — 263
I Wear the Chain I Forged in Life, Replied the Ghost — 264
Patch It Up — 265
The Bottom Line — 266
Teams for the Ages — 267
Play Time — 270

CHAPTER 20
RATPOCALYPSE! — 271
"Willard! There Are Rats in the Basement!" — 271
"Tear Him Up!" — 272
"And Hear Them! Don't You Hear Them Down There?" "It's Just the Wind" — 273
"Our Time Will Come" — 275
Challenging the Critics — 275

CHAPTER 21
UNSETTLING TREATMENT OF *UNSETTLED* — 277
The Book — 277
Gary Yohe — 278
Permission to Speak — 280
Error Types — 281
Greenland — 283
Rehashing Heatwaves — 284
Three Little Words — 285

CHAPTER 22
DIVERSITY + EQUITY + INCLUSION = BETTER PERFORMANCE? — 287
Yes, Virginia, There Is a Study — 288
Helmer and Hector — 289
H&H Juries — 290
Harrison White — 291
Performance Measurement — 293
Back to p-Values — 294
Beyond Is Where We Begin — 295
Do the Right Thing — 296
Good Stories — 298

CHAPTER 23
21ST-CENTURY MUCKRAKING — 299
The First Investigative Journalists — 299
It's the Capitalists, Stupid — 300
Welfare for the Rich — 301
Greed Is Bad — 302
Tradeoffs — 303
Eviction — 305
I Haven't Forgotten You — 306

CONTENTS

CHAPTER 24
PHILIP TETLOCK — 307
Modern Financial Risk Management — 307
What's in a Name? — 308
The Median Quiet Voice — 309
Kelly — 310
What You Probably Get Wrong — 311
Binary Betting — 312
The Results — 314
Movies and Marriage — 317
Prohibition and Crime — 318

CHAPTER 25
SEX AND TRAFFIC COPS — 319
Secret Police — 319
Prohibition and Trafficking — 320
The Study — 321
End Democracy Now! — 322
Fact Versus Fiction — 324

CHAPTER 26
WHAT IS THE INTEREST RATE IN HELL? — 325
Best American Novel — 325
"Willa Cather Steeped in Rotgut—and Armed with A .45" — 327
Rotgut, A .45 and … Calculus? — 328
The Getaway — 330
The Math — 331
What Then? — 332
Is There Really Calculus in a Crime Thriller? — 333
Politics and Life — 334
How Do Cigarettes Harm You, Let Me Count the Ways — 335

CHAPTER 27
THE 5% SOLUTION — 337
Jumping the Gun — 337
Surgeon General's Warning — 339
Mother's Milk: The Gateway Drug to Everything — 340
Psychology of Vaping — 341
The Natural — 342
Football or, in American English, Soccer — 343

CHAPTER 28
FOOTBALL FIXES — 345
Soccer Betting 101 — 345
The Bell Curve Strikes Again — 346
Fixes Change Everything — 347
Testing the Match-fixing Explanation — 349
Betting the Fix and Anti-fix — 351
Private Equity and Public Inequity — 353

CHAPTER 29
PRIVATE ROOMS AND PRIVATE EQUITY — 355
The Art of the Deal — 355
Always Look on the Dim Side — 356
Avoiding Falls — 357
Statistical Significance — 358
Pure Wrong Number — 360

CHAPTER 30
THE REASON THAT THEY DON'T TEACH AT SCHOOLS LIKE WHARTON — 361
Really, a Business School Professor? — 362
The Real Issue — 363
Fermi Problems — 364
Home Stretch — 365

CONTENTS

CHAPTER 31
    CONCLUDING THOUGHTS   367

REFERENCES   371
ABOUT THE AUTHOR   389
INDEX   391

ACKNOWLEDGMENTS

Many of the chapters in this book originated as articles or videos, which have been revised and expanded with additional material here. Chapters 4, 5, 6, 7, 8, 12, 13, 15, 17, 20, 21, 23, 25 and 27 began life as Wrong Number videos for Reason Television. Chapters 2, 16 and 29 were the subject of short articles for Reason Magazine. Chapters 14, 19, 26 and 28 are descended from articles in Wilmott Magazine. Chapters 3 and 30 cover topics addressed in articles on Real Clear Markets.

CHAPTER ONE

THE STORY OF *WRONG NUMBER*

A aron Steinberg, the marketing director at the libertarian opinion magazine *Reason*, came up with the title for this book, but that's starting the story at the end. Let's go back to the beginning.

LAST CENTURY

In 1997, I overheard my students referring to "riding the Chinatown bus," or the "Fung Wah," which was the name of a company that provided service between New York City's Chinatown and Boston's Chinatown for just $10. Started by Pei Lin Liang, a Chinese immigrant and former noodle factory deliveryman, Fung Wah inspired scores of imitators. Even Greyhound eventually got into the game, partnering with Peter Pan to launch its own version, "Yo! Bus." I take pleasure that "Fung Wah" (meaningless to most riders, but the inspiring "magnificent wind that brings flowers" in Cantonese) instantly entered common speech while the presumably focus-group-tested marketing creation, "Yo! Bus," induced cringes and was perhaps never used by an actual rider. The replacement "Bolt Bus" was inoffensive but uninspiring.

Convenience was as important as price. The Chinatown buses picked up in front of a storefront (such as 88 East Broadway under the Manhattan Bridge in New York, in the case of Fung Wah), which beat navigating the Port Authority Bus Terminal on the West Side of Manhattan with its dirt, crime, and long lines. Plus, Fung Wah never ran out of seats. When there were more riders than seats, Fung Wah chartered more buses. Eventually, curbside busing became the fastest-growing form of intercity transit in the United States.

Around 2011, federal safety regulators began imposing new rules on the industry following a tragic accident that drew widespread media attention. In March of that year, a casino bus run by a company called World Wide Tours crashed, killing 15 passengers and injuring 18. World Wide Tours was not a curbside carrier like Fung Wah; it was a charter bus company hired by the Mohegan Sun to bring gamblers to and from the casino.

The media labeled it a "Chinatown bus" anyway. There were xenophobic undertones. A satirical piece in *College Humor*, titled "An Important Safety Message from Fung Wah Buses," joked that a company manager had been telling drivers in broken English that if a bus catches fire, "pull over at either the first sight of flames or the first smell of burning flesh, whichever comes later."

NEVER LET A CRISIS GO TO WASTE

The World Wide Tours accident provided ammunition for New York Senator Charles Schumer and Congresswoman Nydia Velázquez to request that the National Transportation Safety Board (NTSB) investigate curbside bus safety. Schumer and Velázquez, who had been trying to restrict or shut down smaller bus operators since 2005, went so far as to dictate the study's conclusions: "There is ample evidence that the incident involving World Wide Tours is not an isolated incident but rather just one example of an industry that, in many cases, is operating outside the bounds of city, state and federal transportation safety guidelines," they wrote.

Fung Wah and other companies did skirt some rules. I use "skirt" advisedly. Many of these rules were vague or unenforced, or were pure technicalities. Some were passed or enforced specifically to suppress competition. But some companies did violate some rules and were less safe as a result. In general, the established, corporate providers find it easier to navigate red tape, while the immigrant-owned services that had built the curbside industry were landing in legal trouble. Low-cost carriers sometimes cut corners on maintenance, driver selection, or work rules to make ends meet. However, it's not at all clear that the big companies are always safer.

Fung Wah was forced off the highways in 2012. Twenty-six more Chinatown companies would be shuttered by regulators in 2013. The NTSB study justified the crackdown. The agency had delivered exactly what Schumer and Velázquez had asked for: It claimed that curbside bus companies were seven times more likely to be involved in an accident with at least one fatality than conventional bus operators. This finding was reported without skepticism by *The New York Times*, the *Los Angeles Times*, *Businessweek*, *USA Today*, the *New York Daily News*, *WNYC*, and *Reuters*, among others. The study did not single out Chinatown bus companies, but reporters did. The headline in *Businessweek* read: "Chinatown Buses Death Rate Said Seven Times That of Others."

I GET INVOLVED

I had been writing *Wrong-Number*-style articles for various outlets since the 1980s. When I read about the NTSB study in the paper, it set off my alarm bells. There's ample data on fatal bus accidents, and it couldn't possibly support the claim that curbside service was seven times more dangerous than conventional carriers. Moreover, the study did not meet the standard level of statistical significance. The NTSB refused to make its data public. It also used a poor measure of safety—number of fatal accidents per company divided by number of buses the company owned. Fatalities per mile traveled, or per passenger mile, are more meaningful.

Rather than dividing all curbside fatal accidents by all curbside buses, it computed a ratio for each company and then averaged them. If you do things the former way, you get the same fatal-accident-to-bus ratio for traditional and curbside carriers: 0.2 fatal accidents per 100 buses over the study period. But one curbside company, Sky Horse Bus Tour, owned one bus involved in one fatal accident. That 100% ratio alone, even divided among 71 curbside companies in the study, was responsible for most of the 1.4 average fatal accidents per 100 buses.

If that objection seems technical, consider averaging the same way in baseball. Batting average is the number of hits a player gets divided by the number of at bats. In the 2024 season, teams ranged from a low of 0.221 (hits in 22.1% of at bats) to 0.263. That's taking total team hits and dividing by total team at bats.

If you average the batting averages of the individual players on each team, you get a much larger range, from 0.192 to 0.298. The New York Yankees, for example, had a team batting average of 0.248. But they had two batters, Duke Ellis and Kevin Smith, who each had one plate appearance during the season and one hit. Those 1.000 batting averages brought the average of the team batting averages up 0.050 to 0.298, far higher than any actual team batting average.

At the other extreme, the Houston Astros were one of the top batting teams with a 0.262 team batting average. But their seldom-used batters (Jacob Amaya with one at bat, Aledmys Díaz with four, and Cooper Hummel with eight) got no hits. The three 0.000s brought the average of their team batting averages down 0.060 to 0.202, far lower than any team batting average.

The average of team batting averages depends mostly on the performance of the least-used batters—who have lots of 0.000s and 1.000s, while your regular players are generally between 0.200 and 0.300. It tells you very little about the overall team performance.

I'm not going to critique the NTSB study in detail because it's old news and anyway you can read my Minyanville articles explaining why "seven times" was the wrong number if you're curious. Suffice to say that the study was filled with statistical errors. Moreover, like many official reports, its 78 slickly printed and illustrated pages were filled with puffery about how great the NTSB is and how much work was done to produce the report. Buried in the middle was the seven times claim, which is a simple calculation given that the NTSB already had data on all fatal bus accidents.

IT GETS WORSE

Jim Epstein, a reporter and video producer at *Reason*, was covering the regulatory crackdown on curbside buses. (He later published an investigative piece exposing that Fung Wah's shutdown had been triggered by an error made by two Massachusetts state inspectors, and, in fact, the company had an excellent safety record.) Jim thought the NTSB study's conclusions were questionable, but he lacked the background in statistics needed to critically evaluate them. He saw my piece in Minyanville, and I ended up serving as a source for his reporting on the topic.

Jim filed a Freedom of Information Act request for the NTSB's data, and fought with the agency for six months. Shockingly, his request was denied. Think about that for a moment. The agency responsible for transportation safety figures out that some bus companies are seven times more dangerous than others—but the identities of the dangerous companies must be kept secret.

Jim eventually did manage to obtain a list of the bus companies that the NTSB had categorized as "curbside" and "conventional" carriers anyway, probably by accident. It turned out that the NTSB had miscategorized the companies, even classifying Greyhound as a curbside carrier! That company's 24 fatal accidents were nearly two-thirds of the 37 that the NTSB blamed on curbside carriers. Jim discovered that 30 of the 37 fatal accidents attributed to curbside carriers actually involved traditional providers, such as Greyhound and Peter Pan.

The NTSB included in its list of traditional bus station carriers the Hampton Jitney, which picks up and drops off curbside, and New Jersey Transit, which runs commuter buses and is not a comparable business. (And if New Jersey Transit was to be included, why not include all other commuter bus providers that cross state lines?)

When Jim presented the NTSB with these glaring errors, its spokesperson said that the agency "stands by its report." *Bloomberg* picked up the story, and again the NTSB defended its study, despite having committed statistical malpractice and used incorrect data. The agency's response was typical of how institutions, confronted with glaring errors, will almost always dig in.

CORRUPTION AND INCOMPETENCE

I want to call your attention to some non-obvious aspects of the NTSB story, not to argue the points here, but to alert you to look for them in the many other Wrong Numbers in this book.

The first point is "conspiracy theory" is an inadequate explanation. If you're partial to conspiracy theories, you might imagine that big traditional bus companies paid their tame people in Congress to pressure the NTSB to put upstart, low-cost competitors out of business.

But this study was too incompetent to be a pure conspiracy. Conspirators would make one carefully hidden error. Once you decide to stuff the ballot box by putting traditional carrier fatal accidents in the curbside bucket, you don't need all the other statistical missteps. Moreover, conspirators don't even need the Wrong Number in the first place, NTSB inspectors could just close down the low-cost competitors for vague violations.

Moreover, while you might believe that big businesses, politicians, and bureaucrats are corrupt, how about all the journalists covering the story? There was extensive, serious, and insightful coverage of the Mohegan Sun bus disaster; why would those same reporters turn lapdogs for an NTSB report? Moreover, when the reporters discovered they had been lied to, why did none of them launch an investigation of that scandal—or even correct their earlier misreports?

On the other hand, you might try to explain things by incompetence. But the tale is too conspiratorial to be pure incompetence. Incompetence would lead to errors in both directions, but all the statistical missteps worked to make curbside carriers look more dangerous. Moreover, incompetent researchers who thought they had done a good job would have no need to hide the identities of the companies.

Therefore, as you peruse the many other Wrong Numbers in this book, don't jump quickly to conspiracy or incompetence as explanations. There is something more complicated, something systemic, going on.

BRICKS

A more subtle point is that this Wrong Number was not embedded in any established body of work. Many people—including many at the NTSB—study bus and highway safety. They do it for bus and highway design, for regulation, and for insurance analysis. The NTSB study did not draw on any of that, and other researchers did not build on the NTSB study.

Had the NTSB tried to integrate this study into established knowledge, other researchers would have pushed back, since the conclusion was clearly inconsistent with existing data and knowledge. And if that had not happened, other researchers would have tried replicating and building on the study, which would have exposed its errors.

An individual study is a brick, and it only proves itself when incorporated into a useful structure. Bad bricks either get rejected as not fitting into the structure, or exposed when things built on them collapse. But the Wrong Numbers you'll find in this book do not try to fit into structures, they are used to throw through windows instead. They go direct to the public, claiming the authority of science. But it's cargo-cult science. It looks like science, with equations and data and references and peer review and jargon, but it was never exposed to critical scrutiny, never cross-checked with related work, never used to build structures of understanding.

THE MOVE TO VIDEO

Jim became the executive editor of *Reason*'s video team, and he recruited me to create a series that dissects influential-yet-flawed studies that impact policy or that are blindly amplified by reporters.

I've also written on the same themes for *Reason* and other publications, but video is what allows us to use animated charts and graphics to explain complex concepts, and to show video clips of well-known figures confidently asserting nonsense. The project has proved staggeringly popular, thanks largely to the expert production and editing of the *Reason* team, including, in alphabetical order: Natalie Dowzicky, Cody Huff, Ian Keyser, Regan McDaniel, Justin Monticello, Isaac Reese, Adani Samat, Adam Sullivan, Lex Villena, and Nathalie Walker, in addition to Epstein and Steinberg. Almost half the chapters in this book are based on studies I examined for *Reason* videos, and include some phrasing and research contributed by the team.

Bill Fallon, my editor at Wiley, noticed the attention generated by the videos and suggested that Wrong Number was a good theme for a book. Wiley had published three of my previous books, and I enjoyed working with the company, so I agreed.

You hold the result in your hand.

A BRIEF WORD ABOUT SELECTION

How did I pick the Wrong Numbers you'll meet in the coming chapters? If I picked the silliest quantitative claims I could find, the book might be amusing but it wouldn't have much educational value. If I picked studies in which I found subtle errors, interest would be limited to specialists in the fields.

I picked highly influential studies, either from top researchers published in top journals or from respected think-tanks, government agencies, international organizations, or policy groups. These numbers made headlines in major media sources. They were cited in legislation, court filings, regulations, and political speeches. They're taught as fact in classrooms and textbooks. You'll find them in AI summaries, on Wikipedia, and asserted as common knowledge.

All these studies have obvious, glaring errors that skeptical readers will spot instantly without any specialized knowledge. If you doubt your ability to do that, this book provides some useful tips and—more important—the knowledge that the most respected, credentialed experts on the largest stages frequently spout total nonsense.

The Wrong Numbers in this book are not clever attempts at deception. They are too obviously wrong to be serious attempts to deceive anyone. They rely on the reputations of academics, journals, referees, and major media reporters to generate unthinking trust and the hope that Toto will not pull aside the curtain.

I did not select the Wrong Numbers for partisan reasons. Like everyone, I have my political opinions, and some of them will emerge in the book. But I don't judge numbers by whether I like them, or even by whether they're accurate, only by whether they represent credible and sincere efforts to uncover truth.

Nevertheless, my choices will suggest both populist and libertarian biases. Populists distrust mainstream experts and official sources, and mainstream experts and official sources are the promoters of my Wrong Numbers. Populists promote plenty of Wrong Numbers of their own, but they don't get the academic or media respect of establishment claims. One simple rule is to expose claims by trusted sources to the same skepticism you would apply to someone in a tin-foil hat shouting on a street corner. A business suit or academic gown should not disarm your bullshit alarms.

I am no populist, but I am a libertarian. Libertarians do not distrust experts, in fact most libertarians I know consider themselves experts. In a few cases, that's even justified. Libertarians often promote their own Wrong Numbers, and you'll find a few examples in this book. But libertarians are treated with more skepticism than mainstream experts, so their Wrong Numbers only occasionally achieve enough amplification and influence to make this book.

Showing a public health study is a Wrong Number does not prove quack medicine claims, and debunking an article in an economics journal does not mean the economy is controlled by shape-shifting lizard people from another dimension who consume human misery. Showing that the NTSB, egged on by some politicians, used government power to bankrupt innovators, destroy jobs, and raise the cost of bus transportation does not mean you should vote Libertarian in the next election. Wrong Numbers are warnings of places not to go, not directions of where to go.

You won't find much fraud or other academic crime in this book. Some creeps in, but my main targets are flawed methods that graduate students are taught to use, that journal editors and granting agencies reward, that serious science journalists promote, and that drive public policy and legal decisions.

Let the Wrong Numbers begin.

CHAPTER TWO

DID USAID REALLY SAVE 90 MILLION LIVES? NOT UNLESS IT RAISED THE DEAD

The *Lancet* is generally ranked as the world's most influential general medical journal. Founded in 1823, it is also among the world's oldest surviving ones. It claims to have the "highest standards for medical science." Its "expert editors" scrutinize each article, before sending it out to independent peer "reviewers with different expertise and from different locations, deliberately seeking reviews that provide an in-depth critique." Then it enlists a "statistical reviewer" and gets opinions from "modelers, data scientists, health economists." *The Lancet* boasts, "We select only the best research papers."

Not.

LIFESAVERS: THE CANDY WITH A HOLE—OR THE STUDY WITH A HOLE

On July 19, 2025, *The Lancet* published "Evaluating the Impact of Two Decades of USAID Interventions," by 15 authors, 9 with PhDs, representing some top medical institutions including UCLA and the Barcelona Institute for Global Health. Nine major government health funding organizations paid for the work.

How could an obvious Wrong Number slip through this impressive set of gatekeepers? And get widely publicized without skepticism by major news outlets such as NPR, the BBC, the Associated Press, and NBC? And quickly find its way into the Congressional Record and court filings, not to mention Wikipedia, political stump speeches, and editorials?

I can't answer that. I can only tell you that it did happen and that when the absurdity was exposed in public, no action resulted. The article was not retracted and no corrections were issued for the news accounts or other downstream uses of the number.

I picked this example as the first Wrong Number not because it was the most important, but to smash any illusions you might have that the most respected sources in the world would notice or care about obvious false claims. Don't trust the most prestigious gatekeepers to block even the most absurd and unsupported assertions. To navigate the blizzard of disinformation in the world today, you need to think for yourself. Reading this book is only a first step.

What was the absurd claim? That 91,839,663 "deaths were prevented by USAID funding over the 21-year study period" from 2001 to 2021.

U SAID, I SAID

USAID is the United States Agency for International Development. It is a relic of the Cold War. In 1961, the John F. Kennedy administration established it to counter the Soviet Union. The idea was to purchase goodwill in non-aligned countries by giving money for economic development, democracy, and health.

When Donald Trump took office for his second term in 2025, he ordered most USAID programs eliminated. Speaking for the administration, Secretary of State Marco Rubio said:

> *USAID viewed its constituency as the United Nations, multinational NGOs, and the broader global community—not the US taxpayers who funded its budget. Too often, these programs promoted anti-American ideals and groups, from global DEI, censorship and regime change operations, to NGOs and international organizations in league with Communist China and other geopolitical adversaries. That ends today.*

The programs Trump spared were transferred to the State Department, the entity responsible for managing US interests in foreign countries.

These cuts touched off academic and media interest in how successful USAID had been in the past, including *The Lancet* paper.

Significantly, neither *The Lancet* paper nor the media accounts provided any context for the 91,839,663 figure. Many readers likely understood only "big number of lives saved," and would have interpreted the story the same if the claim had been 9 million or 900 million.

You might compare the 92 million claimed lives saved over 21 years by USAID to 1.5 million lives saved by the

> *"The most pervasive fallacy of philosophic thinking goes back to neglect of context."*
>
> *– John Dewey*

polio vaccine over 70 years. Roughly 8 million people were murdered in the world from 2001 to 2021. These things make *The Lancet* claim seem pretty bold—60 times as valuable as the polio vaccine, 11 times as valuable as stopping all murders?

For better context, I produced Figure 2.1 from UN global mortality data. The thick solid line shows the number of people who died each year in the world from 2001 to 2021. The thin dashed line shows how many would have died had the global death rate in 2001 remained constant. The thin line increases in a near-linear fashion due to population increase; the number of deaths per 1,000 population stays the same.

The chart shows that actual global deaths increased from a bit over 52 million in 2001 to a bit over 58 million in 2019, before rising sharply due to COVID in 2020 and 2021. So, if USAID saved 92 million lives, that

Figure 2.1 Global mortality.

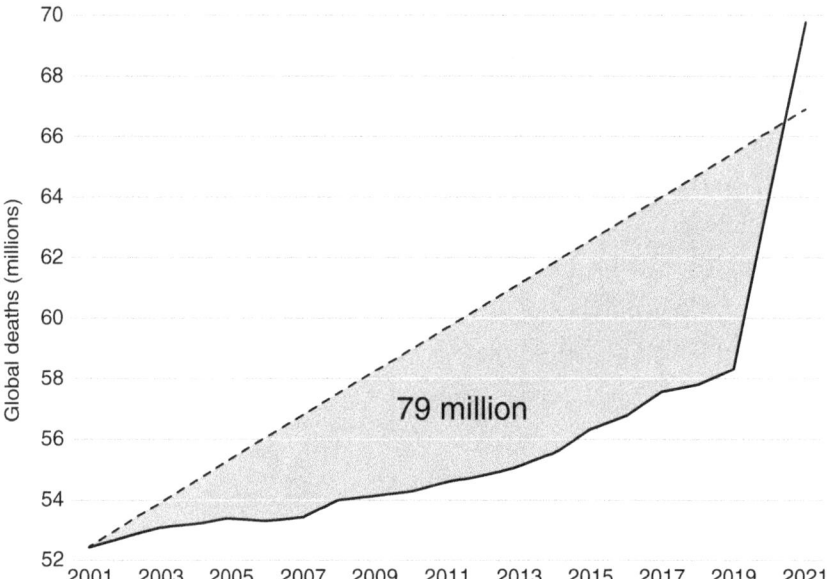

represents well over one year's total global deaths, even in the worst COVID year. It's 8% of all world deaths over the 21 years. Here's another reason to regard *The Lancet* claim as bold. If one foreign aid program, representing less than 8% of all foreign aid, saved 8% of all deaths, and other foreign aid programs were equally effective, there would be no one left to die.

The difference between the two lines is 79 million people. In 2001, the United Nations reports, there were 52.43 million deaths, or 8.4 per 1,000 people. In 2002, the death rate fell slightly; if it hadn't, 370,000 additional people would have died. In 2003, if the 2001 death rate had stayed constant, 750,000 more would have died, and so on. If you add up all the people who would have died over 21 years if the 2001 death rate had remained constant, you get 79 million lives saved.

That's the total number of lives saved by declining global mortality from 2001 to 2021, from all causes: rising GDP; advances in medicine, agriculture, and technology; improved public health; all government and charitable domestic and foreign aid programs. *The Lancet* claims that USAID alone was responsible for 116% of the global decline in mortality. That means all those other things you thought reduced global mortality actually caused 13 million extra deaths for USAID to save.

DRILL, BABY, DRILL!

If you drill down into the numbers, the claim gets even more absurd. Most of the mortality decline (47 million of the 79 million) occurred in China, which received only 73 cents per capita annually from USAID. Less than a quarter of the USAID budget is for health initiatives, although some of the other spending could reduce deaths indirectly. The least developed countries—the ones with the highest per capita USAID spending—actually saw an increase in mortality of 8 million during the study period, thanks to increased average death rates from 2001 to 2021.

Even if you believe that foreign aid is the primary cause of the declining death rate, these numbers make no sense. USAID comprises about 60% of US foreign aid, and the United States contributes about a third of all government aid worldwide. Private cross-border charity dwarfs the USAID budget, and private cross-border charity is dwarfed by domestic programs to promote health. Was all that money wasted while USAID funds were well spent?

I admit that it's not logically impossible for USAID to have saved 92 million lives while all other foreign aid and efforts to reduce global mortality backfired to the tune of killing 13 million people. But then you'd expect *The Lancet* article to begin something like: "While it may seem hard to believe that USAID is the only reason global mortality has fallen since 2001, and that it also prevented 13 million other deaths that would have been caused by other aid programs and medical advances, we have extraordinary evidence to back up our extraordinary claim." You would expect extensive discussion of what USAID did that made it so dramatically positive when all other foreign aid programs were counterproductive. There should be mentions of how it's possible that improvements in economic production, public health, agriculture, medicine, and technology were net killers in the world. Those should be the first questions from any reporter covering the study.

Nothing like this was in the paper or the downstream discussions. There was no suggestion that 91,839,663 was a large or surprising figure, nor that it was greater than the entire decline in global mortality over the study period. The authors were not even trying to convince anyone that their claim was correct.

This last is an important point I want to belabor. The Wrong Numbers in this book are not clever deceptions that require heroic investigations to spot. They are absurd claims based on arguments that wouldn't convince intelligent and mildly skeptical readers. They rely entirely on popular faith that peer-reviewed articles by top academics in top journals have some kind of support. Major media sources don't bother to ask basic questions, like "Isn't that more lives than were saved by all aid and advances since 2001?"

WHAT DID THEY KNOW, AND WHEN DID THEY KNOW IT?

All of the authors, plus the expert editors at *The Lancet*, all the expert reviewers and the journalists who cover scientific papers about global mortality, should have known the figure was absurdly large. I recognized it immediately, and I don't claim expertise in global mortality. I just have a general familiarity with numbers like the global population and mortality trends.

Anyone who didn't know from general knowledge could have quickly checked the figures. They're all based on public data, and population and mortality figures are easily found on the Internet. All the gatekeepers should have questioned the figure, demanding the strongest evidence. And if the claim really could be established, it should have been the headline in both the paper and the articles about the paper. Not the actual NPR headline, "USAID has saved 91 million lives, study finds," but "USAID caused the entire decline in global mortality since 2001 and all other efforts backfired." In addition to calling for USAID cuts to be restored, editorialists should have been agitating for the abolition of those killer other programs.

What's going on here? Are academic researchers, top journal editors, peer reviewers, and science journalists clueless about their alleged fields of expertise? Do they not bother with even the simplest sanity checks or do they just see "big number" and turn off their brains? Do they really believe their claims but have no interest in convincing anyone else by offering context and addressing obvious implausibility? Do they cynically publish and report things they know to be false? I'm going to postpone these questions until much later in the book, after we've seen more Wrong Numbers.

FALSE PERSPECTIVE

Interestingly, *The Lancet* authors did provide one bit of context. UCLA health policy researcher and paper co-author James Macinko told NPR: "We found that the average taxpayer has contributed about 18 cents per day to USAID." That "small amount," Macinko estimated, had prevented "up to 90 million deaths around the world."

I call this anti-context, a comparison meant to confuse rather than illuminate. It compares USAID spending divided by the 7,670 days in the 21-year period, then again by the number of US taxpayers, and compares it to the total claimed lives saved over 21 years. That doesn't give meaning to the 91,839,663 figure; it waves it as a bloody shirt. It's meant to suggest supporting the Trump administration cuts means you value $0.18 more than 92 million lives.

Incidentally, Macinko's claim implies there are over 500 million US taxpayers, when the population of the United States is only 340 million and only about 90 million pay the federal income taxes that fund USAID. Numbers are not his strong suit.

MIDDLE-SCHOOL SCIENCE-FAIR PROJECTS, AND NOT WINNERS

How did the authors get things so wrong? The most important error takes a bit of explaining.

Suppose you were to do this study yourself. You'd likely download data on USAID per capita spending by country and check to see if mortality declined faster in countries with more USAID per capita spending. All of this is easy to do; the data are easily available in useful form and all you need is a spreadsheet or basic statistics program. It's about the effort I see when I judge middle-school science-fair projects. If you imagine that academic researchers are super geniuses using methods beyond the ken of ordinary mortals, and that the authors (often a dozen or more) are working night-and-day for months on the research, you'll often be disappointed when you read the actual studies, and strip out pages of impenetrable jargon meant to muddy the waters that they may appear deep.

Anyway, I did this in a couple of hours one afternoon after reading the paper. I found that USAID spending does not seem to save lives; if anything, mortality increased or declined less in the countries with more USAID spending. That doesn't prove USAID kills people, because correlation does not prove causation. But it does cast doubt on any great causal reduction in mortality from USAID spending.

Although my study was easy, it was not very reliable. USAID spending is a complex process, from Presidential requests through Congressional appropriations through spending plans through agreements with various foreign partners to actual disbursements. Many programs result in spending in multiple countries by multiple entities over multiple years after the cash leaves USAID. It takes some guesswork and approximation to assign actual dollar amounts spent per capita per year by country.

Mortality and population data are low quality. Most countries do not have reliable recent censuses. Estimates from surveys and other methods yield significantly different values in different sources. No countries count all deaths, and one-third of countries miss more than 10% of deaths. Of course, the problems are the biggest in the least-developed countries that are the focus of much USAID activity. Both the study authors and I were forced to fill in missing or inaccurate data with guesses.

Aside from data problems, there are many potential confounding variables. These are things that change the outcome (global mortality) without being caused by the treatment (USAID spending). The most troublesome confounding variables are ones that are correlated with the treatment. For example, most foreign aid tends to go to the same countries, so per capita USAID spending in a country is correlated with total aid spending. Another major one is some USAID spending is disaster relief, and mortality naturally falls after a high value in a year with a major humanitarian disaster.

CONFOUND IT!

To adjust for confounding variables, you put "control" variables in your model. This allows you to subtract out the effect of per capita aid spending by non-USAID sources, disasters, and other noise. Otherwise, you'll give USAID credit for all aid spending and for the return to normal conditions after a disaster and other factors.

The authors mentioned 48 potential control variables in their paper, and chose nine to use to get their result. They did not even mention using non-USAID foreign aid or natural disasters, the most obvious and probably largest confounders. In fact, none of the 48 candidates would have reduced the estimated effect of USAID, and most were things at least partially caused by USAID, which should rule them out as control variables.

An important research safeguard is to pre-register your proposed control variables to avoid consciously or unconsciously choosing a set that gives you the answer you want. Pre-registration has been a best practice for decades, but only in the last 10 years or so has it become common. Despite *The Lancet*'s boast of the "highest standards for medical science," it did not require pre-registration for this paper.

Despite all the problems of data and confounding, the paper authors claim a 95% confidence interval (see Chapter 11 for more on confidence intervals) for the lives saved by USAID, from 85,690,135 to 98,291,626. We don't know the global population or the number of people who died from

2001 to 2021 to that degree of accuracy with 95% confidence; it's absurd to claim that much certainty for USAID mortality reduction. But this study has bigger problems.

UNIT OF ANALYSIS

The authors claim in the paper to have used country as the unit of analysis, as I suggested in the study I sketched out above. But the authors' claim was not true. You have to download a separate appendix document to realize that. On page 13 of that 49-page technical appendix, you discover the actual unit of analysis was years. It's not stated explicitly; you have to decode an equation. It's a major red flag when authors hide the fundamental meaning of their study in this manner.

The authors do not compare mortality declines in countries with different levels of USAID per capita spending to get their 91,839,663 figure. Instead, they look in each country at mortality in years with different levels of per capita USAID funds. They do not compare countries to other countries in the same years; they compare years to other years in the same countries. This is the key to the paper's methodology, and the only reason for the absurd conclusion.

In a minute I'll explain why this forced the conclusion of an absurd number of lives saved. But aside from that, it's not a reasonable way to conduct the analysis in the first place. Suppose USAID writes a check in 2010 to an international organization that builds piped water supplies in poor countries. That money may not even start a project in a particular country until 2011 or later, and it is still later that it will be completed. When clean water first flows through, it won't immediately save everyone dying from water-borne illnesses, nor resurrect people who died earlier in the year. It will prevent some future water-borne illnesses, which could save lives in future years. But the authors only consider reduction in mortality in the year USAID wrote the check, even if the check was written on December 31.

PICK 133 NUMBERS FROM 1 TO 4

Next, the authors pick 133 countries in the world and assign each a number from 1 to 4 each year from 2001 to 2021 based on per capital USAID disbursements. The categories were as follows:

Category	USAID per capita spending for the year
1	Under $1.97
2	$1.97 to $3.96
3	$3.97 to $7.09
4	Above $7.09

The key point that drives the paper's results is that the category limits are fixed; they do not increase with inflation or USAID budget growth. As a result, countries tend to migrate to higher categories over time. In 2001, 81 of the 133 countries were in category 1, but by 2021 only 54 remained. Category 4 had only 14 countries in 2001 but 43 in 2021.

Why does this matter? Because global mortality was falling over the period. In the authors' methodology, countries that remain in the same category do not affect the 92 million estimate one way or the other. When a country changes categories, the old category is penalized for the high mortality of the earlier years, and the new category gets credit for the lower mortality of later years. The penalties and credits are not confined to that country, but are extrapolated to all countries, including those that didn't change categories. The authors have baked in the assumption that the entire reduction in global mortality is due to USAID spending.

GETTING TECHNICAL

This and the next two paragraphs are a bit more technical, and you can skip them if you like. Say we want to get a back-of-the-envelope estimate of the size of this bias. We know 81 countries started in category 1 in 2001, and only 54 remained by 2021. Only the 27 countries leaving matter for the analysis. The study will estimate the harm from being in category 1 by the average mortality rate in the 27 countries that left before they left, minus the average mortality rate after they left. If these 27 countries experienced the global average mortality decline on average, then we'd expect the study to show all countries in category 1 were harmed by half the global decline in mortality.

Similarly, the study will find that the 29 countries that started in lower categories but ended up in category 4 gained an amount similar to half the worldwide decline in mortality. So, the study will conclude that if all category 4 countries had been moved to category 1, they would have had no mortality decline—so USAID gets credit for the entire mortality decline in these countries. It gets credit for about half the mortality decline in category 2 and 3 countries. But it actually gets even more credit, because it doesn't compare everything to category 1, but to an extrapolated zero-USAID country. Anyway, you can see how this error alone meant that USAID was going to get credit for something in the ballpark of all global mortality reduction.

USAID spending has nothing to do with the analysis; the authors could equally well have chosen anything that increases over time: stock market prices, US federal debt, the distance of the Voyager 1 spacecraft from Earth. Any or all of these could be cited as the cause of saving around 79 million lives.

EXCLUDING INCONVENIENT TRUTH

The authors weren't done with the tricks. In four of the 21 years, global mortality rose rather than fell, which reversed the effect the paper relied upon. So, the authors added special variables to exclude the effect of those years: 2015, 2019, 2020, and 2021. In one other year, 2008, more countries moved down in category than up, also reversing the effect. So, 2008 got tossed into the trash as well. Five of the 21 years were discarded because they didn't fit the narrative, but the authors reported results as if they had included all years. They even extrapolated results from the years when global mortality dropped and the USAID budget increased to claim additional savings in the excluded years.

The authors did not even try to justify these exclusions. They blandly remarked they excluded years "to adjust for major economic and health shocks."

It's not just years that were excluded. USAID funds went to 250 different countries and territories since 2001; the authors selected 133 to use for their study. You had to download the 49-page supplementary file to find on page 8 the reason they excluded 71 high-income countries because it was "crucial for ensuring the internal validity of the study, maintaining a more consistent and relevant scope for the countries under analysis," whatever that means. More proof that the paper was written with jargon to intimidate rather than useful information to convince a skeptical and intelligent reader. There's no hint at all about the other 56 exclusions. The only clue about which countries were included or excluded is from a color-coded global map.

For the year exclusions, it's not at all clear that 2015 and 2019 had larger economic and health shocks than other years. Moreover, if USAID saves lives only in calm times, and costs lives when there are shocks, we care about the total lives saved or lost over all years, not just the results in calm times. Nevertheless, none of *The Lancet*'s peer "reviewers with different expertise and from different locations, deliberately seeking reviews that provide an in-depth critique" appear to have questioned the authors' data censorship, nor insisted on a better justification. The authors did not even follow the standard practice of disclosing what their results would have been had the years been included.

For the country exclusions, the authors did provide a table on page 21 of their supplementary materials that allows readers to compute the effect if 59 of the 117 unselected countries had been included, but no clue about which 59. The results do not change dramatically; their claimed mortality reduction in low-funding countries drops from 5.8% to 5.4% and in high-funding countries from 4.9% to 4.7%.

ISAAC ASIMOV

I want you to think about this for a minute to see the low state of academic research. The authors found, even with all their tricks, that USAID reduced mortality in 16 of 21 years and increased it in five, in 133 countries and territories selected out of 250. None of this was described in clear terms; it was buried in jargon and tables deep in the paper or supplementary materials and no good reasons were given.

We'll find unexplained or unmentioned data exclusions in most Wrong Numbers in this book. Moreover, when I replicate papers, I very rarely match the authors' results even when the paper is basically sound. The most common reason is that the authors excluded data and didn't mention it in the paper. When it is mentioned, as in the USAID paper, it's generally buried with no mention that the paper's result would fail if all data were included. A few papers mention that the results hold if you include all data, but I check and find when authors say this, it's usually not true. An even smaller number of papers actually present the results with all the data in an appendix or supplementary file, as the USAID paper did for about half of its country exclusions, in which case about half the time the main paper results hold, as they did in this case.

Clearly, the authors are not trying to convince anyone who actually reads the paper and has an ounce of skepticism. Clearly, the peer reviewers and other gatekeepers either aren't reading the papers or have less than an ounce of skepticism.

But that's not the worst of it. Scientist and science fiction author Isaac Asimov famously wrote: "The most exciting phrase to hear in science, the one that heralds new discoveries, is not 'Eureka' but 'That's funny.'" Data that don't fit your hypothesis are the things that lead to new discoveries, but researchers are engaged in an "emperor's new clothes" pretense that every paper is a Eureka. Anything casting doubt on the simple hypothesis must be suppressed to maintain the fiction.

In this case, the five years that broke the pattern merely pointed to the rigged methodology to force the conclusion. But suppose this were a good study and actually showed USAID spending saved lives in quiet times but cost lives when economy or health was disrupted. This would be an exciting and useful finding. It would generate conjectures.

For example, USAID spends money on economic aid, healthcare, and support for democracy. Maybe, after financial or health disasters, money is redirected from democracy to the crisis. If that results in USAID killing people instead of helping, it could be that USAID saves lives with its democracy spending, but costs lives with its other programs.

Another conjecture is that, like generals always ready to fight the last war, USAID programs attack the problems of the recent past. In quiet times, with relatively little change, this is effective, because today's problems are similar to yesterday's. But in chaotic times, perhaps looking backward is counterproductive.

Researchers seeking truth would keep looking until they had a good explanation. Good explanations usually don't need statistics; their truth is obvious without painstaking calculations. But too many researchers today stop as soon as they get a publishable result, because they're trying to notch publications, not find truth. If that means throwing out data or using other tricks to pretend to find truth, so be it.

A FINANCIAL ANALOGY

Imagine you (Y) have a dialog with a mutual fund salesperson (S) promoting a fund that invests in stocks in some small faraway country, Usaid:

S: The fund made $91,839,663 from 2001 to 2021. You should get in.
Y: That's strange, I looked up the entire Usaid stock market gain over those 21 years and it was only $79 million. Did every other investor lose money?
S: Never mind about that, are you in or out?
Y: Well, show me the performance chart.
S: We don't use performance charts because we don't like to show the results in 2008, 2015, 2019, 2020, and 2021. The $91,839,663 omits those years.
Y: Are those the years the fund lost money?
S: We don't discuss them.
Y: Okay, I can look this up on Bloomberg. Yup, those are the five years the fund lost money. I also see that in the profitable years the fund made only a few hundred dollars, nothing that could add up to a million dollars, much less 92 million.
S: Well, the fund made 250 investments, but we only show results for 133 of them.
Y: Don't tell me, the 133 that made money?

S: We don't discuss our reasons.

Y: Okay, but even so there doesn't seem to be enough profit in any investment in any year in the fund to generate a total $92 million profit.

S: The $91,839,663 isn't the actual profit from the 133 selected investments in 16 selected years. See, we put the 133 positions in four buckets based on how much we invested in each one. Whenever we add money, so an investment moves to a higher bucket, we pretend that every other investment in the old bucket increased in value by the same amount as the investment we added money to. Then we add some additional profit to compare to imaginary investments we didn't make.

Y: Why do you keep repeating $91,839,663? Are you hoping, if you keep saying it, I'll be blinded by greed and ignore the terrible logic of your sales presentation?

S: $91,839,663. $91,839,663. $91,839,663.

When you apply the natural skepticism salespeople—especially financial salespeople—are exposed to, you see how impossibly weak this paper's argument is.

TWO LAST DIGS

I'm going to draw the line here with detailed discussions of the other errors in this paper. I will content myself with two other points we'll see in other Wrong Numbers.

First, causation versus correlation. The authors did an observational study as opposed to an experiment. In an experiment, you control the variable of interest. That would mean finding two similar countries and selecting one at random to get USAID, then observing the mortality trends. With enough experiments of this type, you can get strong evidence for causation—that USAID saves lives.

In observational studies where researchers observe data they do not control, you can only measure association or correlation, not causation. You might find that countries getting more USAID had larger mortality declines but causality could run in either direction or be due to a third factor. Maybe USAID funded projects that reduced mortality. Maybe USAID came in after disasters and just happened to be around as mortality came back down. Maybe USAID identified countries where mortality was going to fall anyway. Maybe mortality falls everywhere due to economic growth, which also means the United States has more money to spend on foreign aid.

Careful researchers note that their observational studies show only association, not causation. Good journals require this, and good science journalists make the point clearly. But this observational study was presented as causal, and the gatekeepers allowed it.

The second dig is about a fundamental misuse of statistics. This paper has literally thousands of statistics in the main text and the appendix, presented as if the statistics themselves are logical arguments. They're not. If you find an argument is logically sound, you can turn to statistics to see if it might be the result of random noise. But if the underlying argument is not sound, it doesn't matter how strongly you can reject the random explanation. In that case, thousands of statistics just bury the important question: the logic.

A famous illustration of this is the calculation done by statistician Charles Cicchetti and used as the basis of a lawsuit claiming the 2020 US Presidential election was stolen. Cicchetti's logic was that the number of votes Joe Biden received in Georgia in 2020 (2,474,507) should have been drawn from the same binomial distribution as the number of votes Hillary Clinton received in Georgia in 2016 (1,877,963). The probability of those two results coming from the same binomial distribution was less than one in one quadrillion (1 followed by 15 zeros, in fact it is far less than that).

Cicchetti did some other calculations as well, some of which were not as absurd. But the one-in-one-quadrillion claim for Georgia and three other states as well is what captured attention. The problem is not in his mathematics, it is indeed virtually impossible to get such a difference in outcome if the same Georgia voters were polled each year, and each one had independent fixed probabilities of voting Democratic. (Cicchetti could have presented exactly the same evidence with the same extraordinary significance claim to support that Donald Trump had stolen the 2016 election from Hillary Clinton.)

This probability Cicchetti computed is called a "p-value" or "significance," and we'll discuss it in Chapter 9. By convention, journals will publish studies with p-values lower than 0.05, a standard that Cicchetti's claim easily met. But the low p-value only demonstrates that Cicchetti's election model is wrong. The voters were not the same in 2016 and 2020, and they didn't select votes as independent draws from a binomial distribution. Hillary Clinton was not the same as Joe Biden, and 2016 was not the same as 2020.

The argument was that unless the absurd election model was accurate, the election must have been stolen is absurd. The strength of the statistical case is irrelevant if the argument is wrong.

This particular claim was treated with skepticism—and derision as a result—as all Wrong Numbers should be.

GOOD NEWS!

If this chapter has left you depressed, take heart. Not all Wrong Numbers are this wrong from researcher through journal to headline. The next chapter will take on a headline from 2020 that the median worker should make $102,000 per year. The number comes from a fine study, but the interpretation it acquired in the media was as absurd as USAID saving 91,839,663 lives.

CHAPTER THREE

SHOULD MEDIAN WORKER PAY BE $102,000? GULLIBLE REPORTERS THINK SO

On September 19, 2020, *Business Insider* ran the headline: "The economy has failed 90% of workers" and suggested a typical full-time salary in America should be $102,000. The figure was picked up in other media, speeches, and policy documents and still pops up as a fact in AI answers, Wikipedia, and web searches.

RIGHT NUMBER, WRONG HEADLINE

This is a different kind of Wrong Number. It's not a false number from a bad study. Unlike the USAID lives-saved claim, the $102,000 number comes from a good study: "Trends in Income from 1975 to 2018" by

Carter Price and Kathryn Edwards, published by the RAND Corporation on September 14, 2020.

This Wrong Number is an example of a published figure that creates the story it purports to report. My guess is almost no one reading the *Business Insider* story had ever imagined there was a specific amount the median worker should earn, but the article attempted to make it a key indicator of social justice. And a little thought demonstrates the number cannot mean what the article claims, that the economy has failed 90% of workers.

Numbers that no one thought of or cared about yesterday, but become hot topics today, when reported, are major red flags of a Wrong Number. The number itself may be accurate, but why would it suddenly acquire importance? It's an example of having an answer, then looking for a click-bait question to fit it. Focus on the question and whether it matters before considering the answer.

PRECISELY!

One quick minor point, the authors of this study avoided false precision by rounding their claim to the nearest $1,000—unlike the previous paper that counted down to the individual life saved. You may recall from grade-school science that numbers should be reported such that only the last non-zero digit is uncertain—so $102,000 means between $101,500 and $102,499, and 91,839,663 means you counted exactly that many people. While proper reporting of significant figures does not guarantee a study is good, it's an indicator that the authors had at least a grade-school science education.

The $102,000 is in 2018 dollars, a year in which the median full-time, full-year, prime-age (FTFYPA) worker earned $50,000. So, $102,000 represents a 104% raise. But worker compensation represents 70% of national income, with 30% going to capital providers in the form of interest and dividends. So, even if all business revenue were paid to workers, with nothing to pay investors, you couldn't double all worker pay.

But I'm getting ahead of myself and oversimplifying as much as *Business Insider* did. Let's start with where the $102,000 comes from and what the RAND study actually said. Since the study used data through 2018, and I'm writing this in 2025 with 2024 data available, I'm going to use updated numbers. The argument is the same as the one made in the RAND paper.

BACK TO THE FUTURE

Back in 1975, US national income per capita was $6,300. By 2024 it had grown to $74,500. In 1975, the median full-time (35+ hours per week), full-year (40+ weeks), prime-age (25–54 years old) worker made $10,200. By 2024 this had grown to $64,000. I should point out that these numbers are all estimates, with some errors. You can find somewhat different values in different sources reflecting both estimation error and differences in definitions. I've rounded them to the nearest $100 (1975 numbers) and $500 (2024 numbers) to avoid false precision.

The RAND authors noted (in my updated formulation) that if the median FTFYPA worker's pay had gone up in proportion to national income, it would have been $10,200 $\frac{\$74,500}{\$6,300} \approx \$121,000$ in 2024 instead of only $64,000.

You may notice that $121,000 is "only" 89% higher than $64,000. This is in line with the authors' number of 84%, using data through 2018. The $102,000 used for the 104% *Business Insider* claim is not found in the paper itself. You have to scroll through a lot of numbers to find it in Appendix C on page 42. It's not relevant to this discussion. I suspect someone searched the paper for the largest number to make the most impressive headline.

So, here's the puzzle—if workers as a whole are getting about the same share of national income in 2024 as 1975, why is the median FYFTPA worker's pay not keeping up with gross national income per capita? Is more money going to below-median or above-median workers? Are there more FYFTPA workers as a fraction of the population in 2024 versus 1975? Is more worker compensation being paid in forms other than wages? These are the questions that interest the RAND authors.

$121,000 is not a Wrong Number, nor is the $94,000 2018 version found in the paper. Using it to suggest workers have been robbed of nearly half their wages, or that "the economy has failed 90% of workers," is wrong. You can't rob people of half their entitlement and leave them with 70% of everything.

The authors are clear they are not making a normative point—what workers should earn—merely investigating a counterfactual: What would the world be like if the median FYFTPA worker's income had risen with per capita gross national income? The counterfactual illuminates major social and labor-market changes since 1975—changes that some people will like and others will dislike—not a simple story of workers getting cheated.

ROSIE THE RIVETER

In 1975, FYFTPA workers made up 20% of the population. In 2024, they represented 35%, mainly due to more women working full-year and full-time, and to a lesser extent, more participation by racial and ethnic minority workers of both sexes. While it's impossible to adjust for this fact precisely, we can do a back-of-the-envelope comparison. In 1975, 10% of the population made more than the median FYFTPA worker. In 2024, if 10% of the population makes more than you, you are about the 70th percentile FYFTPA worker. 70th percentile workers make about 64% more than median workers, or $105,000 in 2024. So, if instead of comparing median-wage FYFTPA workers in 1975 and 2024, we compare the 90th percentile wage earner within the entire population in both years, we get closer to the $121,000 counterfactual.

Is this good or bad? Was it a problem in 1975 that most women and minorities were blocked from FYFTPA employment? Or is it a problem in 2024 that so many people are forced to take FYFTPA employment to make ends meet? While nearly everyone will agree that more diversity of economic opportunity is good, is it fair that women and minorities are paid less than white men, and therefore drag down median wages? If the new entrants are just as productive workers, shouldn't they earn the same median income?

My expertise is numbers, not social justice. I will say only that 2024 is quite different from 1975. Personally, I vastly prefer things today, but that's irrelevant because labor markets are restructuring since 2020 even faster than they did from 1975 to 2020. In 2025 we may see gig jobs grow to outnumber traditional jobs. In five years there may be fewer FYFTPA jobs than there were in 1975.

The quantitative point is that most of the reason FYFTPA wages have not gone up as much as national income—even though total worker compensation has gone up at the same rate as national income—is that there are more FYFTPA workers to share the compensation.

We're still $16,000 short, the difference between the $105,000 the 70th percentile FYFTPA worker earned in 2024 and the $121,000 figure from the 1975 median FYFTPA wage, grossed up by the growth in national per capita income. That is explained by benefits, mainly health insurance. In 1975, benefits were only a few percent of total compensation; in 2024, they were almost 20% for FYFTPA workers. That $105,000 annual income worker probably got benefits that cost their employer around $16,000 more than 1975 benefits.

Does this represent a real benefit? Are medical services $16,000 better than 1975 services? Personally, I think so, but opinions differ widely. Some people will say much of the $16,000 was stolen from workers by rapacious insurance and drug companies, with government complicity.

On the other hand, many other people like compensation shifting from cash wages to benefits, because benefits are more egalitarian—there's usually little or no difference in health insurance options for a company's low-paid and high-paid workers. Also, health services and other benefits like disability and paid leave are distributed on the basis of need rather than productivity.

I've only scratched the surface of the RAND study, but you can see the numbers provide a lot of food for thought. If you are interested in these things, by all means read it. It won't tell you what to think, but it will provide you with facts to shape your opinions. Don't rely on shallow interpretations and misrepresentations from partisan media.

REALITY BITES

One point that will be important in future chapters as well as this one is that it's important to focus on real goods and services, not just paper figures. When people earn more money, they spend more money. Overall, a 3% increase in income leads to a 1% increase in purchases of real goods and services. An 89% increase in all workers' wages would create demand for 30% more goods and services to be produced in the economy. Where would those goods and services come from? Or would the extra demand just drive up prices so workers were getting the same goods and services as before?

To make it specific, consider cars. If workers made 89% more income, and followed the same car-consumption patterns as the current population, they would demand 50 million more cars—about four years' US production. And 50 million additional cars would demand more roads, gas stations, and repair shops.

I suspect most people reading the $102,000 claim imagined it meant that median workers could enjoy the lifestyles of people earning $102,000 in 2018, meaning they implicitly assumed 50 million additional cars would wink into existence along with the necessary supporting infrastructure. The point is, if you want the median FYFTPA worker to enjoy more goods and services, not merely enjoy seeing six figures instead of five on line 1a of their annual 1040 income tax form, either they have to produce more goods and services, or they have to take them from someone else.

I don't say it's impossible for median workers to have more goods and services. Perhaps the economy could run at a higher level with more work done, more people hired, higher wages, producing the extra goods and services demanded by more workers earning more money. There are reasons to doubt the economy's capacity for this, but that's a question of empirical economics. Perhaps goods and services can be taken from above or below-median-wage workers.

BACK TO POVERTY, DISEASE, AND DEATH

If it bleeds, it leads seems to be true of Wrong Numbers as well as news headlines. Our next chapter had a trifecta—evictions, pandemic, and lives lost. Worse, while Chapter 2 and this chapter concern exaggeration and gullibility, Chapter 4 introduces darker motives for Wrong Numbers.

CHAPTER FOUR

COULD MORE COVID EVICTION MORATORIUMS HAVE CUT US COVID DEATH RATES BY 41%? NO

The point of the chapter on USAID (Chapter 2) was that you cannot trust even the most prestigious researchers and gatekeepers to avoid obvious Wrong Numbers, nor to correct them when exposed. The chapter on median worker pay (Chapter 3) emphasized that even good studies are twisted in media accounts to make claims that defy logic and common sense. You have to think about what numbers mean, not accept a reporter's slant uncritically.

ABANDON HOPE, ALL YE WHO ENTER

This is the last of my chapters designed to remove any preconceptions you might have that widely reported numbers with credible pedigrees and expert testimony are reliable, or that numbers cited in serious media accounts, legislative proceedings, court cases, and political speeches make any sense.

This chapter is darker than the previous two, because it shows how the most prestigious institutions close ranks to block questions about research, even when that research is used to justify government actions affecting millions of people's lives and livelihoods.

On September 4, 2020, the Centers for Disease Control and Prevention (CDC) halted residential evictions in the United States for non-payment of rent due to the COVID-19 pandemic. Many states and municipalities got there first, imposing at least partial eviction moratoriums starting in March and April 2020. The theory behind these emergency orders was that if Americans were forced to leave their homes and move into more crowded settings, it would increase transmission of COVID-19.

A moment's thought exposes the error. When someone is evicted, the residence does not disappear, it is rented to a new tenant. Crowding is the number of people divided by the number of residences. Eviction moratoriums do nothing to decrease the population; in fact, they are intended to keep it from falling. But they do cause landlords to remove properties from rental markets since they cannot be confident of collecting rent. For the same reason, they discourage new rental construction and conversion. The same number of people with fewer residences means more crowding due to eviction moratoriums, not less crowding.

The federal ban was supposed to expire at the end of 2020. Then it was extended a month, then two more months, then through the end of June, and again until the end of July 2021. Many states and cities also extended their moratoriums—in some cases through the end of September 2021, even as COVID-19 infection and death rates fell.

DUKE OF EARL

"Housing Precarity & the COVID-19 Pandemic" was authored by five Duke University researchers in January 2021 as the eviction bans were being extended. It was co-authored by a team of academics with prestigious credentials, including a professor of economics with a PhD from Stanford University and a quantitative epidemiologist who is an assistant professor of medicine. It got widespread media attention and was cited twice by the Consumer Financial Protection Bureau (CFPB) in the federal register as justification for its rulemaking. The paper was cited in an amicus brief at the fifth Circuit Court of Appeals to support legal arguments that eviction moratoriums have prevented COVID-19 deaths.

The Duke researchers claimed that 40.7% of US COVID-19 deaths between March and November 2020 could have been prevented by a universal eviction ban for non-payment of rent beginning in April 2020. Is that number reasonable?

Data on evictions are terrible. There is no useful aggregated reporting. We have some data on eviction filings, but one-third of jurisdictions don't report, and reporting for the other two-thirds is often erratic. Moreover, most filings don't result in an eviction, and one eviction proceeding can involve many filings. In normal times, evictions may have amounted to about 25% of filings, but a survey from the summer of 2020 by *The Post and Courier*, a South Carolina newspaper, found that the ratio of orders to vacate to filings was under 10% during the pandemic. On the other hand, forced moves—many forced by threat of eviction—easily outnumber evictions.

The hundreds of local COVID-19 temporary eviction bans are difficult to classify because they take different approaches with different terms and restrictions, and some were enforced while others were ineffective.

CENSUS TO THE RESCUE

The best source we have is the biannual American Housing Survey by the Census Bureau. The latest pre-COVID survey showed 264,000 court-ordered evictions in 2017. Not all of those were for non-payment of rent (although most were) and not all resulted in actual evictions—tenants sometimes settle their issues with the landlord.

However, for every legal eviction for non-payment of rent, the American Housing Survey suggests another seven tenants make forced moves. In many but not all cases, these moves are forced because the tenant fears eviction. So, an effective nationwide eviction moratorium for 10 normal months could prevent something on the order of a million forced moves. There's no good data on this question, but a number between 500,000 and 2 million seems plausible.

However, March to November 2020 was far from normal. In the first place, as mentioned above, eviction moratoriums were in place for many places much of the time. For another, courts were closed in most jurisdictions for months, and open only for limited proceedings for other months. Many judges refused to issue eviction orders due to public health concerns, even if there was no official ban.

Eviction filings dropped to near zero during March and April 2020. Starting in late April, places without moratoriums gradually rose to about 40% of normal levels by August. Places with moratoriums did the same thing with about a two-month lag. The most effective moratoriums were lifted; the less effective ones were eroded away. There was a jump everywhere to beat the deadline as the federal moratorium went into effect in

September, after which filings ran at about 50% of normal levels in both local-moratorium and non-local-moratorium places.

All these figures are uncertain. They rely upon filings tracked by the Eviction Lab, which covers only about 70% of jurisdictions, with considerable error. Moreover, eviction filings are only loosely related to forced moves for the reasons above. All we can say is a ballpark guess that a universal moratorium in March might have cut 20% of normal forced moves for four months in half the country—or about one-thirtieth of a normal year's forced moves. That's perhaps 40,000 forced moves. Of course, it could have been half that or twice that or outside that range. There's simply no data available to make a better estimate.

CENTERS FOR DISEASE CONTROL AND PREVENTION

Now, 40.7% of US COVID deaths from March to November 2020 is 116,951 according to the Centers for Disease Control. So, the study's claim amounts to every forced move causing two or three COVID deaths.

The average US household size is 2.5 people (there is no good data for the average size of an evicted household). It's true that a forced move could cause infections in other households if the evictees moved in with others. But this should be offset because some other tenant will move into the vacated residence, reducing crowding in other households. So, the 40.7% figure means something like 100% of evictees and forced movers dying of COVID.

The overall COVID death rate in the United States during this period was 0.09%. Yes, evictees are poorer than average and forced moves are a stress that could increase the chance of infection and death. But even the most vulnerable populations—elderly people with comorbidities in crowded nursing homes—had COVID death rates below 10%. Therefore 100% is simply not credible. Even if my numbers are way off, 20% or 10% is not credible.

Moreover, lots of people study COVID deaths. They would have noticed quickly if 40.7% of them represented recently evicted tenants. And many researchers study evicted people. They would have noticed quickly if there weren't any to study because all of them were dead from COVID.

Admittedly there's a lot of guesswork to the numbers above, but it's simply not plausible that a universal eviction moratorium could have saved anything like 117,000 lives. If the authors were correct, they would have arrived at one of the greatest public health discoveries in history. It took over a year, a major scientific breakthrough, an unprecedentedly successful government-encouraged research project, and perhaps $100 billion to reduce COVID-19 death rates by 40% with vaccinations. The Duke researchers claim that if a universal eviction moratorium had been implemented six months earlier, it could have reduced death rates by over 40%. Researchers have struggled to demonstrate any benefit at all of masks, social distancing, and lockdowns with high levels of certainty. Yet these eviction moratorium researchers claim a gigantic immediate effect from a legal change affecting a tiny subset of the population. In defiance of good statistical practice, they don't give a standard error or confidence interval for their estimate, but it appears to be about 5% based on a graph at the end of the paper. That's impossibly small given the data issues and other uncertainties.

DO IT YOURSELF

If you were to study this question, you would likely start by comparing COVID death rates in places with and without moratoriums. You would immediately run into the huge data problems mentioned above. There's another problem as well. All the places that were hit hard by COVID deaths in March and April 2020 enacted moratoriums. You can't find any similar places without moratoriums for controls.

Among places that were not hit hard early, the ones that enacted moratoriums had much higher subsequent COVID death rates than the ones that didn't. But while moratoriums might have increased crowding by removing housing units from the rental market, they cannot plausibly explain the size or timing of the COVID mortality increases. It's much more likely that places that anticipated increased COVID death rates, due to increasing infections or other indications, enacted moratoriums, while places that seemed less threatened did not.

The Duke authors took an entirely different approach, with the advantage of bypassing the data issues with evictions. While the overall design was complicated, the basic idea was simple—compare counties within states based on the number of days they had eviction moratoriums in place. If counties with few moratorium days had higher-than-state-average COVID death rates, and counties with many moratorium days had lower-than-state-average COVID death rates, it would show an association between eviction moratoriums and COVID death rates. No data on evictions or the fate of evictees is needed.

There are disadvantages to this research design as well. It ignores timing. You could give a country credit for low COVID death rates in March, based on eviction moratorium days the following November. Another is that it ignores whether or not a moratorium was effective. Many moratoriums were during periods when courts were closed anyway, or when a state or federal ban made them redundant. Some were sweeping, others had lots of loopholes. Some were in places with few or no evictions, even without moratoriums.

CONFOUND IT, AGAIN

The biggest problem is by eschewing eviction data, you pick up the effect of everything correlated with eviction moratoriums. Places with more moratorium days probably had lots of other COVID policies that could have affected death rates, and were likely different in other ways as well.

For example, they were wealthier, with younger populations and a higher ratio of urban to rural residents—all things correlated with reduced COVID deaths.

Observational studies can never prove causation (a fact that the study authors ignore), but this kind of indirect observational study has an even larger gap between correlation and causation than direct measures.

That's why this approach can give absurd numbers like 100% of evictees dying of COVID. You'd never claim that working with eviction data, unless it happened to be true. So, if you take this kind of approach, it's essential to sanity check your results against your assumed causal mechanism.

BUT THAT'S NOT MY POINT

One more absurd number promoted by prestigious experts and institutions and used for government policy is not the main point of this chapter. It's too common to merit a Wrong Number chapter.

The Duke researchers made my book because of what happened when I tried to replicate the authors' numbers. This is my standard practice; I don't understand a study until I can reproduce the results. Invariably there are details the authors forgot to disclose, or that were ambiguous in the paper, or that I misunderstood when I read it.

The best practice for academic research is for authors to make available all their data and code on-line. Failing that, precise disclosure of where the data came from and precisely what it was, and the technical details of the statistical methods used, are basic requirements. Given the shocking amount of research fraud that has been exposed in the last two decades, including in seminal papers from the most celebrated researchers and respected institutions, data disclosure has become a practical necessity for anyone to trust research, and is a requirement for many research and funding institutions as well as journals.

But beyond fraud protection, data disclosure is necessary for anyone to understand the paper. If you don't know the source of the data, you don't know how evictions are defined, how they are measured, and dozens of other crucial details.

The paper discloses the source for only one of their many data items. "We use a panel of daily observations of the confirmed infections and deaths in each of 3,141 U.S. counties from March 1st to November 28th (COVID Tracking Project 2020)." The problem? The COVID Tracking Project doesn't have county-level data. There's no hint about where the researchers got the rest of their data.

A lesser problem is the paper uses a lot of data stitched together in different ways. To understand the paper's numbers, you have to know precisely which data field the researchers used, and when they downloaded it, since revisions were frequent. There are a lot of different ways to count COVID deaths—COVID as the cause on the death certificate, COVID mentioned on the death certificate, guesses based on causes of death related to COVID, excess deaths over pre-COVID numbers in the same place. The same thing is true of all the other variables used in the paper. Some of the authors' data are not available at the county level even conceptually. Housing courts and local housing authorities are not all organized at the county level. Other data are not available daily. You don't understand the paper without understanding the data.

If researchers and institutions want to inform and convince readers, they need to disclose data. In this case, the goal of the research was clearly something other than informing or convincing.

Another problem is how to match data up. A person evicted in one county might die in another, either because she had to move to another county for her new residence or because she sought healthcare out of county. Much of the data probably come from the American Community Survey, which polls 60,000 households. That's fewer than 20 households per county, with many counties not represented at all. How did the authors fill in data for counties without data, or with too few households surveyed for reliability? These details matter a lot when you try to replicate the study.

DUKE: THE WRONG NUMBER SCHOOL

In this case, all I needed was a set of links to the public sources from which the authors downloaded their data (they did claim all their data were public). I emailed the authors and they didn't respond. So, I asked an editor at *Reason* magazine—which was publishing my review of the paper—to ask. The authors did respond, and refused to give the link or even to identify the sources.

In the last decade, Duke University has become the poster child for a top research institution tainted by coverups of major academic frauds. In 2019, Duke paid $112.5 million to settle a whistleblower lawsuit that accused the university of protecting a medical researcher found to have used falsified data in 39 academic papers. Superstar Duke behavioral economist Dan Ariely had to retract a paper—on dishonesty of all topics—for fabricated data, but the university took no action against him.

Following the whistleblower lawsuit and other issues, Duke set up its Office of Scientific Integrity to avoid repeats. My *Reason* editor reached out to the office's assistant dean, Lindsey Spangler, for help in getting answers for the data used in the Duke study. He also reached out to Associate Vice President for Research and Vice Dean for Scientific Integrity, Geeta Swamy. Neither responded.

The paper was published by the National Bureau for Economic Research (NBER). A spokesperson for NBER told *Reason* that it "encourages researchers to make data and code available to other researchers, but it does not require them to" for working papers. This is a relic of the day when scientists never discussed work in public until it had been published in scientific journals, and when disclosure of data and code could represent significant work. It allows NBER to publish work, but to deny it is the publisher, and to disclaim any responsibility for the quality of the research. Disclosing the data sources requires trivial effort, especially in this case when it was simply a set of Internet links. The Duke authors used the obvious loophole in this system by never publishing in a peer-reviewed journal.

And yet the authors gave interviews in which they promoted their findings. They influenced public policy, court decisions, and popular opinion. Duke trumpeted the findings in a press release that encouraged "members of the media interested in speaking with the authors" to get in touch—though apparently not if that meant asking questions about where they got their data.

THE GREATEST PUBLIC-HEALTH DISCOVERY OF ALL TIME

If the findings of the Duke paper on COVID-19 and eviction moratoriums are correct, the authors have made an historic public health discovery—sharing their data and methodology would ensure that the world isn't deprived of an idea that could save millions of lives. Instead, their refusal to share data has led to the work being disregarded by working researchers, but taken as gospel by political partisans.

This is what won the paper a Wrong Number chapter. If you think an institution badly burned by its coverups of academic fraud would demand answers to simple questions—"How did you get county-level data from a source that doesn't have county-level data?"—or that its Office of Scientific

Integrity would respond to questions from the media about scientific integrity, or that prestigious publishers like NBER will take basic steps to avoid fraud and allow readers to understand the papers they publish, guess again. Many of the top research institutions close ranks to defend researchers from anyone questioning their results.

I did my best to replicate what I think the authors did, and I found no significant relation at all, much less anything of the size and certainty the authors claim. Even if the authors' results are correct regarding the differences among counties within a state, since they are inconsistent with differences among states, they cannot be used to predict the effects of nationwide adoption.

To the extent we are going to involve scientific researchers in policy discussions, we should concentrate on issues that have been studied by many people who are openly sharing data and arguing back and forth until there is a consensus among experts. These shoddy one-off studies are just ammunition for people who want to put a link saying "studies prove" in their otherwise completely speculative articles.

HIGH TIMES AND HEART ATTACKS

Our next Wrong Number isn't absurd, it's an entirely plausible claim. The paper is written to convince, unlike most Wrong Numbers. On casual reading, the problems are not obvious. Yet it manages to make almost every mistake possible. It would be comic, except that it offers completely unsupported medical advice—quack medicine.

CHAPTER FIVE

IS MARIJUANA BAD FOR YOUR HEART? THE HEAD SAYS "NO"

Thirty years ago, the sociologist Craig Reinarman observed that there's something "woven into the very fabric of American culture" that makes us susceptible to believing that a "chemical boogeyman" is to blame for "society's ills." He added that every moral panic about drugs since the 19th century has been fueled by "media magnification" in which the danger of a particular substance is dramatized and distorted.

HE'S BAAACK

Now that recreational marijuana is legal in about half of US states, and more Americans are consuming weed than ever before, the chemical bogeyman is back, and he's armed with a new paper in the *Journal of the American Heart Association* by researchers from Harvard and the University of

California, San Francisco, claiming that marijuana use increases the risk of coronary heart disease, myocardial infarction, and stroke.

This study, which was amplified in *The New York Times* and *The Washington Post*, commits so many egregious statistical errors that it's a poster child for junk science.

This Wrong Number comes with a huge caveat. Marty Makary, who is now Commissioner of the Food and Drug Administration, wrote a great book, *Blind Spots*, in which he exposed many of the same Wrong Numbers I had written about in the past, plus some ones that were new to me. I eliminated the studies he covered from this book to avoid duplication. However, this *Journal of the American Heart Association* study was mentioned favorably in *Blind Spots*. At least one of us must be wrong. So, take that as a warning not to accept anything uncritically, even from people like Makary and me, who claim to be exposing other people's errors.

This paper contains no fraud or misconduct. The authors did exactly what researchers are taught to do, and are rewarded for doing. Because the paper uses conventional methods to arrive at false conclusions, it speaks to the profound crisis in academic research. Too many researchers have forgotten that the point of scientific studies is the pursuit of truth, not seeking the approval of institutions.

PANEL STUDIES AND A MAGIC NUMBER 3

The best studies linking behavior like marijuana ingestion to health outcomes like heart disease and stroke are based on panel studies that follow large groups of people over many years with full medical records and periodic behavioral questionnaires. Many of these are done by national health services with centralized records. Others follow healthcare workers who use the same providers over long periods.

The results of these studies are typically described by "odds ratios." An odds ratio of 1 means the health outcome—say having a heart attack—is equally frequent in the two behavioral groups—marijuana users and non-users. An odds ratio greater than 1 means the health outcome is more common among users than the overall study population. For example, this study claimed a 1.16 odds ratio for coronary heart disease among marijuana users, meaning they had 16% more risk of heart disease than average.

Most of this book uses arguments of logic and mathematics, but here I'll just give you a piece of practical advice used by many statisticians—ignore any odds ratios below 3. Long experience shows that anyone can get odds ratios above 1 but below 3 for any hypothesis with apparent statistical significance, and these usually evaporate after a few days of sensational media accounts.

One reason is these panel studies have hundreds or thousands of variables, which can be combined or adjusted to create millions of hypotheses. Many of these will produce odds ratios different from 1, and that satisfy conventional statistical tests for significance. But this is true even if there are no associations between the behavior and the outcome.

Most important, when researchers find an elevated odds ratio, they should try to refine it. For example, the odds ratio for cigarette smoking and heart disease is about 2. But you can easily find subgroups of smokers, or specific types or patterns of heart disease, with odds ratios of 10 or more. You can look at the heaviest smokers, or those who smoked for the most years, or those who had the most severe heart problems, or those who had both heart and lung problems.

Moreover, the non-smokers with these conditions often have characteristics like long-term exposure to inhaled industrial toxins. These are the kinds of odds ratios that strongly suggest a causal relation. Once you have them, you can take the lower odds ratios—like the 2 for cigarette smoking and heart disease—seriously.

The refining process is important not just to validate the causal finding. It gives you clues about why there is a relation. If a condition affects both cigarette smokers and people who inhale industrial toxins, it points to the cigarette smoke as the culprit, rather than, say, the nicotine.

But if someone tries hard to refine the analysis to get an odds ratio of 3 or more and fails, that's pretty good evidence that there isn't a strong causal effect. And if the researcher didn't try to refine the result, and just wanted to notch a publication without validating the finding or trying to understand it, you can dismiss the work out of hand. Too many researchers stop work when they get a publishable result, rather than keeping on the trail until they actually learn something.

NO SUBSTITUTE FOR EXPERIENCE

A point I'll discuss in greater depth later is that rules of thumb like "ignore odds ratios of less than 3 regardless of statistical significance" are learned by long experience working with many different kinds of data and getting objective feedback about predictions—or at least by apprenticing under an experienced person. It also helps to note lots of research findings and track which ones hold up and which ones dissipate like morning dew. Too many researchers learned just enough rote statistics from a cookbook course to be dangerous.

Getting a statistically significant odds ratio of 3 or more is just the start. It's also important to show that the behavior—marijuana smoking—began before there were symptoms of the health outcome—the heart disease. It helps a lot if you can show a plausible mechanism for the causation. For example, most behavioral contributors to heart disease take decades to develop. That makes it plausible that, say, 30 years of marijuana use causes heart disease symptoms that show up at age 50. It's less plausible that marijuana caused a first-time marijuana user on Sunday to have a heart attack on Monday. Not impossible, of course, but less plausible.

There's another major problem with that 1.16 odds ratio. The authors report a 95% confidence interval of 0.98–1.38. I have an in-depth discussion of confidence intervals in Chapter 11, for now I just note that confidence intervals that include the odds ratio 1—meaning you don't have 95% confidence that marijuana makes coronary heart disease more likely—are usually called "not significant statistically at the 5% level." The usual procedure is not to publish these results at all, although that creates problems of its own. But what's certainly true is these results should not be used to give medical advice to patients without the caveat that they fail to meet normal standards of significance.

ANSWER THE PHONE

This marijuana study did not use one of the major health panels that underlie the best behavioral health work. Instead, it relied on the Behavioral Risk Factor Surveillance Surveys. These are annual telephone surveys conducted by the Centers for Disease Control. They're big, 400,000 interviews, but they have major disadvantages compared to panel studies. At most they can suggest associations, correlations; they're useless for determining causes. I'll go into the reasons for that below.

Most researchers are transparent about the limitations of their data. The standard wording when working with this type of data is, "We find an association between marijuana use and heart disease." Not in this case.

The authors went so far as to derive a "clinical implication" from their finding, writing that patients should be "advised to avoid smoking cannabis to reduce their risk of premature cardiovascular disease and cardiac events." The media took them at their word. I assume many doctors did as well.

Observational studies can only show correlation, not causation. And in this case, we can be certain there is no causation because the phone survey measured marijuana use that occurred after the onset of disease. It asked participants about their marijuana use over the last 30 days and about their cardiovascular problems at any point in the past. How could a bong hit a week ago, or a THC gummy last Saturday, possibly cause someone to have a stroke 10 years ago? Yet the authors claimed this as a causal relation.

Another problem is that the data don't show the people who had cardiovascular problems; they show the people who survived cardiovascular problems. Let's say hypothetically that marijuana reduced cardiovascular mortality (warning, this is not medical advice, I know of no evidence that getting high reduces heart attack and stroke mortality). We'd expect the study to show more marijuana users with heart disease and stroke because they would be alive to report their cardiovascular problems in the phone survey. More of the non-users who had cardiovascular problems would be too dead to answer the phone.

The authors could equally well have presented their findings as marijuana users have a 1.16 odds ratio for surviving cardiovascular problems, and a clinical implication of patients should be advised to use marijuana to improve their chances of surviving heart disease. This advice would be no better and no worse than what they did publish, but I'm pretty sure the *Journal of the American Heart Association* would have rejected it.

There is a similar issue with the observation that people who wear motorcycle helmets are hospitalized more often for accidents—because three times as many non-helmet wearers die before they get to the hospital.

The classic example of this effect dates to World War II, when Britain's Royal Air Force (RAF) presented the great statistician Abraham Wald with data on where their bombers were most often hit by projectiles from enemy fighter planes and anti-aircraft guns. They wanted to know the best places to reinforce planes. Each additional pound of armor meant two fewer pounds of bombs (armor has to be carried for a round trip, bombs are one-way), meaning more missions. The RAF wanted to know the optimal amount of armor and where the most frequently hit areas were to put it.

Wald presented them with a plan for armor in the places that were never hit. When asked why, he replied: "Because planes hit in those places never returned."

WHO CAN YOU TRUST?

Though the data come from phone surveys, the authors make no allowance for the unreliability of what people might tell a stranger on the phone about their health and drug habits.

The researchers even had the gall to assert that surveys of this kind tend to be accurate, while referencing only two studies in support of that claim—a 1982 paper that found such data are "so unreliable" as to be almost impossible to interpret and a 2004 study showing that over a third of self-reported cardiovascular problems were fictitious. Worse, the fictitious self-reports weren't random, but were much higher for some groups than others, which would distort any findings.

This is a distressingly common problem in academic studies, more evidence that gatekeepers like editors and referees do not even do minimal checking. Authors will include citations on points crucial to their findings—as in this case, if the phone data are unreliable, the entire paper is worthless—citing papers that say the opposite. Referees and editors cannot be bothered to click on links and glance at the cited papers' abstracts.

CONFOUND IT AGAIN!

The researchers also had to deal with the other behaviors that correlate with marijuana use and are known to impact cardiovascular health. Marijuana users were more likely to be current and former tobacco smokers, more were men, and they drank more, all of which you'd expect to correlate with cardiovascular problems.

In fact, despite these increased risk factors, marijuana users in the study had fewer of all three types of cardiovascular problems measured in the study—an inconvenient point that the authors only mention in one jargony sentence late in the paper: "Coronary heart disease, for example, afflicted more nonusers of marijuana than either daily or nondaily users."

This doesn't necessarily negate the authors' thesis. To drill down into the data, they should have tried to find a meaningful subgroup—such as unmarried Asian female college graduates with pets—in which people who used marijuana had more cardiovascular problems than non-users. This analysis could illuminate why and how marijuana use affected cardiac health. It might produce a statistically solid result—ideally a subgroup in which marijuana users had three times the risk of non-users for some outcome. The failure to identify even a single subgroup and outcome for which marijuana use seemed to make things worse is a reason to ignore the study.

LOGISTIC TORTURE

So, how did the researchers claim to back up their thesis? They tortured the data until they offered a false confession. Their rack was multivariable logistic regression, and their thumbscrew was data censoring.

Logistic regression is a complex tool for forcing data into a shape you want. For a simple example, consider the data on strokes by educational attainment and marijuana use shown in the table below.

Education	Stroke frequency (%)	
	Marijuana user	Non-user
No school	22.2	5.9
School but no high school	6.9	8.0
Some high school	7.3	7.9
High school graduate	4.4	5.1
Some college	3.4	4.3
College graduate	2.8	2.8

You can see that stroke frequency declines with education for some reason, and for every level of education, marijuana users report fewer strokes than non-users—except for the 0.07% of the sample that reported having no schooling of any kind, and for college graduates where the stroke frequency is the same for users and non-users.

Now, as I keep saying, correlation does not prove causation. The data do not prove that marijuana protects against stroke. But they certainly do not support the authors' opposite claim, that marijuana increased the risk of stroke.

The authors use logistic regression to make the data conform to a specific mathematical pattern, that stroke frequency for marijuana users in every educational category is 88% of the stroke frequency for non-users. Eighty-eight percent is the fraction that best fits the data. That results in the table below.

Education	Stroke frequency (%)			
	Marijuana user		Non-user	
	Data	LR replacement	Data	LR replacement
No school	22.9	6.7	5.9	7.5
School but no high school	6.9	7.0	8.0	7.9
Some high school	7.3	7.0	7.9	7.9

(Continued)

(Continued)

Education	Stroke frequency (%)			
	Marijuana user		Non-user	
	Data	LR replacement	Data	LR replacement
High school graduate	4.4	4.5	5.1	5.1
Some college	3.4	3.8	4.3	4.3
College graduate	2.8	2.5	2.8	2.9

Why would someone replace real data with imaginary data? There's some justification for the first row, the people who report never having been to school at all. This is 0.07% of the sample, and a handful of extra strokes among marijuana users gives an unlikely high value, while the value for non-users looks implausible, if not as much of an outlier. The logistic regression replacement values seem more reasonable and the tiny sample size in the first row means there's considerable uncertainty about the population frequency.

But why mess with all the other values? They are based on very large sample sizes, and there's no reason to doubt the observed frequencies. It's implausible—virtually impossible—that the logistic regression frequencies are correct and that the observed frequencies differed only due to random noise.

There's no theoretical reason to assume the ratio of strokes in each educational category between users and non-users of marijuana is the same. The authors don't even mention this as an assumption, despite the fact that if it's false it invalidates their entire paper. They just applied a cookbook statistical technique that made the assumption implicitly for them.

So far, this doesn't make a big difference. Marijuana users had 88% of the stroke frequency of non-users. It doesn't matter much—except to people reporting no school at all—whether they had exactly 88% of the risk for every level of education, or rates varying from 79% for people with some college to 100% for college graduates; and 378% for the 0.07% of people with no school.

VARIABLE EXPLOSION

The trouble is the distortion from logistic regression increases dramatically as you add more variables to the equations. In addition to educational attainment, the authors use age, sex, race, alcohol use, smoking history, body-mass index, physical activity, and diabetes. All nine of these, plus marijuana use, are assumed to have independent multiplicative effects on cardiovascular health. Forcing this to be true transforms the actual data into unrecognizable form. This assumption, not the actual data, drives the authors' conclusions.

In fact, although multivariable logistic regression is the go-to tool for causal studies in medicine and social sciences—whenever you see an odds ratio it's likely derived from this tool—it's a basic statistical error to use it for a causal study. It's a tool of prediction, not analysis of cause. You might use it to predict the number of strokes in some region and time period, but it cannot tell you what causes strokes.

The reason multivariable logistic regression is unsuited to causal study is its main assumption—that the odds ratio for an observation is the product of the odds ratios for the individual variables—is often true of coincidental factors, only very rarely for causal factors. Therefore, the model only gives reliable results when you feed it noise data. It's damned if you do, damned if you don't. If you feed it noise, the results are meaningless because you started with noise. If you feed it causal factors, the results are meaningless because the assumptions are wrong.

This will be easier to explain with an example. Suppose I want to explain how baseball players make it to the Hall of Fame. I start with two noise factors: whether the player was born on an even or odd day of the month, and whether his first name has more than four letters. I get an odds ratio of 1.026 for being born on an even day of the month, and 1.014 for having a first name of five or more letters. Players born on even days of the month are 2.6% more likely to make the Hall, players with longer first names are 1.4% more likely.

Since these are accidental deviations—noise, rather than causal factors—we expect them to be uncorrelated. That means the odds ratio for a long-first-name player born on an even day of the month should be around 1.026 × 1.014, or 1.041. That's close to true, the actual odds ratio is only slightly less, at 1.038.

Now suppose I start with two causal factors: whether a player had a career batting average of 0.300 or better, and whether he played for at least five seasons. Now I get an odds ratio of 1.737 for batting over 0.300, and 2.028 for playing at least five seasons. Their product is 3.522, but the actual odds ratio for players with both achievements is 8.281. This is typical of causal factors; they can have synergies that make their combined odds ratios much greater than the product of the individual ratios. That violates the core assumption of multivariable logistic regression.

For those of you who are wondering how any baseball players make the Hall of Fame with fewer than 10 seasons of play—the normal minimum to be admitted as a player, although it was waived for three players—some make it as managers or executives.

Incidentally, this is further support for my rule to ignore odds ratios below 3. If you have accidental factors, it's pretty hard to combine them to get an odds ratio above 3, unless you take a very large number. But with causal factors, odds ratios can explode with only two factors.

Causes can work the opposite way as well, where odds ratios of 1.737 and 2.028 combine for an odds ratio much less than their product of 3.522. But in that case, the odds ratio of the inverse case—someone with below 0.300 and fewer than five seasons making the Hall—will have an odds ratio above the product of the two individual odds ratios.

Think of a test given in a class and two causal factors—whether the student is smart and whether she studied. If the test is hard, such that only smart students who study have much chance of success, we'll find that the odds ratio for smart studiers is much higher than the product of the odds ratios for smart students and studiers individually.

But if the test is easy, such that smart students pass whether or not they study, and studiers pass whether or not they're smart, we'll find that the odds ratio for smart studiers is much lower than the product of the odds ratio for smart students and the odds ratio for studiers.

The only way these two causal factors will match the multivariable logistic regression assumption is if the test is exactly Goldilocks hard. That won't happen often with real data.

THE RESEARCHER'S FRIEND

In addition to the theoretical issue of using multivariable logistic regression for causal studies, there are a number of practical objections. Another piece of empirical wisdom is to treat any alleged odds ratio from this technique with extreme skepticism, and any field of study that relies heavily on it with the same.

The older and more common form of multivariable regression is the linear model. This has issues as well, but long experience with use by truth-seeking investigators has mitigated many of them. There are robust estimation techniques that reduce sensitivity to violations of assumptions, and extensive diagnostics automatically printed out by standard statistical software to identify problems. Causal researchers limit variables to those with plausible causal relations to the dependent variable, and exclude those that do not add to explanatory power. Researchers distinguish between the variables of interest ("treatment" variables) and the "control" variables, included only to refine the estimate of the effect of the treatment.

Before these reforms came into general practice in the 1970s, multivariable linear regression had acquired a tainted reputation among serious investigators, similar to the one held by multivariable logistic regression today. Results from these studies never seemed to pan out in further analysis, never seemed to lead to useful progress. Fields that embraced multivariable linear regression enthusiastically fell by the wayside or drifted into sterile ideological bickering.

In multivariable logistic regressions, you seldom see robust estimation techniques or rigorous diagnostics applied. Investigators typically throw in a fishing expedition of things that might be causally related, and exclude nothing. On the other hand, they more often than not exclude inconvenient data with either no mention, or brief allusions without sound reasons given.

I am actually surprised when I find that authors highlight their largest odds ratios from these regressions, which you would expect if authors were interested in reporting their biggest findings. Usually, the papers pick out the effect the authors like for abstracts and summaries, and only mention the rest in tables or brief notices in the text.

A publishable, "statistically significant," result is virtually guaranteed by undisciplined multivariable logistic regression, making it tempting for academics under publish-or-perish pressure.

UNLEASH THE CENSORS

The error of using multivariable logistic regression for causal studies is so common that we might forgive the authors for it. But what they did next is impossible to justify. It's the single most obvious error in this paper, and the most shocking.

I'm proud to say that our brave data resisted the rack of logistic regression and refused to say that marijuana use resulted in more cardiovascular problems. So, researchers brought out the thumbscrews.

Consider the control variables the authors used in addition to the treatment variable (whether or not the subject had used marijuana in the last 30 days): education, age, sex, race, alcohol use, smoking history, body-mass index, physical activity, and diabetes.

At one extreme, education is unlikely to be causal—attending a course is unlikely to prevent a stroke. Most likely educated people had more money, better healthcare, less stress, or other differences. At the other extreme, age is very likely causal, both because older people have had more years in which to have strokes, and because age increases vulnerability to strokes. The other variables fall in between, with likely some causal and some non-causal associations.

The problem for anyone trying to use these data to claim marijuana was bad for your heart is that most of the cardiovascular problems were found in older people—75 or more years old—and very few people in this group used marijuana.

The solution? The authors threw out the data for people over 74. How did they explain that decision? They asserted that people older than 74 didn't use enough marijuana to be suitable for the study. But that's precisely what makes them valuable for controls. To get reliable results you need lots of users (treatment population) and non-users (control population). And why throw out only old non-users? Why not all non-users? The answer is that people older than 74 didn't use enough marijuana *and* had too many cardiovascular events. That's what made them unwelcome for this paper.

Think back to the hard-test/easy-test story about odds ratios. Getting a stroke when you're young is like passing a hard test. It's unusual; a lot of stuff has to go wrong. In this situation, we expect the individual odds ratios—and specifically the one on marijuana use—to be inflated by multivariable logistic regression.

Getting a stroke when you're over 74 is more like an easy test. It's common; any one wrong thing might tip the balance. Therefore, multivariable logistic regression might underestimate individual odds ratios. By throwing out the easy test data, the authors biased their results to show harm from marijuana.

While the effect of throwing out people over 74 years of age is not obvious to a non-statistician, the fact of throwing out data without any sort of rational explanation is among the most obvious red flags.

THERE'S MORE

I could keep going. For example, the authors excluded all the survey data from 1988 to 2015 and after 2020 without explaining why; they failed to distinguish between edibles and smoking; they didn't pre-register their hypothesis or use a holdout sample, which makes it impossible to evaluate if their findings were statistically significant; and so on.

The point of this Wrong Number is it's possible to do everything wrong, from start to finish, and still publish in top journals and get widespread uncritical media coverage. You can even fool professional skeptics like Marty Makary. You can get your Wrong Number out to every doctor, where you can be confident it will be given to hundreds of millions of patients.

IT GETS WORSE

So far we've looked at studies that torture and misrepresent data. But at least these studies have data. The next chapter is a change of pace, we'll look at several studies that had no data at all.

CHAPTER SIX

NO DATA? NO PROBLEM

After surviving a disastrous congressional hearing, Claudine Gay was forced to resign as the president of Harvard for repeatedly copying and pasting language used by other scholars and passing it off as her own. She's hardly alone among elite academics, and plagiarism has become a roiling scandal in academia.

STUDIES IN FICTION

There's another common practice among professional researchers that should be generating even more outrage: making up data. I'm not talking about explicit fraud, which also happens way too often, but about openly inserting fictional data into a supposedly objective analysis.

Instead of doing the hard work of gathering data to test hypotheses, researchers take the easy path of generating numbers to support their preconceptions or to claim statistical significance. They cloak this practice in words like "imputation," "ecological inference," "contextualization," and "synthetic control."

They're actually just making stuff up.

There are times when it's justifiable to make up data. When you need to make a decision and you cannot get the necessary data, or cannot get it in time, you have to do the best you can. But this is almost never the case in academic studies. Academics make up data to answer questions nobody cares about, and certainly for which there is no pressing demand for immediate low-quality answers. Data are usually available, just more trouble than the researcher wants to take—or perhaps the researcher doesn't want to risk getting an unwelcome answer. The nice thing about making up data is it always says what you want it to say.

But even if making up data is justifiable, the papers doing it should carry a clear warning label in large type: "The results of this paper derive from data the authors imagine is true, or wish were true, not actual research."

THE ECOLOGY OF VOTER PARTICIPATION

Claudine Gay was accused of plagiarizing sections of her PhD thesis, for which she was awarded Harvard's Toppan Prize for the best dissertation in political science. She has since requested three corrections. More outrageous is that she wrote the dissertation on White voter participation without having any data on White voter participation.

In an article in the *American Political Science Review* that was based on her dissertation, Gay set out to investigate "the link between black congressional representation and political engagement," finding that "the election of blacks to Congress negatively affects white political involvement and only rarely increases political engagement among African Americans."

To arrive at that finding, you might assume that Gay had done the work of measuring White and Black voting patterns in the districts she was studying. You would assume wrong.

Instead, Gay used regression analysis to estimate voting patterns. She analyzed 10 districts with Black representatives and observed that those with more voting-age Whites had lower turnout at the polls than her model predicted. She concluded that Whites must be the ones not voting.

She committed what in statistics is known as the "ecological fallacy"— you see two things occurring in the same place and assume a causal relationship. For example, you notice a lot of people dying in hospitals, so you assume hospitals kill people. The classic example is how Jim Crow laws in the century following the Civil War were strictest in states that skewed Black. Ecological inference leads to the false conclusion that Blacks supported Jim Crow.

Gay's theory that a Black congressional representative depresses White voter turnout could be true, but there are other plausible explanations for what she observed. The point is that we don't know. The way to investigate White voter turnout is to measure White voter turnout.

To better appreciate Gay's error, consider a scenario in which her approach would be justified. You're director of election analytics for the re-election campaign of a first-term Black Congresswoman who was the first person of color elected to Congress from her district. The national party provides you with its election model that predicts turnout and voting tendency by demographic group.

You notice that the national model does not take into account whether a Black candidate displaced a White candidate in the previous election, and you think that's likely relevant to voter behavior in the next election. You check the model's historical predictions for that situation and discover that it systematically overestimates turnout, and further, that the higher the proportion of White voters in a district, the greater the overestimate.

You don't need any fancy statistics to alert your candidate that turnout could likely be below the national party's model estimate. This will affect decisions of messaging, ad spending, appearances, and other campaign matters.

Ecological inference allows you to make a further prediction, that White voters are likely to be the ones with reduced turnout. Your rationale is that since the effect is larger when there are more White voters, it's probably the White voters who aren't showing up to the polls as often as in the past. But as you know from the examples I cited above about the ecological fallacy—like hospitals killing people because so many people die there—this kind of inference can be wrong.

I can't tell you whether or not you should make the guess about White voter turnout, but it's not unjustified. You have to advise your candidate one way or the other. You don't have time or resources to rework the national party model after gathering more national data on White voter turnout in historical elections. All you have is the aggregate data, and you have to make your best guess. It's a matter of judgment whether you consider the most plausible explanation is that White voters disengage when a Black is elected. Is that more likely than Black candidates who win in White-majority districts cause Black voters to lose interest—they've accomplished an important goal and the new candidate is favored by Whites anyway—while Black candidates who win in Black-majority districts energize Black voters for further gains?

Because you have to make a decision and cannot get the necessary data, any basis for a guess is justified. But when no one is clamoring for an answer to a question and it's straightforward to get the data, there's no excuse for publishing a paper without the data, relying on a dubious logic that is often wrong. Moreover, if you choose to do it, you should put a clear disclaimer that you're guessing rather than reporting on data.

SHE IS NOT ALONE

Gay is hardly the only culprit who makes up her data. Because she was the president of Harvard, it's worth making an example of her work, but it reflects broad trends in academia. Unlike the academic crime of plagiarism, students are taught and encouraged to invent data under the guise of statistical sophistication. Academia values the appearance of truth over actual truth.

You need real data to understand the world. The process of gathering real data also leads to essential insights. Researchers pick up on subtleties that often cause them to shift their hypotheses. Claudine Gay might have learned more talking to a few dozen real voters than from making ecological inferences from aggregate data collected by others for a different purpose. Armchair investigators build neat rows and columns in their spreadsheets that don't say anything about what's happening outside their windows.

IMPUTING GREEN

Another technique for generating rather than collecting data is called "imputation," which was used in a paper titled "Green Innovations and Patents in OECD Countries" by economists Almas Heshmati and Mike Shinas. The authors wanted to analyze the number of "green" patents issued by different countries in different years. But the authors only had data for some countries and some years.

"Imputation" means filling in data gaps with educated guesses. It can be defensible if you have a good basis for your guesses and they don't affect your conclusions strongly. For example, suppose you are missing occupation for a subject who lives at 1600 Pennsylvania Avenue and earns

$400,000 per year. Imputing "president" is sensible. But if you're studying the number of green patents, and you don't know that number, imputation isn't an appropriate tool for solving the problem.

The use of imputation allowed the authors to publish a paper arguing that environmentalist policies lead to innovation—which is likely the conclusion they had hoped for—and to do so with enough statistical significance to pass muster with journal editors.

A graduate student in economics working with the same data as Heshmati and Shinas recounted being "dumbstruck" after reading their paper. The student, who wants to remain anonymous for career reasons, reached out to Heshmati to find out how he and Shinas had filled in the data gaps. The research accountability site Retraction Watch reported that they had used the Excel "autofill" function.

According to an analysis by the economist Gary Smith, altogether there were over 2,000 fictional data points, amounting to 13% of all the data used in the paper.

The Excel autofill function is a lot of fun and genuinely handy in some situations. When you enter 1, 2, 3, it guesses 4. But it doesn't work when the data—like much of reality—have no simple or predictable pattern.

When you give Excel a list of US presidents, it can't predict the next one. I did give it a try though. This was in 2024, when Kamala Harris was running against Donald Trump. Excel picked William Henry Harrison to win and predicted he would take the White House in 1941. Why? Harrison died in office just 31 days after his inauguration, in 1841—the first elected president not to finish his term. Most likely, autofill figured it was only fair that he be allowed to serve out his remaining years. Why did it pick 1941? That's when Franklin D. Roosevelt began his third term, which apparently Excel considered to be illegitimate, so it exhumed Harrison and put him back in the White House.

When does imputation make sense? Suppose you are studying graduation rates by gender at a university. For one student, Susan Smith, there's no entry for gender. If you guess "female," you're probably right. He might be the boy named Sue or xe might be non-binary. But most Susans check "female" on forms.

Another example is if you're studying stock market prices. One stock closed on Monday at $50.00. On Tuesday it was $5,020.00 and on Wednesday $50.40. Prices of other stocks in its industry were overall flat for the three days and there was no news about the company over the three days. If you replace Tuesday's price with $50.20, you're likely pretty close.

You're using imputation for convenience, not to improve the analysis. Missing values complicate statistical analysis, and some packages may not give an answer. If you have pretty good guesses for your missing values, and there aren't too many of them, and your conclusions don't change much if you repeat the analysis excluding all observations with missing or unlikely values, then the practical benefits of imputation can exceed its theoretical defects.

However, an essential point is that the significance levels and confidence intervals you claim should be adjusted for all your imputations. This was not done in "Green Innovations and Patents in OECD Countries" and is usually neglected in my experience.

KILLER FILINGS

In a paper published in the *Journal of the American Medical Association* and written up by CNN and the *New York Post*, a team of academics claimed to show that age-adjusted death rates soared 106% during the pandemic among renters who had received eviction filing notices, compared to 25% for a control group.

The authors got 483,408 eviction filings and asked the US Census how many of the tenants had died. The answer was 0.3% had death records, and 58.0% were still alive. The status of 41.7% was unknown—usually because the tenant had moved without filing a change of address. If the authors had assumed that all the unknowns were still alive, the COVID-era mortality increase would be 22% for tenants who got eviction notices versus 25% who didn't. This would have been a statistically insignificant finding, wouldn't have been publishable, and certainly wouldn't have gotten any press attention.

Some of the tenants that the Census couldn't find probably did die, though likely not many, since most dead people end up with death certificates—and people who are dead can't move, so you'd expect most of them to be linked to their census addresses. But some might move or change their names and then die, or perhaps they were missing from the Census database before receiving an eviction notice.

But whatever the reality, the authors didn't have the data. The entire result of their paper—the 106% claimed increase in mortality for renters with eviction filings versus the 22% observed rate—comes from a guess about how many of the unknown tenants had died.

How did they guess? They made the wildly implausible assumption that the Census and the Social Security Administration are equally likely to lose track of a dead person and a living one. Yet the government is far more interested in when people die than when they move, because they don't want to keep cutting them Social Security checks. If they send your check to an old address, that's your problem. Also, dead people don't move or change their names so they're easier to find.

Whether or not their assumption was plausible, the paper reported a guess as if it reflected objective data. That's considered acceptable in academia, but it shouldn't be.

When is guessing justified? Suppose the authors had taken a sample of eviction filings for which the Census database did not return data and tracked the individuals down. They wouldn't have to check all 200,000 people with missing data. This is an appropriate use of capture–recapture analysis that will come up in Chapter 11, and would not have taken great effort. In addition to correcting or validating the study's claim, this exercise would give considerable insight into what happens to people after an eviction filing, and how the Census Bureau loses track of them.

SYNTHETIC CONNECTICUT

"Association Between Connecticut's Permit-to-Purchase Handgun Law and Homicides" was published in the *American Journal of Public Health*. It cooked up data to use as a control. The study claimed to show that a 1994 gun control law passed in Connecticut cut firearm homicides by 40%.

The authors did have data from the Centers for Disease Control and Prevention (CDC) on firearm homicides in Connecticut. The gun control law at issue went into effect in October 1995. In the first year, firearm homicides in Connecticut increased 16% versus the year prior. But after that, they began to decline and were 6% lower on average for the three years following implementation.

Moreover, firearm homicides had been declining rapidly in Connecticut before the law was implemented. The three years after implementation averaged 22% fewer firearm homicides per 100,000 population than the three years before.

To be meaningful, we need a control for comparison with these figures, a guess as to how many firearm homicides there would have been in Connecticut without the law. An obvious control is nationwide firearm homicide rates. These fell 12% in the year after Connecticut's implementation, compared to a rise of 16% in Connecticut. The national rate fell 16%, averaged over the three years after implementation, compared to Connecticut's 6% decline. The national rate was 28% lower in the three years after implementation compared to the three years before; Connecticut had a 22% decline. So, using a national control we'd conclude there is no evidence that the Connecticut law reduced firearm homicides over what they would have been without the law, and perhaps the law actually increased firearm homicides.

So, the authors decided to make up a synthetic control. Not any real place, but a statistical aggregation pieced together from bodies dug up from a cemetery and blasted by lightning in a hilltop laboratory. Okay, not that. Actually, the authors used a weighted average of the homicide rates from California (3.6%), Maryland (14.7%), Nevada (8.7%), New Hampshire (0.5%), and Rhode Island (72.4%). This fictional state had 40% more homicides than the real Connecticut.

Rhode Island is a small state with 10–15 gun homicides per year prior to Connecticut's gun law going into effect. It experienced a spate of gun homicides, with 19–27 for eight years afterward. Because Rhode Island represented nearly three-quarters of the synthetic control, and its firearm homicides nearly doubled, Connecticut looked great by comparison. But any other state would have also looked great. The result was driven by Rhode Island's misfortune not by Connecticut's gun law.

Moreover, Rhode Island is such a small state that the CDC labels its firearm homicide rates "unreliable." Connecticut had about 120–150 gun homicides per year. That's a human tragedy, but a statistical benefit; there's less random noise in the gun homicide rates.

The synthetic control is made-up data, because no state resembles it, and it certainly doesn't resemble Connecticut in any meaningful way. California, Maryland, and Nevada are not like Connecticut. New Hampshire has some similarity to northern Connecticut, but it's only 0.5% of the control. Rhode Island has some similarities to southern Connecticut, but it's so small that its firearm homicide rates are unreliable.

The ideal control is a state identical to Connecticut in all respects except a different gun law. Of course, this does not exist. One reasonable second-best control is the entire United States. Another one is the neighboring states of New York, Massachusetts, and Rhode Island. Connecticut is not the same as any of those three, but areas of Connecticut are similar to areas in those states, and perhaps the combination of the three states is a decent control.

A key distinction is the national rate, or the rate from neighboring states, is a real control. You're adding up the firearm homicides and dividing by the total population. You're dividing real homicides by real populations. With the synthetic control in "Association Between Connecticut's Permit-to-Purchase Handgun Law and Homicides," each Rhode Island firearm homicide counts as three Connecticut firearm homicides, because Connecticut has three times the population. On the other hand, a California firearm homicide counts as only 0.1 Connecticut firearm homicides because California has 10 times the population of Connecticut. This is the same error the National Transportation Safety Board made in Chapter 1. The result is a firearm homicide total that does not represent actual homicides, merely statistical extrapolations from data, and unreliable extrapolations.

GOING TO WAR

When can a synthetic control be justified? One of the best-known examples, at least if you're a baseball fan, is wins-above-replacement (WAR). This is a metric for evaluating player quality. It compares each player's production with a hypothetical replacement player that a team could easily call up from its minor-league affiliates or sign from players waived by other teams or free agents. The only cost is the league-minimum salary.

Most sports statistics of this type use an actual control, usually the league-average player. This is based on actual production of real players, averaged over the league. Using a hypothetical replacement player as a control is synthetic. The replacement players, by definition, aren't playing, so there are no real statistics to aggregate. Moreover, we don't even identify specific replacement players. We just make up a theoretical composite.

In baseball, if we use the league-average player as a control, we call the result wins-above-average (WAA). But this is a relatively obscure statistic, nowhere near as well known as WAR.

WAR is useful because if you trade two 2.0 WAR players for a 4.0 WAR player, you break even—at least if your WAR estimates are accurate. You can pick up a replacement player with zero WAR (by definition) to fill in the extra player at no cost. But if you traded two 2.0 WAA players for one 4.0 WAA player, you'd need to go out and find a league-average player to fill out your team, and league-average players are hard to find and expensive. Similarly, if you pay $10 million above league-minimum salary for a 6.0 WAR player, you should be willing to pay $5 million above league-minimum salary for a 3.0 WAR player and $15 million for a 9.0 WAR player. You can't do the same math with WAA.

Another nice thing about WAR is it allows you to compare an injury-prone star, who would be an 8.0 WAR player if he were healthy every day but plays only half the team's games, to a healthy 4.0 WAR player who plays every day.

The disadvantage of WAR is the difficulty of estimating the production of a replacement-level player. The league average player is easy to measure objectively, hypothetical replacement-level players are a matter of opinion, and opinions differ.

Synthetic controls are more trouble to estimate, and require subjective judgment. They have more room for researchers to consciously or unconsciously shape results to their liking. This is especially true for the synthetic control in "Association Between Connecticut's Permit-to-Purchase Handgun Law and Homicides," with its five states picked out of 50 with big weight differences and most of the weight on a state with unreliable data.

The offsetting advantage occurs when the synthetic control is a true natural baseline, a zero point. In baseball, the hypothetical replacement player is a natural zero point because there are always lots of them you can find for free (other than the league-minimum salary you'll have to pay to whomever occupies the roster spot). That makes WAR a more meaningful statistic than WAA, which makes up for its subjectivity. Another point is we actually have quite a bit of data to estimate the performance of a replacement player, because players get replaced all the time.

In the gun control study, two natural baselines would be a hypothetical state with no gun regulation at all, or alternatively, a state that completely outlawed civilian possession of firearms. Neither of these are practical, because it's impossible to find any places remotely like Connecticut that are close to either extreme. Moreover, since the authors' synthetic control was not a natural baseline, they did not gain the advantage that can offset the subjectivity and uncertainty of using synthetic controls. And unlike WAR, they did not have reliable data to estimate their control.

If a natural baseline were possible, it would be valuable. You could estimate the absolute effect of every state's package of gun laws every year, instead of being limited to the relative effect of single states in years with major changes in gun laws.

The gun control study needed a different synthetic control for each effect of the Connecticut law they studied. When looking at non-firearm homicides, the synthetic control was 72.4% for New Hampshire (New Hampshire numbers are even less reliable than Rhode Island's). That means you can't tell if the increase in non-firearm homicides relative to synthetic control offsets the decline in firearm homicides, because the two are measured against different baselines. More generally, you can't form an overall picture of all the effects of the law—including possible increases in crime due to disarmed civilians.

So synthetic controls can be a powerful tool but, like firearms, a powerful tool that is dangerous when misused. These authors have shot themselves in the foot.

WHY IS THERE PROGRESS?

At this point you could be forgiven for wondering how science makes progress. Shouldn't all the Wrong Numbers drive fields into endless paths of error? That will be the subject of our next chapter.

CHAPTER SEVEN

A WOVEN WEB OF GUESSES

The gods did not reveal, from the beginning,
All things to us, but in the course of time
Through seeking we may learn and know things better.
But as for certain truth, no man has known it,
Nor shall he know it, neither of the gods
Nor yet of all the things of which I speak.
For even if by chance he were to utter
The final truth, he would himself not know it:
For all is but a woven web of guesses.

—Xenophanes

If teachers, journals, granting institutions, and others are not even trying to avoid Wrong Numbers, why is there so much progress in at least some academic fields? The main answer is a woven web of guesses does not require each thread, or even most threads, to be strong (I made the same point with the bricks metaphor in Chapter 1).

Xenophanes used the Greek word δόκος for what was translated as "guesses." I'm no scholar of ancient Greek, but I prefer the alternative translation of "conjectures" in this context—as more accurate, if not necessarily a better indication of what Xenophanes meant. Random guesses are poor material for weaving strong webs. Biological evolution does things this way and it is extremely slow. Inspired conjectures—rigorously and skeptically tested—can drive progress in understanding on a human time scale.

SIX DEGREES OF SEPARATION

Modern science is not communicated by journal articles. Most articles are published long after the work is done and has been transmitted via personal messages, working papers, and presentations. Most science is in the collective web-weaving, rather than generating individual findings.

Researchers in a field know whom to trust, and in what ways. They build up personal networks and can reach out to check on work from outside their network. Most important, academics know which of their papers are sound, and which ones were churned out for career reasons. The good work they promote within their network, and by presentations and seminars, and follow up. The other stuff is seldom mentioned. There are further levels of filtering as similar good work coalesces into generally accepted facts that reach beyond narrow fields and rise up to influence textbooks, policies, and standard instructions in the field.

The system does not work perfectly, of course—especially when topics get political or media attention. Moreover, in some fields it does not seem to work at all.

Most of the Wrong Numbers in my book are not conjectural attempts at web-weaving but end runs around the existing web to promote specific findings directly to reporters, policymakers, judges, partisans, and others without expertise in the field or familiarity with its established web. They are often cloaked in impenetrable jargon or use data the researchers refuse to reveal. This makes their authors more like pre-Enlightenment priests—prophets and mystics claiming to pass along divine revelations—rather than scientists investigating conjectures to be woven into rational webs. More on this point in the final chapter.

In this chapter I'll shift the focus from individual Wrong Numbers to how they influence entire fields of study.

GRIM TEST

One attempt to investigate this question goes by the scary name of "the GRIM test," which is an acronym for the intimidating but not scary "granularity-related inconsistency of means." It's actually simple and friendly.

Consider the free-throw percentage of a basketball player, the ratio of the number of free throws made to the number of attempts. If a player has 50 attempts, she could make 35 of them, for a free-throw percentage of 0.700, or 36 for a free-throw percentage of 0.720, but she couldn't have any percentage greater than 0.700 and less than 0.720. A paper that reported a free-throw percentage of 0.710 for a player with 50 attempts would fail the GRIM test.

In 2016, researchers Nick Brown and James Heathers selected 260 recent empirical papers from top journals and ran the GRIM test. A total of 71 papers reported means of whole numbers with specified denominators, 36 of which—slightly more than half—failed the GRIM test. Some 16 of the papers had multiple failures. Nine authors of failed papers supplied the researchers with the original data, and all GRIM failures were confirmed. Three of the nine papers required extensive corrections as a result. If we assume the authors who did not supply original data were as bad as the ones that did (a conservative assumption), it means at least 12 of 71 papers should have made extensive changes to correct elementary data errors.

Now this is not a very large sample, and the majority of GRIM failures were relatively minor and did not require extensive corrections.

Nevertheless, this is only one possible error, and one that should have been instantly obvious to any author or reviewer. If 12 of 71, 17%, of papers require extensive correction due to authors incorrectly dividing two whole numbers and no one catching it, it's not hard to believe that most published research findings are wrong.

STATCHECK

Statisticians Michèle B. Nuijten and Jelte Wicherts built a more sophisticated tool, "Statcheck," around a similar idea. Statcheck looks for inconsistent reported significance levels. The authors studied over 30,000 articles with 250,000 reported p-values (p-values are discussed in Chapter 9). They wrote: "we found that half of all published psychology papers that use NHST [null hypothesis significance testing, the standard statistical approach used in many studies] contained at least one p-value that was inconsistent with its test statistic and degrees of freedom. One in eight papers contained a grossly inconsistent p-value that may have affected the statistical conclusion."

Statcheck is available free on-line, and some journals have added it to their review process on submitted articles. In a follow-up study, Nuijten and Wicherts studied 8,814 articles from four major psychology journals. Journals that introduced Statcheck into their review process saw their average number of inconsistencies per paper drop from 1.2 to 0.9, and their fraction of inconsistent reported p-values drop from 8% to 4%. A control group of journals that did not implement Statcheck averaged 1.9 inconsistent results per paper, and 7% of reported p-values were inconsistent.

This is only one field, psychology, and a field that has been more discredited than most by Wrong Numbers. But Statcheck only catches gross inconsistencies, and it's easy for authors to run it on their papers before submission. And even journals that claim to use it in their review process let an astoundingly large number of inconsistent results slip into print.

CARLISLE DEVIATIONS

Another field that has had more than its share of problems is anesthesiology, with both the number one and number two slots on the *Retraction Watch* leaderboard for researchers with the most retracted articles.

Back in 2000, a group of researchers including Peter Krenke noticed discrepancies in papers published by a star researcher in anesthesiology, Yoshitaka Fujii. For example, in one study he divided 270 women into six groups of 45 prior to operations and reported afterward exactly three women in each group reported post-operative headaches. His point was the six different anesthesiology regimes did not affect the probability of headaches.

The problem is that getting exactly three women in each group of 45 is an unlikely event, about one chance in 623, assuming that there was no effect of the anesthesia regime and the assignments were random (if the regime had any effects, good or bad, the probability of getting exactly three women in each group is less). By itself this is suspicious (we would easily reject at the 5% level that the assignment had been random), but Fujii's papers were filled with similar anomalies. This made it virtually certain that something was wrong, and the most plausible explanation is he was making up the data. It would be almost impossible to rig an experiment such that it produced exactly three women in each group of 45 with headaches, even if you tried. It took 12 years of stonewalling and foot-dragging by journals, which continued to publish Fujii's work, before his papers began to be retracted.

Incidentally, it's worth pointing out that Krenke miscalculated the probability as one chance in 4,499. That's just another reminder not to take anyone's word for things, not even debunkers of other people's work, and especially not mine.

If you don't care about the calculation, you can skip this and the next paragraph. You may know that Powerball requires players to pick five numbers from 1 to 69, and the chance of getting them all correct is one in 11,238,513. The mathematical formula for that is $\binom{69}{5}$, which is read "69 choose 5," the number of ways to choose five distinguishable objects without replacement from among 69.

There are $\binom{270}{18} \approx 5 \times 10^{27}$ (5 followed by 27 zeros, the squiggly equals sign means "approximately equal to") or five octillion ways to choose 18 women from 270. Some $\binom{45}{3}^6 \approx 8 \times 10^{24}$ or eight septillion of them result in exactly three women in each of the six groups of 45. So it's like playing a super Powerball with odds about the same as picking four perfect Powerball choices (just the five regular numbers, not the Powerball) in a row. But in this super Powerball, you get eight septillion tickets. Your overall chance of winning is about one chance in 5 octillion divided by 8 septillion or 625 (it would be closer to the 623 I quoted above if you carried more decimal places).

In 2017, another researcher, John Carlisle, decided to see how common statistically improbable events were in allegedly randomized control trials. Instead of looking for results that were too perfect, like exactly three women in each group, he looked for highly improbable deviations. For example, suppose a researcher has a sample of 1,000 patients with an average age of 50 and a standard deviation of 10 years. She randomly divides them into two groups of 500, and one group has an average age of 48.2 years, while the other group's average is 51.8. In a random assignment, this much difference should occur only about one time in 35,000. This could easily affect the study's results. For example, if the treatment group was 3.6 years younger than the control group, its improved outcomes could be the result of age rather than treatment.

Out of 5,087 randomized control trials reported in six top medical journals—four in anesthesiology plus the *New England Journal of Medicine* and the *Journal of the American Medical Association*—Carlisle found 135 had deviations that should happen less than one time in 500 (about 10 expected), 158 had deviations between one time in 50 and one time in 500 (about 92 expected), and 501 had deviations between one time in 10 and one time in 50 (about 417 expected).

What could explain these excess deviations? It could be sloppiness of various sorts, or researchers could be biasing their samples to make their effects seem bigger with better statistical significance.

BENFORD'S LAW

Two biologists from the University of St. Andrews, Gregory Eckhartt and Graeme Ruxton, published a pilot study: "Investigating and Preventing Scientific Misconduct Using Benford's Law." Benford's law is the non-intuitive result that in many contexts, natural measurements do not have a uniform distribution of first digits.

Eckhartt and Buxton proposed applying this to data submitted for journal articles. I've used it myself for this purpose, and for other investigations of whether purported values are real measurements or made-up values. As proof of concept they applied it to two papers retracted for data issues, and compared them to similar papers without known data problems, selected as controls. Indeed, both retracted papers failed the Benford test, while all control papers passed it.

Consider the populations of the 241 countries and dependencies of the world. These range from Pitcairn Island's 35 residents to India's 1.4 billion. Benford is more reliable when quantities range over several orders of magnitude.

The table below shows the number of countries in each population range by first digit. There is one place—Pitcairn Island—in the 10 to 99 population range, and its population starts with a three. There are two in the 100 to 999 range, Cocos Islands (population 593, which starts with a five) and Vatican City (population 882, which starts with an eight). And so on, up to two countries with over 1 billion population, India and China, which both start with a one.

First digit	10 to 99	100 to 999	1,000 to 9,999	10,000 to 99,999	100,000 to 999,999	1,000,000 to 9,999,999	10,000,000 to 99,999,999	100,000,000 to 999,999,999	1,000,000,000 to 9,999,999,999	Total	Benford prediction
1	0	0	3	7	12	12	30	9	2	75	73
2	0	0	2	1	6	9	15	4	0	37	42
3	1	0	1	5	4	10	12	1	0	34	30
4	0	0	1	5	4	3	7	0	0	20	23
5	0	1	2	5	2	10	6	0	0	26	19
6	0	0	0	3	5	9	5	0	0	22	16
7	0	0	0	0	3	5	0	0	0	8	14
8	0	1	0	4	1	1	3	0	0	10	12
9	0	0	0	0	2	7	0	0	0	9	11

None of the columns individually is close to the Benford relation, but when you sum across all columns (the "total" column), it comes reasonably close to the Benford prediction. It's by no means exact, but it's easy to tell a Benford-like pattern from a uniform distribution of first digits that you would expect if you asked someone to make up 241 numbers.

CANDIDATE GENES

Getting back to woven webs of guesses, are the large number of obvious inconsistencies and errors revealed in the studies above enough to invalidate an entire web, an entire field of scientific inquiry? That's clearly not true in all fields, we know there are advances in physics and computer science, for example—despite plenty of Wrong Numbers.

One example of an "emperor's new clothes" field from the first decade of the 21st century is candidate gene studies. As genetic testing got cheaper, a hot field of research developed testing correlations between specific genes and characteristics like IQ and depression. Hundreds of studies were published claiming suspiciously large effects.

I say "suspiciously" large because it had been well known for almost a century that almost all complex human traits are highly polygenic, meaning they depend on thousands of genes and alleles working in combination with developmental and environmental factors. No individual alleles have large statistical contributions to the characteristics. We know this from inheritance patterns. Looking for candidate genes is a bit like looking for the words that make literature great and deciding that books with "purple" as their 10,321st word are 20% more likely to be great than books that have "life" instead.

Of course, there are certain traits that depend heavily on single genes, such as some genetic diseases. But the candidate gene studies did not look at simple traits like these with obvious inheritance patterns.

The reason for so many false-positive results was simple. Researchers used small samples of individuals and looked only at a small number of genes. Small samples can only detect large effects—real or statistical outliers due to random chance. Since there were no real large effects to find, only outliers got published. As genetic testing got cheaper—so larger samples could be tested and entire genomes became available—nearly all category gene results evaporated, and the field melted away.

I'm going to return to this error in more detail in Chapter 9, as it raises issues common to many Wrong Numbers, even in basically healthy fields.

33,266 GUN CONTROL PAPERS CAN'T BE WRONG, OR COULD THEY?

There has been a massive research effort going back decades to determine whether gun control measures work. A 2024 analysis by the RAND Corporation, a non-profit research organization, parsed the results of 33,266 research publications on the effectiveness of gun control laws. From this vast body of work, the RAND authors found only 182 studies, or 0.5%, that tested the effects rigorously.

Not all the 33,084 other studies were worthless. For example, some papers merely described gun control legislation and what happened afterward. Without a control to compare what might have happened without the legislation, this is not a rigorous test of the effect. But the article could be useful to someone looking for qualitative or historical information. Other papers had conclusions but no data, or only data but no statistical analysis. But most of the 33,084 were just terrible studies.

The 182 studies that met RAND's criteria may have been the best of the 33,266 that were analyzed, but they still had serious statistical defects, such as a lack of controls, too many parameters or hypotheses for the data, undisclosed data, erroneous data, misspecified models, and other problems. Moreover, these were not 182 independent studies. Many used the same data sets or had the same authors.

The 182 papers identified by RAND tested 1,873 separate hypotheses about the impact of gun control policies. Only 12 papers produced any high-quality statistically significant results. So, what does the evidence show?

- Six studies tested 11 hypotheses about shall-issue gun permit laws. Nine hypotheses failed to find a significant effect at the 5% level. One estimated shall-issue laws were associated with a 9% increase in the violent crime rate, another a 20% increase in the violent crime rate excluding rape in large cities.
- Two studies showed statistically significant 8% increases in firearm homicides in states with stand-your-ground laws after adjusting for confounding variables.
- One study found purchase waiting period laws reduced gun homicide rates by 17%, with no significant effect found for non-gun homicides.
- One study found a 21% reduction in women intimate partners killed by firearms due to red-flag laws, but an increase (statistically insignificant) of male intimate partner firearm victims.
- One study found a 26% reduction in firearm murders by offenders under age 18 from child access prevention negligent storage laws, but child access prevention reckless endangerment laws had no statistically significant effect.

TAKING STOCK

That doesn't seem much for 33,266 papers. Moreover, the effect sizes are improbably large (I'll have more to say about this issue in Chapter 9). The studies had to estimate between 79 and 289 parameters for each model, and there's simply not enough data available to do that reliably.

All the high-quality studies and most of the rest come from only two databases, maintained by the FBI and the Centers for Disease Control and Prevention (CDC). Both have significant issues. The FBI compiles reports from local police forces, not all of which participate, nor report on the same basis. It misses a lot of crimes and has no data at all about defensive gun use. The CDC is pretty good at tracking deaths but has limited context about each one. In both cases the errors are systematic rather than random, which can undermine results.

However, it's not fair to say this is all we know about gun control legislation. Someone who knows a lot about the field can extract some information from the 33,266 papers, just not the kind of clear-cut, simple hypotheses with high confidence RAND looked for. Carefully sifting through 100 low-quality studies to figure out where they agree and why they differ can produce insight. In a healthier and less politicized field, with more emphasis on finding truth and less on generating publications, all that knowledge might be distilled into a few hundred high-quality papers that combined to paint a meaningful picture.

RAND tried to do this by throwing in another 40 low-quality papers that lacked critical flaws and by loosening the p-value threshold to 0.2 from the standard 0.05. That means, if no gun control regulation had any effect on any outcome, we would expect 20% of the 1,873 hypotheses, 375, to appear significant. If any three or more of these papers, using at least two data sets (which in all cases meant at least one using FBI data and at least one other using CDC data) tested similar regulations and outcomes, and pointed in the same direction, RAND gave that hypothesis its highest designation, "supportive evidence," and made policy recommendations assuming it was true.

On that basis, which seems very thin to me, RAND advocated child access prevention laws (among the least controversial gun control regulations), abolishing stand-your-ground and shall-issue laws, and increasing the minimum age required to purchase firearms.

RAND declared "moderate evidence" if even one high or low-quality publication found a 5% significant effect and at least one other paper of any type—including ones with severe methodological problems—agreed with it. On this basis it recommended firearm prohibitions for individuals subject to domestic restraining orders, dealer and purchaser background checks, and waiting periods for firearm purchases.

Finally, in the lowest category of "limited evidence," requiring only one high or low-quality study, there were recommendations for red-flag laws and prohibitions on firearms for people adjudicated mentally incompetent.

To my mind, none of this comes close to moving the needle on any of these issues. If you are inclined to believe that tighter restrictions on firearms and self-defense rules will reduce bad outcomes, you can take comfort from the fact no good studies contradict you. But the quantity and quality of threads is grossly inadequate to claim there is a woven web of guesses supporting your opinion. The strongest argument for your position remains, "Maybe if the United States had Canada's gun and self-defense laws, it would have Canada's gun violence levels."

If you are inclined to believe that restrictions on the right to self-defense increase bad outcomes, and/or are wrong in principle, you can easily laugh off the pathetic attempts to build a web from bad studies and inconclusive results.

WHY DON'T WE KNOW MORE?

The reasons that we have no good causal evidence about the effectiveness of gun control are fundamental and unlikely to be overcome in the foreseeable future. The data on gun violence are simply too imprecise, and violent events too rare, for any researcher to separate the signal from the noise, or, in other words, to determine if changes in gun violence rates have anything to do with a particular policy.

One common research approach is to compare homicide rates in a state the years before and after gun control legislation was passed. But such legislation can take months or years to be fully implemented and enforced, if ever. Most modern gun control measures only affect a minority of gun sales, and new gun sales are a small proportion of all firearms owned. Very few of the people who would be prevented from buying guns by the legislation were going to kill anyone, and many of the people who were going to kill someone would do it anyway, with another weapon or by getting a gun some other way.

Therefore, the most optimistic projection of the first-year effect of most laws on gun homicides would be a reduction of a fraction of a percent. But gun homicide rates in a state change by an average of 6% in years with no legislative changes, based on FBI Uniform Crime Reporting (UCR) data going back to 1990. As a statistician's rule of thumb, this kind of before-and-after study can only pick up effects about three times the size of the average year-to-year change, meaning that such studies can't say anything about the impact of a gun law unless it leads to an 18% change or greater in the gun murder rate in a single year. That's at least an order of magnitude larger than any likely effect of the legislation.

One way to try to get around these limitations is to use what statisticians call "controls," which are mathematical tools that allow them to compare two things that are different in many ways, and isolate just the effect they're looking for (Chapter 6 described one flawed attempt to invent a control). In this case, gun control studies often compare the violence rates in two or more states that have stricter versus more lax gun laws, and they try to control for all the differences between the states except for these policies.

Another option for researchers is to compare violence rates in a single state with national averages. The idea is that factors that change homicide rates other than the legislation will affect both state and national numbers in the same way. Comparing changes in the state rate to changes in the national rate supposedly controls for other factors that are affecting rates of violence, such as a nationwide crime wave or an overall decline in shootings.

The problem here is that national violence rates don't track well with individual states' violence rates. Based on the FBI's UCR data, annual changes within states have only about a 0.4 correlation with national rates when there is no change in legislation. That means the difference between any individual state's rate and the national rate is more volatile than the change in the state's rate on its own. The control adds noise to the study rather than filtering noise out. The same problem exists if you try to compare the state to similar or neighboring states. We just don't have good controls for state homicide rates.

To find an effect large enough to be measured, gun control researchers sometimes group together dozens or hundreds of state legislative initiatives and then look for changes in homicide rates. But states with strong gun control regulations are different from states with weaker gun control regulations: they're generally richer, more liberal, more urban, and they have lower murder and suicide rates. The cultural differences are too big and there's just too much uncertainty in the data to say anything about what would happen if we enforced Greenwich, Connecticut laws in Festus, Missouri. The problem is even larger when researchers attempt cross-country comparisons.

Researchers try to avoid the pitfalls of before-and-after studies or inter-state comparisons by using longer periods of time—say, by studying the change in gun homicide rates in the 10 years after legislation was enacted compared to the 10 years before. Now you might plausibly get an effect size large enough to be distinguished from one year's noise, but not from 20 years' noise.

GARBAGE IN, GARBAGE OUT

Another limitation on the usefulness of all gun control studies is that the underlying data are incomplete and unreliable. Estimates of the number of working firearms in the United States differ by more than a factor of two—from around 250 million to 600 million—and most uses of firearms go unreported unless someone is killed or injured. We have some information on gun sales, but only from licensed dealers, and on gun crimes, but not all crimes are reported to the police, not all police report to the FBI, many non-crimes are reported, and reported crimes often have missing or erroneous details.

Even if you could somehow assemble convincing statistical evidence that gun violence declined after the passage of gun control legislation, there are always many other things that happened around the same time that could plausibly explain the change.

The solution is more basic research on crime and violence, rather than more specific studies on gun control legislation. We don't know enough about the effect of gun control regulations on outcomes to even make usefully testable guesses, much less to start building a woven web of conjectures. In fact, it's implausible there even is a coherent stand-alone web on gun control regulation—it almost has to be part of a larger web explaining crime, violence, and law enforcement.

Better understanding can lead to precise experimentation and measurement to detect changes too small to find in aggregate statistical analyses. We need better crime and violence webs before we can make much progress on a gun control web.

SMOKING GUN

By way of comparison, take the contribution of cigarette smoking to cancer. For years, smoking was alleged to cause cancer on the basis of aggregate statistics, and the studies were deeply flawed. Eventually, however, medical researchers—not statisticians or policy analysts—figured out how cigarette smoking affected cells in the lungs, and how that developed into cancer. Certain types of cancer and other lung problems were identified that were virtually only found in smokers. With this more precise understanding, it was possible to find overwhelming statistical evidence for each link in the chain.

In terms of studies on gun violence, suppose someday psychological researchers can demonstrate empirically the effect that being abused as a child has on the probability a person will commit homicide. This more specific understanding of why violent crime occurs would allow precise, focused studies on the effect of gun control legislation. Instead of comparing large populations of diverse individuals with low homicide rates, researchers could focus on specific groups with high propensities for lethal violence.

Only when we know much more about why people kill themselves and each other, and how the presence or absence of guns affects rape, assault, robbery, and other crimes, can we hope to tease out the effect of gun control measures.

It's not just gun control. Nearly all similar research into the effects of specific legislation suffers from the same sort of problem: too much complexity for the available data. Political partisans yearn for statistical backing for their views, but scientists can't deliver it. Yet researchers flood to favored fields because there is plenty of funding and interest in results, and they peer review each other's papers without applying the sort of rigor required to draw actual policy conclusions.

RACE TO THE BOTTOM

Tellingly, the studies that have gotten the most media or legislative attention aren't among the 182 that met RAND's approval, nor the 12 with high-quality results. The best studies made claims that were too mild, tenuous, and qualified to satisfy partisans and sensationalist media outlets. It was the worst studies, with the most outrageous claims, that made headlines.

We already mentioned one prominent study in Chapter 6, which was touted from the debate stage by Senator Cory Booker (D–N.J.) when he was running for president in the 2016 election. It made the astounding claim that a permit requirement for handgun purchases in Connecticut reduced their gun murder rate by 40%.

This study is typical of the field: strong claims based on complex models and uncertain data. Worse, researchers often cherry pick outcome measures, time periods, and locations to get their preferred results.

For example, take the studies that look at whether bans on assault-style weapons and large-capacity magazines, which are often passed together, have reduced the frequency or deadliness of mass shootings. Researchers define basic terms like "assault weapons" and "mass shootings" differently. They limit their data by time, place, or other factors, such as classifying an event as an act of terror or gang violence, and therefore not considering it a mass shooting.

These studies suffer from even greater data issues than other gun violence research. Mass shootings are extremely rare relative to other forms of gun violence, and most of them don't involve assault weapons. Though estimates vary depending on the definitions used, mass shootings involving assault weapons constitute a small fraction of 1% of all gun homicides.

The US federal ban on assault weapons and large-capacity magazines, which was the subject of numerous studies that reached widely varying and often contradictory conclusions about its efficacy, was in place for 10 years, from 1994 to 2004. Before, during, and after the time the law was in effect, many societal factors caused crime rates to vary widely, making it impossible to draw useful conclusions about the effect of the ban on anything, and in particular on something as rare as mass shootings. But with all the noise in the data, it is easy for researchers to find weak results that support any conclusion they hope to reach.

Moreover, states and countries with bans define assault weapons and other key elements of laws differently. Combined with the data problems inherent in comparing different populations of people over different periods of time, comparisons between states and countries are almost meaningless.

THE WISDOM OF CROWDS

Maybe the problem is we're asking the wrong question. Maybe it's possible to extract some information from gun control studies even if they don't weave a strong web of conjecture.

The problem is analogous to trying to decide if a runner set a world record in the 100-meter sprint—where top times are hundredths of a second apart—using a handheld stopwatch accurate only to the second. The median gun control error range for gun control hypotheses—excluding the large majority with critical flaws—was 24%. For example, if it found waiting periods for gun purchases reduced gun suicides by 14%, any result from an increase of 10% to a decline of 38% was plausible.

That's not useful information. From general principles it seems unlikely a waiting period for gun purchases would increase gun suicides, but it's also hard to credit a first-year reduction more than perhaps 1%. So, we know a lot more from common sense than we can learn from the study.

However, there is another approach. From 1964, when Bob Hayes set a record of 10.06 seconds, to 2009, when Usain Bolt set the current record of 9.58 seconds, there have been 23 new records, an average improvement of 0.02 seconds. A stopwatch accurate to the second might give the correct answer—whether or not a new world record was set—52% of the time. But if we have 1,001 (an odd number to avoid ties) independent monitors with stop watches, we can get the correct majority verdict 90% of the time.

The sensible justification for gun control is not that any one law has a measurable—given the available data quality and sample sizes—effect on any one outcome over short periods of time. Rather, it's that the combination of many such measures over a generation or two will change the gun culture so many fewer civilians want guns and there are strong social pressures on the others not to own, sell, or carry guns. This is what happened to tobacco smoking from a combination of science, regulation, taxes, public service campaigns, and cultural shifts.

Of the 1,081 hypotheses tested by studies labeled "high quality" by RAND, 703, or 65%, went in the pro-control direction. That means a restriction on guns that led to a decline in a bad outcome or an increase in a good outcome, or a law making self-defense easier to claim that led to an increase in a bad outcome or a decrease in a good outcome. If hypotheses were independent and unbiased, this would be overwhelming statistical evidence that the pro-control position was more often correct than the anti-control position.

Unfortunately, the results are certainly not independent. They were made in only 12 studies, using only two data sources. Many were quite similar, like testing the effects of two different types of child access prevention rules on gun accidents involving minors, or the effect of a magazine limit on both gun homicides and all homicides. Moreover, given how much of the gun research is financed by partisans, it's hard to be confident the results are unbiased.

Nevertheless, in principle we could apply this idea more carefully, looking at correlations among results and classifying for bias, in order to arrive at a firm opinion—not about whether one specific regulation affected one specific outcome—but about whether the general strategy of discouraging gun ownership and use was collectively moving society in a good direction.

There is a big problem with this in practice. This is something we see in many research areas, not just gun control. The most precise studies—the ones with the biggest sample sizes, best data, and most careful analyses—give systematically different results than the less precise studies. Only 7 of the 20 most precise gun control studies favor the gun control position, which would make us 87% confident in the anti-gun control position. Some 32 of the 65 studies that claim error margins of 5% or less favor gun control, providing no statistical support for either position. The statistical evidence for the pro-gun control position comes entirely from the studies with the least precision. Chapter 9 will go into the reasons for this, and why it is a problem that afflicts many fields.

Short of legitimate scientific evidence, belief in the efficacy of additional gun control laws is, and will remain, a matter of faith, not reason. Anyone basing a gun control position on scientific evidence of any kind is building on sand. We have no useful empirical data on the subject, no body of work that rises above the level we would expect based on random chance, either for or against gun control measures. And the claim that there are "simple, commonsense" laws we could pass that we can be confident would significantly reduce gun violence, if only we had the political will to go through with them, is simply false.

NO PAIN, NO GAIN

For all the problems of gun control research, at least guns are loud and murders leave bodies to find. Next we'll take a look at Wrong Numbers involving pain, something without much external evidence.

CHAPTER EIGHT

THE WAR TO MAKE THE WORLD SAFE FOR PAIN

About a quarter-century ago, public health officials began to notice increases in what would later be called "deaths of despair": suicides, deaths from alcoholism, and drug overdoses. The problem traced back to the early 1970s and is not well understood.

DEATHS OF DESPAIR

The phrase "deaths of despair," coined by Princeton economists Anne Case and Angus Deaton, is woefully imprecise: different types of deaths often get muddled statistically and even definitionally. Is increasing mental illness a cause of the deaths, or another symptom of the same social pressures, or an unrelated problem? Who can determine the intentions of drug and alcohol abusers to distinguish accidental deaths from suicides? Who knows if social pressures, mental issues, or the substances involved were the ultimate cause of death? Moreover, many deaths officially ruled as accidental are likely either deliberate suicides or resulted in part from a lowered will to live.

Nevertheless, imprecise and misunderstood as it is, the phenomenon is one of the major social issues facing the United States. It's also a motherlode of material to justify policies including banning guns or pornography, restricting social media use by teenagers, providing more gender-affirming care, replacing armed police officers with unarmed social workers, among many others.

Public health officials and legislators have often blamed drugs for the deaths of despair. Around 2010, as a result of a dramatic increase in opioid overdoses in the prior decade, the problem was renamed the "opioid crisis." A concerted effort began to limit opioid prescriptions for non-cancer chronic pain. The tactics included violent raids and criminal charges against doctors deemed to overprescribe pain relief. Opioid prescriptions for non-cancer chronic pain fell dramatically.

The war on pain drugs turned out to be a colossal failure. So-called deaths of despair rose even faster, and millions of Americans with chronic pain have had trouble obtaining prescriptions that would ease their suffering because doctors feared losing their medical licenses. Meanwhile, the government expanded failed policies, citing deeply flawed statistical studies and misrepresenting data.

The crackdown coincided with—and perhaps caused—a rapid growth in heroin overdose deaths, and later, an explosion in illegal synthetic opioid deaths, primarily fentanyl, an illicitly manufactured substance added to or substituted for heroin to meet the increasing demand for illegal opiates. Fentanyl is cheaper than heroin and more potent, making it easier to smuggle.

Overdose deaths from commonly prescribed opiates increased rapidly from 1999 to 2010, but we lack data on how many of the victims obtained the opiates legally. Drug overdose deaths have been increasing at a fairly steady rate since 1979, with no obvious changes associated with the rise and fall of opioid prescriptions for chronic pain. Overdose death rates from commonly prescribed opiates did not decline much after 2010, although legal prescriptions went down dramatically. This suggests that these deaths may have involved individuals who bought illegally manufactured opiates, or that the people who lost pain medication as a result of official actions were not the ones liable to overdose.

The increase in deaths of despair obviously merits some policy attention, but labeling it an "opioid crisis," as is common nowadays, profoundly misstates its nature, timing, and likely causes and solutions. Restricting opioids for non-cancer chronic pain patients should require specific evidence that people prescribed opioids for pain are the ones dying of overdoses. There's quite a bit of negative evidence on this score, but public health officials have seized on a few positive studies to support their claims.

THE VHA STUDY

One influential and heavily cited 2011 study published in the *Journal of the American Medical Association*, "Association Between Opioid Prescribing Patterns and Opioid Overdose-Related Deaths," uses a classic prohibitionist tactic. The authors use a sample of 750 Veterans Health Administration (VHA) patients who received opioid prescriptions for pain and later died of opioid overdoses, and compared them to a random sample of 155,000 other VHA patients who received opioid prescriptions and did not die of overdoses.

Since all subjects in the study were prescribed opiates for pain, this analysis can't tell you anything about whether those prescriptions are associated statistically with an increased risk of overdose death. Determining that connection would require comparing patients with similar pain diagnoses and matching them for factors such as age, sex, and prior substance abuse. But doing so might not be very informative anyway. Forty percent of the patients who died of overdose had been diagnosed with substance abuse disorders in the 12 months before getting an opiate prescription. Sixty-six percent of them had been diagnosed with some psychiatric disorder. These individuals were more likely to die from overdose or suicide than other patients in the sample. If someone is at risk of overdosing or committing suicide and has opiates, they are more likely to use them than someone without opiates. It's plausible that many opioid overdose deaths are substitutes for other methods of overdosing or suicide.

The authors did find that patients who were prescribed larger amounts of opiates were more likely to die of overdoses than patients with lower doses. This discovery was used to support Centers for Disease Control and Prevention (CDC) guidelines strongly discouraging larger doses. However, the evidence should be interpreted cautiously since the study does not use any controls: the patients prescribed higher doses presumably were in more pain than lower-dose patients, and may well have differed in other ways, such as type of pain or the length of time they had suffered from it. Controls matched as closely as possible to subjects are a basic requirement of good science.

The study has an even more fundamental gap in its analysis: it did not account for quality of life increases in the 99.96% of opioid patients who did not overdose, nor the bad things that might have happened to the many patients with chronic pain who were denied opioid prescriptions, or given doses too small to control the pain.

THE COHORT STUDY

Another influential study was "Opioid Prescriptions for Chronic Pain and Overdose: A Cohort Study," which was published in the *Annals of Internal Medicine*. Almost comically, it had nine authors but only six patients who died of opiate overdoses—a sample size too small to reach any broad conclusions. The study was funded by the National Institute on Drug Abuse (another comic note is the article mislabels its sponsor as the National Institute of Drug Abuse, suggesting it is made up of junkies rather than researchers). While sponsors do not dictate methods or results, patient treatment issues should be the province of health researchers (like the Veterans Affairs Health Service Research department that funded the previous study), not people focused on fighting drug abuse.

The article begins by rejecting prior work in the field: "The association between prescription opioid exposure and overdose risk has been inferred from uncontrolled case series of autopsies subject to selection bias or from ecological time series studies in which individual-level associations cannot be examined." It criticizes studies like the prior one, which fails to use controls, and flawed statistical analyses, like the CDC's claim that if opioid prescriptions and opioid overdose deaths are simultaneously rising, the prescriptions must be causing the deaths.

Despite the small sample size, the authors claim statistically significant results after adjusting for smoking, depression, substance abuse, comorbid conditions, pain site, age, sex, recent sedative–hypnotic prescription, and recent initiation of opioid use. This is logically impossible. There are not even enough observations to estimate the adjustments, much less make any conclusions with statistical confidence. In any event, the authors conclude that whether their results "were due to patient differences or direct effects of higher doses was not established."

STRONG WORDS BASED ON WEAK STUDIES

These studies continued to be cited by public health officials and policymakers long after better ones using more data became available. For example, the 2017 President's Commission on Combating Drug Addiction and the Opioid Crisis relied on studies published before 2014—usually with data collected before 2011—to claim that opioids prescribed for chronic pain led to abuse. The reason is simple: as the war on opiate prescriptions for non-cancer chronic pain caused prescriptions to decline 60%, the number of deaths from opiate overdoses—and also deaths of despair in general—continued to grow. Moreover, careful, controlled research showed clearly that medically supervised opiate pain management was both safe and effective. The prescription-opioids-caused-the-crisis narrative can only be sustained by relying on old studies.

The cockeyed logic of the President's Commission is illustrated by its section "Pathways to Opioid Use Disorder (Including Heroin) from Prescription," which references a 2017 article, "Psychoactive Substance Use Prior to the Development of Iatrogenic Opioid Abuse: A Descriptive Analysis of Treatment-Seeking Opioid Abusers," that studied people who had sought treatment for opioid abuse. The study's main conclusion was that "Only 4% of those who experienced their first opioid via a physician's prescription were truly drug-naive. Rather, more than 95% had significant psychoactive drug experience prior to being prescribed their first opioid." In other words, people who were prescribed opiates and later sought treatment for abuse had almost always begun taking drugs before their prescriptions.

Instead of interpreting the study as evidence that prescription opioids are not the source of drug abuse, the President's Commission claimed that the study "highlights the need for clinicians to screen patients for prior drug use histories." The commission would refuse opiates for pain relief to people who have used drugs in the past. To draw such a conclusion would require an entirely different study—one that compares drug-using patients with non-cancer chronic pain who were prescribed opiates versus those who were not prescribed opiates.

The only article cited that supports any claim that opioid prescriptions led to opioid deaths was the 2012 article "Opioid Epidemic in the

United States," which summarizes the results of a 2010 drug survey in overheated blustering language.

The underlying argument was that the simultaneous rise in opioid prescriptions, opioid treatment admissions, and opioid deaths must have been caused by opioid prescriptions. Of course, this pattern rapidly reversed when opioid prescriptions fell dramatically and the other two measures continued to increase, but that didn't stop officials from citing it.

Even back in 2009, before the reversal, this data did not support the contention. It only indicates that the three things are correlated, but does not demonstrate causation. Moreover, it only shows that the three things increase in time—lots of things increase in time without any causal interaction: world population, consumer prices, my age, etc.

Although there are still many things we don't know about pain management and drug abuse, we do know that long-term pain management is possible with opiates and that the benefits are extraordinary for people suffering from non-cancer chronic pain, without unacceptable levels of addiction and abuse. Opiate overdose deaths are very infrequent among people given prescription opiates who have no prior history of drug abuse or psychological problems. The rise in opiate overdose deaths seems to be part of a general deaths-of-despair pattern that began at least a decade before increases in opioid prescriptions for pain management and has not been affected by the decline in those prescriptions.

SMILE AND THE WORLD SMILES WITH YOU

Time to return to geekier topics like p-values, power, and priors.

CHAPTER NINE

SMILES MAKE YOU LIVE LONGER?

In 2012, a leading academic researcher named Diederik Stapel published his autobiography, shockingly titled (in English translation) *Faking Science*. He described an entire academic career of making up data. Unsurprisingly, much of the book was plagiarized from novelists James Joyce and Raymond Carver. Why do plagiarism and Wrong Numbers so often seem to go together? I'll discuss that in the next chapter about honesty.

HOW TO SUCCEED IN ACADEMIA WITHOUT REALLY TRYING

Stapel's prominence had been enhanced by click-bait conclusions that got widespread media coverage, such as that carnivores are more selfish than vegetarians, or that disordered environments (specifically a train station under construction) promote discriminatory behavior. He had a flair for arresting titles like "Hot cognition," "What's on our mind and how did it get there?" and "Coping with chaos."

The penalty for over a decade of misapplied research funds and fraudulent publications? Just 120 hours of community service, less than he would have spent actually doing even one of his imagined studies.

Wrong Number is not about this type of wholesale deliberate fraud. The point I want to make about Stapel is he relied on no one really believing or caring about his work. If other researchers had believed his sensational conclusions were relevant to public policy, they would have tried to build on his work and discovered its errors. If they cared about the issues, they would have tried to replicate his studies and failed.

Many other prominent researchers have been caught making up data, although Stapel is the only one to date who boasted so publicly. In nearly all cases the fraudsters were identified by either junior people in the field, or more commonly, people outside the field who specialize in hunting for the most obvious frauds. Journal editors, peer reviewers, academic superiors, granting agencies, and university administrators—the people who claim responsibility for quality control—have pretty much abdicated their duties. That's true even when the frauds are so clear that non-specialists can find them with little trouble. I have little doubt that there are many more clever fakers than the few clumsy and one belatedly honest one that have been exposed.

SCIENCE VERSUS BUSINESS

Think about the accounting statements that public companies publish. They are based on books and records kept in controlled environments with an audit trail. That means every entry and change has a record of who made it, when, and why. Entries have a maker to input the data, and a checker to see that it was done correctly. There are rigorous internal audit reviews, and a strong financial control function to vet the data. An independent external auditor reviews the books, and the CFO and CEO have to personally attest to the numbers. Penalties for violations are harsh—gigantic fines and prison terms. Experienced Wall Street analysts pour over the numbers, tear them apart, and grill executives about them. Well-staffed government agencies investigate and prosecute even minor errors. Yet accounting fraud in public companies is still common.

Compare that to academic fraud. Here is where Stapel's confession is so valuable: he gives us a complete account of his method. He came up with an idea and had weeks of meetings with colleagues and students to refine it. His train station was under construction, so he hit on the idea of giving a questionnaire to people waiting for trains, before and after the construction. He thought that the obstacles, noise, and dirt of construction might change how strongly people held negative stereotypes about other groups.

After the weeks of consultations, he had a bunch of questionnaires printed up. Instead of going with his students to the train station to hand them out, he dumped them in the trash. Then he locked his office door and typed the results he wanted into his laptop. No controlled environment, no audit trail, no maker/checker, no internal or external audit, no controller, no significant penalty for fraud, and no active investigators. A few weeks later he submitted a paper based on his fictional data to a journal.

Unless you think all academics have extraordinary personal honesty, you have to expect that a system run entirely on trust will admit a lot of fraud, at least as much as we find in accounting numbers.

p-VALUES IN FACT

At least Stapel wrote his own papers—and wrote them well, hence his success. Many other researchers use paper mills to buy papers written by others or, more often these days, stitched together from other work by AI algorithms. These papers are fraudulent in both data and analysis.

These and other problems—including the ones I highlight in this book—have resulted in a powerful, slow-rolling scandal in science that has been named the "replication crisis": the observation that a high proportion of published results turn out to be false. One of the major non-fraudulent causes is the practice of journal editors selecting articles by p-value.

In common understanding, a p-value is the probability that the observations in the paper would be obtained if the claimed result were false.

For example, suppose someone claims to be able to predict whether the stock market will go up or down tomorrow. We test her over 100 days. Stocks go up on 60 of the days, and she predicts "up" on 65 days. If she's guessing randomly, 60% of her 65 "up" predictions, 39 predictions, will be correct. But there's a 59% chance she would get 39 or more hits by random guessing, so that won't count as much evidence in her favor.

If she is guessing randomly, there is a 6.7% chance of getting 43 or more hits, and a 2.7% chance of getting 44 or more hits. Here, 6.7% and 2.7% are p-values, the probability of getting the result if she is guessing randomly. By convention in most fields, we demand a p-value of 5% or smaller to regard the results as significant.

If she had 43 hits, we'd say the data showed "no evidence for prediction skill at the 5% level" because the p-value was 6.7%, greater than 5%. If she had 44 hits, we'd say "we can reject the null hypothesis of random guessing at the 5% level."

p-VALUES AS TAUGHT AND THE FOUR Ps

In "Failing Grade: 89% of Introduction-to-Psychology Textbooks That Define or Explain Statistical Significance Do So Incorrectly," psychologist Scott Cassidy and co-authors looked at the definition of p-value in 30 of the most popular introductory psychology textbooks. The most common error by far was to describe it as the probability the result is due to chance. Other studies based on textbooks and polls of professional researchers get similar results.

Okay, I see the student in the back everyone thought was asleep waving her hand and saying, "GRIM test violation!" You can have bad definitions in 27 of 30 textbooks for exactly 90%, or 26 of 30 for rounded 87%, but not 89%.

Yes, thank you. I'm glad someone is paying attention.

However, reading carefully, Cassidy's title refers only to the textbooks that define statistical significance. Two of the 30 did not, 25 of the remaining 28 had bad definitions, which rounds to 89%.

We need some basic statistics 101 definitions here. They're simple, but they confuse many students. In classical statistics reasoning, data cannot prove anything, they can only disprove—or more precisely, show to be extremely unlikely—hypotheses. So, if you want to show something you create a "null hypothesis" of its opposite, and try to disprove that. If you want to prove that taking vitamin C reduces the number and severity of colds, you form the null hypothesis that vitamin C either has no effect on colds or increases number and severity, and try to disprove that. The p-value is the probability of getting your data assuming the null hypothesis is true. It's tempting to argue that if the p-value is small, the null hypothesis is probably false, and so the hypothesis you started with—that vitamin C helps for colds—is probably true.

To see the error of calling the p-value the probability that the claimed result is true, that is, the null hypothesis is false—suppose you go into a casino and bet $1 on number 19 in two-zero roulette. Under the null hypothesis that all 38 slots on the wheel are equally likely, you have one chance in 38, 2.6% probability, of winning. If you win, would you say there was only a 2.6% chance that the null hypothesis is true and the roulette spin was random? That there is a 97.4% chance that you won by skill?

Or consider NBA star Stephen Curry who has hit 91.1% of his free-throw attempts over his NBA career, never less than 80% in a season. If your null hypothesis is that his free-throw percentage is 80% or higher, seeing him miss two free throws in a row has 4% probability or less, so you could reject the null hypothesis at the 5% level. Would you really say, based on observing only two misses, that there is a 4% or less chance that his free-throw percentage is 80% or better?

The point is that the probability of getting your results assuming your null hypothesis is true (the p-value) is an entirely different number than the probability the null hypothesis is true, given your results. The probability the result is due to chance is what we want to know, but not what the p-value tells us. We need four Ps: P-values, Prior Probability, and Power, to answer the meaningful question.

To illustrate prior probability, suppose we run the *Journal of Predicting Tomorrow's Stock Market Direction* (JPTSMD). We get one true result submitted by serious researchers per month. But 1,000 charlatans and nuts try 10 experiments per day, 5% of which generate p-values below 5%. So, we get 500 false results per day, around 15,000 per month with only one true result. Over 99.99% of our published results are due to chance.

To combat this, we introduce filtering criteria to exclude most of the charlatans and nuts. Now we get only one false submission per day, and one per month has a p-value below 5%. We also get one legitimate submission per month. Does this mean 50% of our published articles will be true? No, because we also have to consider the power of the test, the chance of the legitimate submission getting a p-value under 5% assuming the result is true.

To calculate the effect of power, we need to know something about the size of true results we expect. Suppose for JPTSMD we think the stock market is pretty random, hard to predict, so valid systems will have about 5% more hits than expected. In the case of the example above, with 39 hits expected by random chance, that means we think a valid system will average about 41 hits. However, since we require 44 hits for a p-value below 5%, 75% of true results will fail the significance test—that is, even if a system averages 41 hits it will fail to get a p-value under 5%, 75% of the time. So, we will reject 9 of the 12 submitted true results in a year for failing to be significant at the 5% level, while accepting all 12 false results. Only 20% of our published results will be true.

EVERYBODY KNOWS

Everybody knows that the boat is leaking
Everybody knows that the captain lied
Everybody's got this broken feeling
Like their father or their dog just died

—Leonard Cohen

The four Ps are well known among researchers and journal editors, and not seriously disputed by anyone. Nevertheless, by emphasizing p-values only, most journals have consciously adopted procedures that lead to most of their published results being false. Moreover, by omitting prior probability and power from most papers, researchers and journals are concealing the information rational readers require to evaluate the credibility of the results.

P-values are related to the confidence intervals we discuss in Chapter 11. Suppose we are estimating the proportion of laid-off workers who will find a new job within eight weeks. We get a 95% confidence interval between 50% and 80%. That means we can reject the hypothesis at the 5% (one minus the confidence) level that the true value is under 50% or over 80%, that is, outside the 95% confidence interval. But we cannot reject at the 5% level the hypothesis that the true value is anything between 50% and 80%. There are different ways to define confidence intervals that can make this claim only approximately true most of the time, but this is the general idea.

p-Values share all the problems of confidence intervals, plus one additional issue. A confidence interval tells you the full range of hypotheses that can be rejected—all values outside the interval. A p-value tells you only about one specific hypothesis, usually one that is obviously false and thus easy to refute—such as that your treatment has absolutely no effect on anything and all your variables have independent Gaussian ("normal") distributions.

A SMILE A DAY KEEPS THE DOCTOR AWAY

Let's look at "Smile Intensity in Photographs Predicts Longevity" in *Psychological Science*, a top 10% journal and the flagship publication of the Association for Psychological Sciences. The paper claimed, among other things, that professional baseball players who had full smiles in their *Baseball Register* photographs lived longer than players with ordinary smiles.

The authors did a complex analysis but we can get a similar result simply. Full smilers lived to an average of 79.9 years with a standard deviation of 11.6 years; ordinary smilers died at 75.0 years on average with a standard deviation of 13.2. If both groups actually had the same life expectancy, there's only a 4.7% probability that the observed deviation would be as large or larger than it was, 4.9 years.

This 4.7% is the p-value. Since it's less than 5%, the result is considered "statistically significant at the 5% level." That was enough to get the paper published. But what about the other Ps?

The big-smilers-live-longer hypothesis seems very far-fetched. How people pose for photographs seems to have little connection to their mental state or personality, which in turn likely have a marginal effect on life expectancy. I'd assign something like a 1% chance that you can make significant predictions of lifespans from photographs of young people's smiles. Feel free to substitute your own guess here.

Next, if the hypothesis is true, how much extra life is plausible? I think a very small amount, probably less than 0.1 years. If so, there is only a 5.1% chance that if the hypothesis is true, a sample of the size used in the paper would get a p-value below 5%.

If someone tests 2,000 hypotheses, only 1% of which are true, at the 5% significance level and 5.1% power, you expect the 20 true hypotheses to yield one significant result to be published, and the 1,980 false hypotheses to yield 99 wrong publications. So 99% of published results are false.

Perhaps you are more inclined to take the hypothesis seriously than I am. Perhaps you believe that there was a 20% chance that big smilers lived a full year longer than small smilers. You expect 1,600 of the 2,000 hypotheses to be false, so 80 will get p-values below 5% by chance. Then 5.7% of the true hypotheses will get p-values below 5% (since there are 400 of them, that is 23). You still have 78% false results.

All of this assumes there are no other problems with the paper—no fraud, no data errors, no wrong assumptions, no excluded data, no tricks to make the results publishable. These are the kinds of accuracy ratios the journals are trying to deliver when everything goes right.

THE VALUE OF SURPRISE AND THE SPIRAL OF POWER

Journals exaggerate the problem because they demand surprising results—and these are the ones played up by the media and partisans. Researchers are encouraged to test hypotheses that are likely false, because getting a significant result that is expected is harder to publish.

Researchers are also encouraged to do low-power tests, which also increases the fraction of false results that get published. One reason is power is expensive—it generally means larger samples and more careful measurements. The smiles-make-you-live-longer claim used 87 players to get a power of 5.1%. If the authors had used four times the sample size—348 players—they would expect to double their power to a 10.2% chance of a publishable result if their hypothesis were true. But they would cut in half to 2.35% their chance of getting a publishable result if their hypothesis was false. Since their hypothesis was probably false, that means net less chance of getting a publishable result. But even if that weren't true, even if the increased power increased their chance of a publishable result, doing four low-power studies for the same time and money would pay off in more publishable results.

A related problem of low-power tests is they can only find large results. That means if multiple studies test similar hypotheses, the ones that underestimate the size of the effect are likely to get non-significant results, which are rarely published, while the ones that overestimate the size of the effect report significant results and get published. So even the published results that are not wrong are biased to overestimate the size of their effects.

This leads to a pernicious spiral. Early experiments on a topic tend to be low-power because people do not invest large amounts of time, effort, and money in novel hypotheses. In fact, wise researchers begin with small "pilot" studies, both to test their intended procedures and to get some idea of likely effect sizes. These should never be published, but if the results are spectacular enough, they often are.

In any event, since the only early studies that get published are the ones with very large effect sizes, other researchers design their studies to look for large effects. That means they don't think they need larger sample sizes or better data. In many fields, it can be hard to publish a study that supports a previous study but finds a smaller effect. Therefore, the only new results that get published show even larger effect sizes.

LOSING POWER

A small sample size is not the only way to get a low-power test. Doing sloppy work also reduces both power and the effort necessary for a study. One popular technique is to use a huge sample size—generally a database generated by someone else and available on-line—with low-quality data for your purposes. This is what we already saw in the "marijuana causes heart trouble" paper and will see in the "vaping is worse than smoking" paper ahead.

Clearly, journals should publish not the p-value, which has no meaning on its own, but the proportion of its published claims it expects are false, based on p-value, power, and prior probability. I hope most journals would be embarrassed to claim a goal of 20% or 50% correct results, and so would have to revamp their procedures to at least try for an accuracy around 90% or 95%.

You might recognize the 4P computation as a "Bayesian" view, as opposed to the standard "frequentist" or "classical" view. But that's misleading. Every statistician of whatever school accepts the computation done here, even though it has a Bayesian flavor. The academic world does not have to convert to Bayesianism to make this simple correction to the headline number used to select publications and report results.

The smiling-baseball-players paper is both inconsequential and silly. I chose it because it demonstrates the issues simply and dramatically, not because it did any great harm or wasted much time or money. Over the last 20 years there have been systematic studies of publications in many fields. Findings that 50% of published research findings fail to replicate—and even the ones that do replicate are found to overstate their effect sizes by an average of 100%—are not out of line with this general literature. These studies generally focus on top journals and heavily cited papers. We'd expect worse results lower down the academic pecking order. Of course, some fields and types of research are better and some are worse, but no one can deny it is a massive problem for academic research in general.

An important point is that it is possible to do good work under a p-value standard. Good researchers can pick hypotheses that are both likely to be true and surprising or valuable if verified. They don't have to wander far out into left field to find silly click-bait things to test. They can do rigorous, careful, properly organized work to increase power. They can demand more rigorous (lower) significance levels for unlikely hypotheses—extraordinary claims require extraordinary evidence. They can insist on tests with high power.

While many researchers work to this standard, it requires talent, energy, time, and, in many cases, money. Few academics can satisfy publish-or-perish university requirements or collect enough grant money to support their graduate students and themselves relying only on high-quality research. So even most good researchers have to resort to some low-quality work, and many academics are incapable of anything but low-quality work.

THIS IS YOUR STUDY ON DRUGS

"Predictors of Sustained Prescription Opioid Use After Admission for Trauma in Adolescents," in the *Journal of Adolescent Health*, is another good example. It was cited by the National Institutes of Health as evidence that marijuana is a gateway drug to opioid abuse, and also by the Centers for Disease Control and Prevention.

The study followed 120 patients aged 15 to 18 who were prescribed opioids following accidental trauma at one medical center for a year. Forty-three of the teens reported having used marijuana within the year prior to admission (the data were from 2008 to 2009, when marijuana was illegal in Washington state where the study took place). Eight of the participants reported using opioids in the prior year. One year later, 15 of the 120 were taking opioids. Eight of the 43 marijuana users were taking opioids, twice the rate of the marijuana non-users.

The biggest objection to using this study to argue for criminalizing marijuana to fight opioid abuse is correlation does not imply causation. Perhaps the kind of kid who smokes marijuana is more likely to also indulge in opioids, but that doesn't mean punishing his marijuana use will discourage later opioid use. It could be even more likely that the kind of kid who admits to marijuana use is more likely to admit to opioid use. Also, the study did not distinguish between legitimate medicinal use for pain relief—remember, all these teens were at least initially prescribed opioids for pain management—from dangerous opioid abuse.

Let's forget all that and just consider the likelihood the result is correct—that a kid who admits to marijuana use today is more likely to admit to opioid use a year later. If confessing to prior marijuana use were unrelated to confessing to continued opioid use, there's an 11% chance that eight or more of the admitted opioid users would have been previous admitted marijuana uses. That's the p-value. It's above 5%, but that's not the only problem.

While at first glance the hypothesis—that admitting to marijuana today makes it more likely a teen will admit to opioids a year from now—may seem plausible, recall that marijuana use was illegal and impossible for doctors to check, while opioid use was legal and could be checked by clinic records. Marijuana use might have been hidden from parents, but opioid prescriptions could not be. My guess is teens suspicious of authority or who hid their marijuana use from their parents would be inclined to deny marijuana use but cop to opioids. Trusting teens and ones whose parents knew of the marijuana use would be more likely to tell the truth in both cases. So, I find the results mildly surprising. I'd call it about a 20% chance the hypothesis is true.

If kids who admit marijuana use are twice as likely to admit opioid use, there's a 22% chance that the experiment as described would have had a statistically significant result. So, out of 1,000 studies—200 of true hypotheses and 800 of false—22% of the 200, or 44, would find statistical significance and 11% of the 800, or 88, of the false hypotheses would be confirmed. So, one-third of the published results would be right.

BIG-BOX VERSUS MOM-AND-POP

My final example is "Minimum Wage Employment Effects and Labor Market Concentration," published by the National Bureau of Economic Research. This was highlighted in a glowing press release by the University of Pennsylvania with the dramatic headline "Increasing minimum wage has positive effects on employment" that was copied by news media accounts and has become received wisdom of many people who support higher minimum wages.

This study was complicated. The authors divided the counties in the United States into those in which on-line job postings for stock clerks, order fillers, retail salespersons, and cashiers were dominated by a few big employers versus those with more diverse companies posting these openings on-line. For convenience, I'll call the former Big-Box counties and the latter Mom-and-Pop counties, although that's not precisely what the authors are measuring.

The authors measured employment numbers in the general merchandise store sector relative to overall county employment, adjusted for six factors such as county population and average wages. In the Big-Box counties, a 10% higher minimum wage was associated with 1.12% smaller job losses among store clerks in the general merchandise store sector than overall county jobs. In Mom-and-Pop counties, a 10% higher minimum wage was associated with 1.79% larger job losses among store clerks relative to overall county jobs.

Why would anyone care about this result? If correlation proved causation, it would suggest that raising the minimum wage in Big-Box counties hurts overall employment more than general merchandise store employees, while raising the minimum wage in Mom-and-Pop counties hurts general merchandise store employees more than other workers.

This is obviously unrelated to the headline claims made about the study, and not very interesting (except perhaps to micro labor market specialists). An obvious explanation is in Big-Box counties, store clerks are not the lowest-wage employees—Walmart pays its entry-level employees more than most small retail stores—so they are not as affected by minimum wage increases as, say, fast-food workers or hotel maids, but in Mom-and-Pop counties, many store clerks earn minimum wage.

But let's pretend that we care about whether more store clerks or burger flippers get laid off when the minimum wage increases. The authors report a very low (i.e., highly significant) p-value, 0.000001, on the null hypothesis that Big-Box and Mom-and-Pop counties are the same in this respect. But that's not the result they emphasize. They don't bother to report even a range on the p-value for the null hypothesis that store clerks lose fewer jobs than the county average in Big-Box counties. I estimate 0.02, or a 2% chance, that they could have achieved their result if store clerks in Big-Box counties lost jobs at the country average rate.

I consider this a pretty unlikely result. Store clerks are not particularly well paid, even at Big-Box stores. While I would expect their job losses to be less than the lowest-paid occupations, I'd expect them to be higher than the county average, which includes mostly people earning well above minimum wages. Having big national employers would likely insulate the employees somewhat from the increase, so I'm not surprised about that finding—but it seems unlikely to insulate them to the point that they actually lose fewer jobs than the country average. Having a bigger parachute will slow your descent from an airplane, but no matter how big you make the parachute, it's not going to take you back up. So, I'm going to give this finding a 5% probability.

What is the probability of getting a 5% significant result if minimum wage increases in Big-Box counties actually spare store clerks more than average county employees? I estimate that there's a 16% chance a study of this design would find a statistically significant result.

So, out of 4,000 studies—200 of true hypotheses and 3,800 of false ones—16% of the 200, or 32, will provide true significant results and 1.5% of the 3,800, or 57, will provide false significant results. So, the chance this study's claim is correct is 36%.

YOUR MILEAGE MAY DIFFER

I don't want you to take any of the numbers I've given as precise values. All the studies reported multiple p-values for multiple statistics, and I used rough guesses for prior probability, and had to make some assumptions to estimate power. You might well come up with different numbers in all the cases. You might even decide that some of these studies are more likely to be true than false, although I'm confident no sensible person would conclude that they are as much as 80% or more likely to be true. Also, all these studies were deeply flawed for reasons other than misleading p-values.

These are by no means the worst studies you will find. All were by serious, credentialed researchers and have been given weight in both academic and policy debates. They are poster children for the claim that most published research findings are wrong.

My point in this chapter is not the many errors of data, analysis, and presentation that pollute most published research—it's the fact that researchers and editors don't even try to publish stuff that's more likely true than false. Papers typically report p-values without any mention of prior likelihood or power, and therefore no simple way for readers to estimate the probability that the claimed result is correct. Apologists sometimes pretend that the p-value is that probability, which as you can see from the examples above, is very far from true.

Fixing this would not require overturning the classic hypothesis testing/5% p-value convention in many fields. It only requires reporting the researchers' and journals' minimum threshold for the fraction of true results. If someone claims less than one chance in 20 the result is incorrect, they can't just point to a p-value under 5%, they need to adjust for prior probability and power.

A WINNING SCRIPT

Since researchers and journals will not be quick to do this, journalists should learn to ask the questions themselves, and to avoid reporting on work that refuses to divulge the information. This is especially true when researchers claim an unexpected result has been solidly established.

Let's see how this might play out in the following dialog between a university press officer (UPO) and a reporter (R).

> UPO: Our crack team of researchers has just published a paper proving that people who don't believe climate change is the greatest threat to humanity have twice as good sex lives as people who think it is the greatest threat. This will get you lots of clicks and the opportunity to illustrate the article with some softcore porn pictures and weather disasters.

R: Oh, how did they establish the result?

UPO: The Sociology Department had an assignment in which 10 students each polled 10 of their friends. Out of the 100 responses, 50 said climate change is the greatest threat, and 12 of those said they had a great sex life; 50 others said climate change was not the greatest threat, and 24 of those said they had a great sex life.

R: That seems pretty shaky to me. It's not a big sample, and it's hardly representative of the population. Some of the students might have just made up the answers to save trouble. Many of the respondents might have been less than truthful.

UPO: But the result was statistically significant. The p-value was 4.95%.

R: The p-value assumes the data are perfect, it ignores all the problems I see. How many questions were on the questionnaire?

UPO: 20

R: And how many possible responses for each?

UPO: 5

R: So there were $100 \times 95 / 2 = 4{,}750$ possible pairs of responses. Even if none of them were related in any way, we'd expect 5%, or 238, to have p-values below 5%. How do I know the researchers didn't pick through the 238 to find the result with the most dramatic headline?

UPO: Our researchers don't do that.

R: Okay, before you saw the study, what would you say was the likelihood that believing climate change was the greatest threat cut your sex life satisfaction in half?

UPO: I dunno. Maybe worrying about the climate gets in the way of enjoying sex?

R: But could worrying less about climate double sexual pleasure?

UPO: Okay, unlikely maybe, call it 5%.

R: What was the power of the test? That is, if people who think climate is not the greatest threat really are more likely to have great sex lives, what is the chance that the researchers would have gotten a p-value under 5%?

UPO: I'll have to ask.

(… later)

UPO: I got your answer. The power is 73%.

R: Okay, so if you tested 2,000 hypotheses and 5%, or 100, were true, you'd get significant p-values 73 times. The 1,900 false hypotheses would generate 95 significant values. Even assuming away all the data problems, this result has about a 43% chance of being true. Sorry, my editor wants 95% of our stories to be true.

YOU CAN'T HANDLE THE TRUTH

I try to stick to what I know, math and statistics, but I do need to take a brief digression into moral philosophy, a field in which I have no expertise. We've gotten this far without considering precisely what we mean about a research finding being wrong or false.

CHAPTER TEN

TO TRUTH AND HONESTY, MAY THEY NEVER MEET

If there were no misunderstandings and no perverse behavior, being honest would be synonymous with speaking the truth. But life is messier than that. Is it honest to say things that are literally true you know will be misinterpreted, or lead to bad decisions? Is it dishonest to conceal dangerous truths—such as how to create a lethal pathogen in your kitchen capable of killing millions of people?

DISHONESTY VERSUS LIMITED HONESTY

You have probably seen news stories about Harvard honesty researcher Francesca Gino being accused of faking data in research papers. I'm not going to discuss the details of that story, only note that much of the popular news coverage focused on the irony of an honesty researcher being accused of dishonesty.

If headline writers had looked more closely into the story, they would realize that modern honesty researchers are not uncritical fans of honesty. Indeed, the subtitle for Professor Gino's most popular book reads: "Why it pays to break the rules in work and life." Business school ethics classes do not recommend "the truth, the whole truth and nothing but the truth."

MBA discussions are unsurprisingly focused on business situations. Your board of directors is upset about a complex issue they all misunderstand. Your attempts to explain have only caused more anger and confusion. Is it wrong to say "I agree with you about the problem and I will take care of it" when in fact you don't think there's a problem and plan to do nothing?

Or you're investing in a start-up you think has only a 10% probability of success and has only an expected eight times return if successful, but the investment makes sense because the cost is fully tax deductible and the gains—if any—are tax-free, and also it provides diversification benefits to your overall portfolio, and it will gain you some favorable news coverage. The founder is mercurial and moody. Should you tell her that you're highly confident of the idea's vast success to boost her confidence and chance of success?

Whatever your answers, I think you can see that it's not always obvious that the most honest choice is the best choice. Strict honesty can impede innovation, dishearten people, frustrate teamwork, and stretch out pointless meetings.

All these are examples of limited honesty rather than dishonesty. It may be best to shield newly conceived innovations from the full blast of withering honesty until they can grow strong enough to withstand it, but that does not excuse lying or fraud to attract support. Limited honesty is not precisely lying, but you are not telling the truth, the whole truth, and nothing but the truth.

White lies and diplomatic silence can smooth social frictions and promote harmony and cooperation, but it's important to avoid the "tangled web we weave, when first we practice to deceive." When honesty is complex or hard to understand, simplifications can save effort and improve short-term outcomes, but oversimplification can lead to long-term problems.

GINO AND MENDEL: FUDGING DATA POINTS

Turning from business to research publications, consider the most famous case of questionable research: Gregor Mendel, known as the "father of genetics" for his pathbreaking work on inheritance in the mid-1800s. Since the early 1900s, people have been complaining that his data conformed too closely to his model to have resulted from honest experiments.

Neither Gino nor Mendel—whose ideas were novel and extremely complex for 19th-century biologists—has been seriously accused of making up data. Rather, both are accused of fudging a few data points to make their results stronger, either deliberately or unconsciously. There have also been allegations of overzealous and honesty-challenged assistants in both cases.

If Mendel hadn't fudged the data to simplify and strengthen his argument, it might have taken even longer for his groundbreaking work on genetics to have been accepted—or perhaps it would have never gained attention. This could have delayed progress in biology for decades. For all we know, in the decades that followed Mendel's research, other more honest experimenters could have been overlooked due to messier reported results—even if their findings had been similar to Mendel's.

The neglect of Mendel's work until the 20th century is one of the great what-ifs in scientific history. Had it received attention when published in

1866, the study of both genetics and evolution might have been accelerated by decades. We might even have avoided the horrific eugenics campaigns of the 20th century.

BALANCING USEFULNESS AND HONESTY

Mendel's dilemma is ubiquitous in research. In textbook versions, researchers do experiments that clearly demonstrate their ideas. In reality, experiments are never completely clear. A common refrain from researchers caught fudging data is they knew the result was correct, so they "cleaned up" the results to accentuate the truth.

Scientific credibility comes from correctly judging when the data are strong enough to make a claim, and when more work is needed. Scientists who make premature claims that are later disproved lose respect, whether they reported their results with complete honesty or fudged them a bit by tricks like throwing away an outlier, ignoring a few experimental runs that failed, or choosing a statistical method that exaggerated the certainty.

Scientists whose claims are supported by subsequent work gain prestige and credibility. Distilling results that are too complex to describe in full detail into comprehensible accounts of the key findings—without misleading anyone—is an important skill in research.

Researchers in the private sector face the same issues as academic scientists. Decision-makers lack the expertise and time to wade through the full details of an investigation. They cannot work with the whole truth. Rather, researchers must communicate what they know in simplified form and indicate accurately the uncertainty attached, balancing usefulness and honesty.

I'm willing to leave the ethical debate about limits to honesty to philosophers and psychologists, and the practical debate to top business decision-makers. Honesty is just one part of culture, and there are many different cultures—with different ideas about honesty limits—that can be productive. Here are some modern controversies about scientific honesty that may convince you the issues are trickier than the Book of John's "ye shall know the truth, and the truth shall make you free."

VACCINES

Let's start with vaccines. The simplest model of pandemics assumes that each infected person exposes an average of R_0 (the "basic reproduction number") additional people. Anyone who gets the disease dies or becomes permanently immune. As more people have had the disease, or are missing because they have died, exposures are less likely to result in a new infection. Eventually the population reaches "herd immunity," when $\frac{1}{R_0}$ of the population remains susceptible. At that point, each new infection produces fewer than one additional infection on average, so any new outbreaks die out.

Real diseases are more complicated than the simple model, but the model nevertheless incorporates some general mathematical features that apply to many diseases. Each vaccinated person prevents one infection. Since the vaccinated person might not have gotten the disease anyway, that means part of the benefit accrues to some unvaccinated person.

Consider the disease mumps with an R_0 of around 10. Before a vaccine was available, about $1 - \frac{1}{10} = 0.9$, or 90%, of the population got mumps. The first person to be vaccinated for mumps saved herself an expected 0.9 infections and gifted a reduction of 0.1 expected infection on society. By the time 50% of the population had been vaccinated, the chance for an unvaccinated person to get mumps had dropped to 80%, so newly vaccinated people saved 0.8 expected personal infections and reduced 0.2

expected infections in others. If vaccinations had stopped with 90% of the population, the last person to be vaccinated would have been a pure altruist, deriving no personal advantage but saving one other person from getting mumps.

Of course, public health is not this neat and precise, but for many diseases this describes the general situation. The first people to be vaccinated mainly benefit personally. They could be the people most exposed to the disease, or who will have the greatest negative consequences from getting it. As more people get vaccinated, we should expect the average recipient will be less likely to get the disease, and less likely to suffer serious consequences from it. But as the personal benefits of getting vaccinated decline, the value to others increases. In practice, the vaccine decision will depend more on public-spiritedness than personal advantage.

From a public health standpoint, vaccinations are more important the smaller the personal benefit. As the fraction of vaccinated people increases, each new shot will protect more unvaccinated people, including a vulnerable population of people who cannot get the vaccine due to issues like compromised immune systems, or lack of access to medical care. This latter group is likely to be among the most harmed if they do get the disease.

One moral question is whether to stop vaccinating when the personal benefit to the vaccinated person is less than the cost and risk of the vaccine, or when the social benefit is maximized. In general, these will be different. The greatest good of the greatest number requires some individuals to make personally suboptimal decisions.

This makes it possible to argue researchers should not even ask what the personal breakeven point is for individuals, as this will only aid people in dodging their social responsibility. It could even justify suppressing the knowledge if it is discovered, or lying about the point. On the other hand, aside from moral questions and the reduced progress in medical science, these actions could erode trust in science and public health authorities, and do more harm than good.

There is a much larger issue in practice. Any discussion of personal advantage versus risk of vaccination can trigger a large drop in vaccination rates. The people refusing vaccination will not be the ones at lowest risk, making personally beneficial but socially suboptimal decisions; they will be the people least trusting of the medical establishment and experts. Not only could this inflict great harm on the people who cannot be vaccinated—many of whom will be at great risk if they get the disease—but the holdouts are likely at greater than average risk due to their rejection of medical advice. Worse, in many cases of importance, this will be parents making bad decisions for their children.

Should medical researchers provide a united front about vaccines that are known to have great public health benefits, insisting they have great personal benefits as well, except to a small and identifiable population, and negligible risks? Or is complete honesty the best policy, despite the harms?

ANDREW WAKEFIELD

In 1998, Andrew Wakefield and 12 of his colleagues published a case series in *The Lancet*, which suggested that the measles, mumps, and rubella (MMR) vaccine may predispose children to behavioral regression and pervasive developmental disorder, together with diarrhea and abdominal pain. Twelve children with developmental issues and chronic enterocolitis were referred to a pediatric unit. In 8 of the 12 cases, parents associated the symptoms with their child receiving the MMR vaccine.

This is extremely tenuous evidence against the MMR vaccine. Essentially all children in the United Kingdom get the vaccine, at ages similar to when developmental and digestive issues are often noticed. Moreover, since symptoms can develop gradually over time, it can be hard for parents to pinpoint whether they began before or after the vaccine.

Nevertheless, the observation was worthy of a follow-up, a larger study with a control group of children without the developmental and digestive problems. Several of these were done, the most prominent being "Autism and Measles, Mumps, and Rubella Vaccine: No Epidemiological Evidence for a Causal Association," by Brent Taylor and six co-authors.

The follow-up used a much larger sample: 356 children diagnosed with autism in eight UK health districts. While a larger sample is better, the tradeoff is the authors had to work from medical records, which were not always complete or clear, rather than having actual patients to study. Moreover, the Wakefield study targeted a specific subpopulation—children with combinations of behavioral and gastroenterological issues—whereas Taylor studied a broader population of children with different types of autism.

Despite the Taylor paper's title, it largely confirmed the Wakefield results. Parents noticed symptoms about 50% more often than could be explained by random chance in the six months following an MMR vaccine. This was statistically significant at the conventional 5% level. The authors explained it away, and pointed out that there was no similar pattern based on age of autism diagnosis. Another finding of the paper was that autism diagnoses in the study area were rising slowly in the five years before the MMR vaccine was introduced—from 9 to 12 per year—but exploded to almost 50 per year in the five years after introduction. Of course, there are many possible explanations for that other than MMR, most important that there was more diagnostic attention to autism, but it's another reason to investigate a possible link.

As a result of the misleading title, Taylor's paper was repeatedly cited in the press and by experts as thoroughly debunking Wakefield's result, despite confirming it. Many other papers were published, most—like the Taylor paper—seemed designed to deny any harm from the MMR vaccine rather than to investigate potential harms seriously. None came up with convincing evidence of no link; they merely failed to find statistically significant evidence of a link, possibly due to small sample size, low-quality data, or lack of interest by the researchers.

Whatever the scientific merits of the rebuttals, they completely failed to convince skeptics and MMR vaccine rates continued to fall. There was never strong evidence for any link between MMR and autism or other serious side effects, but there was no strong evidence to disprove it, nor to limit it to a negligible risk.

Vaccine supporters turned their attention from the data to the researcher and began a sustained assault on Wakefield personally. They quickly found ample grounds. He had failed to disclose funding from lawyers representing parents hoping to sue for their children's disabilities, and 6 of his 12 subjects were referred by lawyers. This is particularly important since his main evidence was parents' testimony that the symptoms first appeared soon after vaccination—something they and their lawyers had a strong financial incentive to say. Wakefield did not get proper consent for all his tests. He had a patent that would increase in value if the MMR were replaced with three separate vaccines. Somewhat later, credible allegations emerged that some of the study data were falsified.

All of those are serious violations. However, given the extreme weakness of the Wakefield study in the first place, they're not very relevant to the question of MMR safety. Even a high-quality study finding worrying symptoms emerged in the months following MMR vaccines in 8 of 12 patients would be only mildly suggestive.

What occurred next was an extraordinary campaign against Wakefield, totally out of proportion to reactions to other scientific lapses and frauds. He was stripped of his medical license and publicly vilified by the public health establishment. Science communicator Stuart Ritchie wrote, "The acceptance of Wakefield's study in as prominent an outlet as *The Lancet* will go down as one of the worst decisions in the history of scientific publication." The result was Wakefield became a martyr and far more influential than he could have achieved on his own. The violence of the retribution was proof to vaccine skeptics of how much the authorities wanted to repress dissent.

This is particularly surprising because Wakefield did not question the value of the vaccines, he merely claimed it was safer to administer them individually rather than as a trio (one of his undisclosed conflicts was a patent for a stand-alone measles vaccine), something that is highly plausible as a matter of common sense. Public health authorities disliked this recommendation because it would be more expensive, and lead to more missed shots.

No one is likely to have sympathy for Wakefield, but what about the vilification of parents who claim their children's problems are due to vaccines? No one can know whether or not those claims are true—not the parents, not public health authorities. Generally, we are sympathetic to people who assign blame for their personal tragedies without strong evidence—even to the point of awarding them large sums in tort suits. But parents who seize on vaccines to blame for their children's severe issues are given much less understanding.

WHAT'S WORSE?

Compare Wakefield's paper to my nomination for the worst publication decision in the history of *The Lancet*. Italian surgeon Paolo Macchiarini replaced tracheas with plastic tubes seeded with the patient's stem cells to prevent rejection by the immune system. It didn't work, seven of nine patients died and the other two had the replacement trachea removed. Nevertheless, Macchiarini published two fraudulent articles in *The Lancet* claiming success. But the worst was after the deception had been exposed. *The Lancet* ran an editorial, "Paolo Macchiarini Is Not Guilty of Scientific Misconduct."

Many thousands of researchers have been found guilty of fraud, undisclosed conflicts of interest, and other scientific or ethical crimes. Some, like Macchiarini, killed people. Many are not even fired; in fact, employers have more often threatened whistleblowers (the doctors who first exposed Macchiarini were threatened with prosecution by his institute) than conducted investigations.

The point is that researchers who question vaccine safety or effectiveness are treated far more savagely than even the most egregious scientific fraudsters. Their studies are subjected to withering criticism by people looking for complaint, rather than weighing the pros and cons of the work. The attacks are not just on the papers, but the authors themselves. A 2022 paper by Ety Elisha and three co-authors interviewed researchers who questioned vaccines, "Respondents reported being subjected to a variety of censorship and suppression tactics, including the retraction of papers pointing to vaccine safety problems, negative publicity, difficulty in obtaining research funding, calls for dismissal, summonses to official hearings, suspension of medical licenses, and self-censorship." And it's not just researchers. Doctors who advise patients a certain vaccine might not be in their individual interest risk censure and loss of medical privileges.

On the other side there is remarkably little mainstream vaccine research to help individuals weigh the risks and benefits of vaccines in their personal situation. Much vaccine research compares the harm of vaccines with the harm of getting the disease. It's generally true that you'd rather have the vaccine than the disease due to all the harm of the disease, and the disease also causing an immune system change similar to what the vaccine does. But this is only relevant if you're sure you're going to get the disease without the vaccine, and sure that you won't get the disease with the vaccine. Neither assumption is generally true.

Many other public health studies are done without controls after the initial vaccine approval. That is, they study the health conditions of vaccinated people, but they don't compare to matched control people who did not get vaccinated. You can't learn much from an uncontrolled study.

One problem is it's hard to get good controls. Most people are vaccinated, and the ones that aren't are different in many respects, and often hard to find and enroll in studies. If they do have worse health outcomes, it could well be due to general distrust of medicine; on the other hand, if they seem to have better health outcomes, it could be due to failure to diagnose problems.

Nevertheless, it's hard to escape the conclusion that another reason is mainstream public health researchers don't want clear evidence about vaccine effectiveness and dangers as the public health benefit of vaccines, in their minds, outweighs individual costs and benefits, and because any negative finding for vaccines will be exaggerated by skeptics to cause individuals to make poor decisions from both their personal perspective and social benefit.

A NOTE ON COVID VACCINES

The simple model for pandemics mentioned above failed completely for COVID. The virus mutated quickly, so getting the disease or getting vaccinated did not provide strong or long-lasting immunity. The vaccine mainly reduced symptoms if you got the disease rather than prevented you from getting or transmitting it. Nevertheless, we saw the same public health campaign to promote universal vaccination, and the same backlash from vaccine skeptics.

The issue was particularly fraught for pregnant women. COVID-19 vaccines were not tested on pregnant women prior to approval. The public health advice to vaccinate pregnant women was based on studies in pregnant animals—which cannot address all the potential developmental issues in human children—and data from a few women who became pregnant inadvertently during trials, none of whom had given birth at the time.

Since then, we've accumulated information, mostly reassuring, that the vaccine is safe and effective during pregnancy, and does not lead to a very high frequency of very severe adverse outcomes. But it will take more time, and better data, to rule out less frequent and less severe outcomes that might outweigh—at least for some women—vaccine benefits.

It took five years to notice the severe harm to unborn children from thalidomide—and that was extremely obvious damage. Moreover, thalidomide was not exposed by medical authorities but by dissident doctors who had to battle the pharmacological–regulatory–public health establishment.

Consider a woman who had a COVID infection and perhaps vaccinations before getting pregnant, and who could isolate effectively to further reduce the chance of being reinfected. In 2021, she might quite rationally have decided that the small risk of getting COVID during pregnancy was outweighed by the unknown but potentially catastrophic risks of getting the vaccine to her unborn child. In 2025 that's harder to support, given four years of experience with no evidence to date of harm. But some problems take years to show up in children, and the vaccine has been constantly changing, so even today it's not entirely irrational to forgo the shot (getting vaccinated before trying to get pregnant, however, seems like an excellent bet).

That brings me to "SARS-CoV-2 Infection and COVID-19 Vaccination Rates in Pregnant Women in Scotland," published in *Nature Medicine*, a top-three medical journal, in January 2022. In their abstract, the authors claimed their study showed "Addressing low vaccine uptake rates in pregnant women is imperative to protect the health of women and babies in the ongoing pandemic," and they ended their discussion with "Addressing low vaccine uptake in pregnant women is imperative to protect the health of women and babies." They began and finished with convictions that were not supported by their data.

This was the first major study of the effect of taking the COVID vaccine in pregnancy. Most public health authorities had been strongly recommending COVID vaccines in pregnancy since the vaccines became available in late 2020, but this is the paper that squashed any lingering qualifications or doubts. After this, questioning the wisdom of vaccinating pregnant women was considered "misinformation." The American College of Obstetrics and Gynecology threatened sanctions, including loss of license, for doctors who disagreed with the consensus. Advising pregnant women to think for themselves on the issue got you banned on Facebook and other sites. Fact-checking sites called you a liar.

The most shocking lapse in the paper is the authors had no data on possible developmental effects of the vaccine. That was the main concern of women reluctant to take an entirely novel vaccine. Of the authors' 131,751 pregnant women, only 79,562 had even given birth, and the authors' data ended four weeks after birth in those cases.

The other 52,189 women, 40% of the study population, the authors had lost track of, or were still pregnant, or had abortions or miscarriages, or otherwise were out of the study. These women likely differed in many respects from the 60% with data, which could skew the results significantly.

Another major issue for this study is it failed to control for anything. It looked at outcomes for vaccinated versus unvaccinated women with COVID and attributed the difference to vaccination alone. But we know vaccinated women are richer and healthier than unvaccinated women, and have healthier lifestyles and better healthcare. It seems likely that vaccinated women are more likely to test for COVID, while unvaccinated ones may only be diagnosed when they have some other health problem.

The lack of controls is particularly salient because the calculation is quite different for different women. Older women, and women with COVID risk factors or significant exposures to infections, and no infections or vaccinations prior to pregnancy, weigh the risks and benefits of the vaccine differently from younger, healthier, less exposed women with some prior immune boost from disease or vaccination. Women with family histories or other indications of high developmental risks will rationally decide differently than women without those factors.

Most public health vaccination research I see takes this uncontrolled approach due, in my opinion, to reluctance to allow individuals to make personal decisions. The point of the research is to reinforce the value of everyone being vaccinated, not to provide useful information to individuals who might value their personal health, and their babies, over the greatest good of the greatest number.

Another major control issue with this study is both vaccination rates and COVID infection rates varied widely over the study period. COVID varieties changed as well. If more women got vaccinated at times of lower infection rates with milder varieties, it would overstate the value of vaccination (unlike the first control problem, this one could go either way).

I'll just toss in the last point, the familiar objection that this is an observational study from which the authors are making recommendations that assume a causal link.

These issues should have caused the paper to fail peer review, or at least to have the authors remove the strong, unqualified medical and public health advice. There is some value in publishing the raw data so more careful people could use it to form their own conclusions, but it's not enough to justify a paper, and certainly not the editorial statements in this one.

Let's put all that aside, and just look at what the paper found. Women who had COVID during pregnancy had 10.2% pre-term births, compared to 7.9% of women who did not have COVID during pregnancy. This result was significant at the 5% level. The COVID women also had a higher rate of stillbirths (0.5% vs. 0.4%) and neonatal deaths (0.3% vs. 0.2%), but these differences were not significant at the 5% level. So, getting COVID was clearly bad for pregnancy, at least if we ignore all the problems with the study.

Women who got a COVID vaccine during pregnancy also had a higher rate of pre-term deliveries (8.6% vs. 7.9%), and this was significant at the

5% level. They had lower rates of stillbirths (0.2% vs. 0.4%) and the same rate of neonatal deaths (0.2%), with neither of those being significant differences at the 5% level. Taken at face value, getting the vaccine carried 32% of the risk of getting COVID. However, let me repeat that I take none of these numbers seriously due to defects in the study.

Do you see the crucial figure we're missing, even if we trust the study results? It's 3%. That's the fraction of pregnant women who got COVID. So, if you're an entirely average pregnant women, getting the vaccine is accepting a certain 0.7% increase in the chance of a pre-term birth for a vaccine that might help you reduce a 3% chance of a 2.3% increase. No casino would dare offer such a terrible bet, yet the authors of the study, the journal editors, and public health authorities all over the world chose to recommend it to all pregnant women. And those figures are for an average woman, for many women the bet was substantially worse.

Fortunately for the world, by 2025 we can be pretty confident—although by no means sure—that there are no lasting developmental issues in children whose mothers took the COVID vaccine in pregnancy. Bad research did not cause another thalidomide disaster.

My personal guess—based on looking at a large body of research and the opinions of experts I respect—is that the study, for all its flaws, came up with a reasonable ballpark estimate of the damage a COVID infection does to pregnancies. We have a lot of data about women who get different infections while pregnant, and COVID seems pretty typical.

I also think the study exaggerated the extent to which getting the vaccine is associated with pre-term births. That result does not seem to have held up in subsequent studies. One plausible speculation is that the women who got the vaccine in pregnancy were at higher risk for COVID complications—older, more risk factors—and had not been previously vaccinated, which is associated with being poorer and having worse general healthcare.

CLIMATE CHANGE AND OTHER MATTERS

Suppose you sincerely and reasonably believe that climate change poses an existential threat—one capable of causing human extinction in the foreseeable future—and that you know of policies that would significantly reduce the probability of disaster and mitigate its scale. Are you justified in committing scientific misconduct—forging data, lying about results, misrepresenting evidence—to save the human race?

While this is an extreme example, many people caught promoting Wrong Numbers appear to have sincerely believed either that their underlying hypotheses were true, or that getting people to believe them would make the world a better place, or both.

Perhaps the most effective campaign of this sort was kicked off by a 1974 article in *Nature* by atmospheric scientist John Hampson. He chose the provocative title "Photochemical War on the Atmosphere" to suggest that oxides of nitrogen released by thermonuclear weapons could wipe out the ozone layer with disastrous consequences to life on Earth. His article made explicit policy recommendations for limiting nuclear weapons with a goal of eliminating them entirely.

Hampson's claims were based on crude one-dimensional general circulation models and unraveled over the next few years. However, they were replaced by the claim of "nuclear winter," the idea that soot from nuclear explosions would cool the Earth, causing massive loss of human and other life. These were based on slightly less crude models. They were promoted effectively by well-known scientists, most prominently Carl Sagan, and are credited as major influences on the arms-control agreements of the Reagan administration. It is quite plausible that the world is safer today, and perhaps avoided global thermonuclear war, due to this body of research.

The research itself was debunked, most spectacularly by the 1991 oil fires set by Iraq while losing the Kuwait war. The main scientists behind the nuclear winter prediction—Richard Turco, John Birks, Carl Sagan, Alan Robock, and Paul Crutzen—predicted catastrophic global climate effects including sub-freezing summer temperatures in temperate regions and devastating acid rain. Nothing like that happened.

Even before the Kuwait experiment, it leaked out that the senior scientists involved in the effort were engaged in advocacy rather than science. Models were tweaked to give the desired results, and credible journalists and speculators exaggerated the claims further. Years later, a junior scientist on the effort—Stephen Schneider—revealed in his book *Science as a Contact Sport* that Carl Sagan ordered him to suppress the results of his early two-dimensional global circulation model that undercut nuclear winter claims.

One of the arguments against lying and perverting science to cause a good social or political outcome is that it doesn't work. It invites backlash, like the anti-vax movement, and discredits good science. However, in this example, it does seem to have worked, and to have made the world a better place, and not to have discredited the scientists involved, climate prediction as a field, nor science in general.

SHOULD SCIENCE BE A CONTACT SPORT?

I have no useful expertise on when fraudulent science can be justified, but I will say the three examples above—Gregor Mendel fudging data, public health authorities denying any danger to vaccines, and activist-scientists inventing nuclear winter—are unusual in several respects.

All three were presumably done out of sincere altruism, whereas most fraudsters who believe they are right seem to be seeking personal glory and payback of skeptics rather than public good. Mendel was right, public health authorities denying significant long-term risk from vaccines may be right, and anti-nuclear activists were wrong on the science but right on the politics.

In all three cases, the alternative of doing better experiments was not available. Mendel was an amateur working with a single assistant—discouraged by his boss and, when he was promoted, too burdened with administrative responsibilities to continue the work. The work necessary to understand fully the long-term consequences of vaccines is impractical. Nuclear winter proponents did not have the computer power or theoretical knowledge to make useful predictions, and in any event were in a race against time.

Finally, all three examples of arguable justification for limited honesty asked the right questions. In science, the right questions are more important than the right answers. If Mendel had not been ignored, his work would have touched off a serious investigation of heredity that would have led to the same useful conclusions even if Mendel had been wrong. Public health authorities may not have the data necessary to prove there are negligible long-term risks from vaccines, but they are in fact gathering what data they can and making it available for others to analyze.

The early general circulation models, crude as they were with results hijacked for partisan purposes, made one crucial point that has never been rebutted. Making simple physical assumptions, human impacts on the environment could result in devastating consequences in the foreseeable future. While those simple assumptions are certainly false, there's no reason to believe that reality is more favorable for humans. This justifies the enormous research effort devoted to the question, even if it has yet to produce consensus about the best environmental policies.

RESTART THE BABBAGE ENGINE

The second great what-if of 19th-century science, after Mendel's work, was the failure of Charles Babbage's computers to gain traction due to personal conflicts and lack of funds. In particular, if his mechanical creations had been more successful, someone might have had the idea of using electric relays—which had been invented and were available in large supply and high quality at reasonable cost due to mass production for use in telegraphs. While such a machine would have been inferior to the vacuum tube machines of the 1940s, it nevertheless could have revolutionized research.

Should Charles Babbage have exaggerated the success of his machines in order to attract the funding and interest necessary for continued improvement?

When I was in college, novelist Clive Cussler had a tremendous bestseller with *Raise the Titanic!* In the story, it became necessary to salvage a rare element thought to have been on the ship. There is a tangled 64-year backstory, a beautiful marine archeologist missy-who-was-ready-to-play, French assassins, spies, Soviet agents, a hurricane, and other expected features of this kind of book.

I decided to try my hand at imitation with *Restart the Babbage Engine!* In my story, astronomers spot a faraway asteroid that might impact the Earth, but its orbital parameters are too uncertain to predict if or when. It's outside the plane of the solar system, so it would approach the Earth from the North Pole. Because that region is relatively empty, its orbit would be less affected by planets.

When the asteroid last approached the Earth a century earlier, an expedition had been sent to the far north of Norway to observe it. The expedition never returned but its data could establish the orbital parameters to determine if the Earth was safe or if drastic countermeasures were needed. Our intrepid heroes find the expedition's camp. Of course, an elaborate backstory was uncovered with sinister agents whose modern descendants were intent on sabotaging the restart. I did not include any marine archeologists.

No paper notes remain at the expedition's camp, but there is a Babbage Engine that had been calculating the orbit. It stopped midway as the expedition members died (the machine required a hand crank) and the machinery became embedded in ice. The task is to melt the ice without damaging the machine and restart it so it can run to completion and reveal the orbital parameters.

The novel was terrible and never published, fortunately. One big issue is I started to write a parody and ended up getting interested in the story. The reason I mention it now is that my research for the book led me to the Dudley Observatory in Albany, which had purchased a knock-off Babbage Engine by Swedish inventors Georg and Edvard Scheutz in 1857. The machine had been used for astronomical calculations of the type I imagined for my novel. The information I had said that the Dudley Babbage Engine was ineffective and soon abandoned. But I wanted to see one because the one strength of my book was geeky accuracy about computer technology and astronomical math rather than plot, character, or literary style.

When I got to the observatory, I was told that the machine had been shipped to the Smithsonian years ago. But a helpful woman at the visitors' desk told me that two boxes of papers about it had been packed up which the Smithsonian refused to take. I was welcome to look through them.

I was shocked to learn that everything I had read about the machine's value was wrong. It had been used extensively for decades, and researchers had developed tricks and improvements to make it better. It was frustrating to use, but researchers could do a summer's worth of work (most of the work consisted of calculating astronomical tables for navigation, called "ephemeris") in a week, allowing 12 weeks of beach frolic or private research on Navy funds (the Navy wanted the tables). There were lots of starts and stops and repositionings—had the machine worked perfectly it might have been an hour's computation instead of a week's tedious work—but it was still 10 or 20 times faster than human calculations, and more accurate. And I got lots of great characters and anecdotes for my book, lots of hands-on detail about how to use the Engine.

I think if this material had been widely known in the 1880s, someone would have combined Herman Hollerith's innovations in electromechanical tabulating machines—which were reliable and commercially successful—with Babbage's design genius and the computer age would have gotten a 50-year headstart. Moreover, the same advantage could have accrued had a charlatan or visionary invented the material.

PARTING THOUGHTS

What we should demand is honesty about honesty. Traditional science claims zero tolerance for dishonesty. If that is not practiced—and it almost certainly is not—the public statements should be toned down. There may not be a perfect balance, and if there is, I don't know it. But openness and transparency about honesty rules are essential.

We now resume our accounts of death and destruction.

CHAPTER ELEVEN

CONFIDENCE INTERVALS IN WARTIME

I've waited to address the important statistical concept of a confidence interval until I had a Wrong Number based on a very simple statistical calculation. It's much easier to see the problems with confidence intervals in textbook problems about coin flips and dice rolls than complex analyses based on tools like multivariable logistic regression or ecological inference. Some Wrong Numbers come from simple textbook models.

CONFIDENCE GAME

There are two reasons I included confidence intervals in this book. The first is that they're often miscalculated and even more often misunderstood. The second is that they cause more published research findings to be wrong than right. They're related to the concept of statistical significance, which I covered in Chapter 9.

Some statisticians call themselves "Bayesian" and refuse to use confidence intervals. Bayesians have a related idea they call "credible interval." This can be illustrated by a popular sports bet called "over/under," for example that the total number of runs scored in tonight's game between the Seattle Mariners and New York Yankees will be over or under 8.5 runs—that is 9 or more runs ("over") or 8 or fewer runs ("under"). We might say that 0–8 runs is a Bayesian 50% credible interval, because the bookie is willing to bet even money on either side of the proposition that the total number of runs will be between 0 and 8.

Now this is not precisely true because the bookie will build in some "vigorish" (she may demand you put up $110 to win $100 whichever side you pick) and the over/under line represents a market-clearing consensus rather than any one individual's belief. There are some other technicalities I'll get to later. But the key point is, a Bayesian credible is very much like a betting proposition—if the Bayesian statistician had to bet at the odds implied by the credible interval, she would be indifferent between betting the true parameter was inside or outside the interval. For example, a 95% credible interval implies being willing to put up $19 to win $1 to bet that the true value is inside the interval, or $1 to win $19 that the true value is outside the interval.

The example I'm going to use for this chapter may offend some readers. We're going to discuss tens of thousands of deaths, and it may seem inhuman to treat individual tragedies as entries in a spreadsheet for mathematical manipulation. Moreover, the issue of the October 7, 2023 Hamas terrorist attacks and subsequent violence generate strong opinions. I'm not going to consider Israeli deaths, nor the moral rights and wrongs involved. I'm going to ignore whether Palestinian deaths are combatants or bystanders, whether they were killed by Israel or Hamas, whether they were unintended collateral damage of legitimate operations or deliberate targets for evil or cynical purposes.

I believe numbers matter. They don't tell you who's right and who's wrong, nor how to resolve the situation. But this conflict will end with a negotiated settlement. Settlements are not driven by moral responsibility or justice. They occur when the shared interests of the parties become larger than their differences, at least temporarily. Accurate numbers can help demonstrate the size of the shared interests. Accurate numbers accepted by all parties can help negotiations. Inaccurate numbers broadcast for propaganda or virtue signaling only gum up the works.

Statisticians may not do much to bring about world peace, but I have more talent for statistics than peacemaking. So, I use my talents and hope for the best.

MORTALITY IN PALESTINE

A recent paper, "Traumatic Injury Mortality in the Gaza Strip from Oct 7, 2023, to June 30, 2024" in *The Lancet*, the top medical journal we have already seen that boasts the highest possible standards, asserts a 95% confidence interval from 55,298 to 78,525 on the number of Palestinians killed by traumatic injury from October 7, 2023 to June 30, 2024 in the Gaza Strip.

Many people interpret confidence intervals as if they were Bayesian credible intervals. They think that if the authors of the paper were forced to bet on the true number of deaths, they would be indifferent between betting $19 to win $1 that the true number was in the interval, or $1 to win $19 that the true number was outside the interval.

Looking at it another way, people think that of all the 95% confidence intervals published in *The Lancet* articles, 95% of them will turn out to have contained the true value, and 5% will turn out not to have contained the true value. In fact, I'm firmly convinced that the true value was outside more than half the intervals, which is another way of saying most published research results in *The Lancet* are wrong.

There are two distinct issues here. First is that confidence intervals are nothing like credible intervals. They do not even attempt to guarantee that

95% of the 95% confidence intervals contain the true value. Second is that favored academic methodologies and journal publication practices cause confidence intervals to be even more unreliable than they have to be in theory.

The interval given for Gaza deaths, 55,298–78,525, is not implausible on its face. There are hundreds of thousands of people unaccounted for since the October 7, 2023 Hamas attacks. Some have left the region, some have lost contact with friends and family, some are hiding, some are in Israeli prisons, some died of non-traumatic causes, and many died of traumatic injuries. Even when peace comes and the rubble is cleared, a census is taken, records are reconciled, and independent researchers weigh in, we won't know the exact figure, but it will not be a shock if the best guess at that point is within the authors' range.

What's implausible is that anyone could be 95% confident today that the figure will be within that range.

OTHER INFORMATION

One major issue is that Hamas claims 37,877 traumatic-injury deaths over the period. Hamas has access to all the public information the authors used, plus much more information. If there's a 95% chance that the true count is between 55,298 and 78,525, then Hamas must be suppressing the death totals. Now some people trust the Hamas totals, as its totals have been reasonably accurate in past conflicts (where it has lied is by categorizing deaths of fighting-age males as females, elderly, or children). But many other people think Hamas exaggerates the totals to help its foreign friends pressure their governments to punish Israel and recognize a Palestinian state. No one seems to think it's likely—and certainly not 95% likely—Hamas is deliberately undercounting deaths.

Of course, it's possible Hamas has some reason no one suspects for this policy, but would you bet $19 to win $1 on that point? And even if it turns out to be true that Hamas lowballs its death counts, you'd need several other unlikely things to be true for the true number to be in the interval.

Moreover, it's not just Hamas that reports much lower figures than *The Lancet* paper's range. The Euro-Mediterranean Human Rights Monitor counted 45,223. The Armed Conflict Location & Event Data project came up with 39,276. Israeli Prime Minister Benjamin Netanyahu said Israeli analysts believed the figure was around 30,000. All these estimates relied on different data and methodology. Can we really be 95% sure that all of them were so far wrong?

OTHER COUNTRIES

Next, let's turn our attention to a more peaceful and developed country, Canada. There's no war, and there's a national healthcare system to track all medical data. *The Lancet* claims 43,700 excess deaths due to COVID in the first two years of the pandemic in Canada. The World Health Organization says 22,018. eLife, a publishing service established by major medical research organizations, says 13,474. It's not just Canada, comparing the numbers in these three major databases used by researchers for the 33 most developed countries in the world showed the highest of the three databases was a median 59% greater than the lowest number. We'd get an even greater range if we looked at more than three databases.

The Lancet paper's claimed confidence interval ran from 55,298 to 78,525 for Gaza deaths. Now, 78,525 is 42% greater than 55,298. Only 13 of the 33 developed countries above had ratios for COVID deaths less than 42%.

Canada is not a war zone, and has an efficient medical establishment with comprehensive records, as did the other 33 countries. Deaths result in death certificates, with doctors certifying cause of death. Most countries had national healthcare systems, with all citizens and permanent residents in a single database. All countries had accurate counts of total deaths; the only issue was determining how many were due to COVID.

Gaza, by contrast, is a war zone, and never had anything like the Canadian level of healthcare or record-keeping. We don't have accurate censuses or vital statistics to track total deaths, much less assign causes. Many deaths in the Hamas total are people missing and presumed dead, or people who were never examined by a doctor under good conditions to determine cause of death (granted, traumatic injuries are usually more obvious than COVID, but not always).

Moreover, Gaza is not a large area, 141 square miles. If the paper's claim is correct, there had to be 124–288 bodies per square mile over a nine-month period that escaped all official attention. Yes, many people were buried under rubble, perhaps more than the 10,000 or so estimated by the UN Office for the Coordination of Humanitarian Affairs. Yes, some people were probably buried quietly without official notification. Yes, there are probably areas no one has been able to examine. Some bodies may have been completely destroyed in explosions. But the sheer number of claimed unnoticed deaths seems unlikely.

THREE STRIKES AND YOU'RE OUT

The last puzzle about the confidence interval I'll mention is the authors actually did three separate analyses that resulted in estimates of 44,130, 52,034, and 79,686. They combined these to get a confidence interval that did not contain any of the three estimates. That suggests they're 95% confident all three estimates are wrong, yet they are 95% confident of an interval derived from them. Whatever happened to garbage-in-garbage-out?

Here's what surprises many people—none of these arguments played any role in the paper's confidence interval. The authors did not claim they believed Gaza deaths were in the range 55,298–78,525, much less that they were 95% confident of that, nor that they would bet $19 to win $1 that the true number was in that range. They rigorously excluded everything they knew about Gaza and figures from all other researchers and authorities. They did not consider plausibility or counterarguments.

Why do such a crazy thing? The answer goes back to a movement in the late 19th and early 20th century to make the social sciences objective. Prior knowledge is subjective and different people start with different prior beliefs. Combining different kinds of evidence and different studies is usually subjective. Only by rigorously excluding all information except the specific quantitative results of the study itself can researchers communicate what they objectively measured. That's true whether the objective measurement is reasonable or absurd, whether it fits in with other estimates or diverges wildly, whether it's plausible or is completely inconsistent with reality.

The idea was the confidence interval was disclosed only to experts in the field, who would know what other evidence was available, and who could form their own subjective estimates based on all information. Think of sending 10 people out to measure something and telling them, "Just report your raw results, don't try to adjust them for reasonability or anything else. I'll do the work of throwing out outliers, adjusting for other evidence and combining the rest to come up with a consensus estimate."

You have to understand that this procedure was invented at a time when researchers did not discuss their work directly with the public. Any public disclosure of results prior to journal publication was a major offense. And after publication, researchers were supposed to explain the consensus of the field, not the isolated results of their study. In this case, a traditional researcher who gave an interview about Gaza deaths would say something like, "Most authorities have come up with estimates from about 30,000 to 50,000, but we've done some recent work that suggests the numbers could be higher, perhaps 60,000 or even 80,000. It will take further work to narrow the range of estimate."

Of course, those old-fashioned rules have been long abandoned by many researchers. Given that, and also journalist preferences for the researchers who make the most flamboyant claims with the fewest qualifications, maintaining the objective model is unjustified.

LAYERS OF RELIABILITY

I don't know where you get your information about the world, but consider a hierarchy:

1. Sources that report baseless or debunked numbers, or no numbers at all.
2. Sources that report numbers without confidence intervals. This is how major media sources reported the Gaza death story, just the point estimate of 64,260. But we learn in grade-school science that statistical estimates without uncertainty ranges are meaningless. And if you don't report confidence intervals you should at least avoid false precision by reporting non-significant digits. A confidence interval of 55,298–78,525 should be reported as "about 50 to 80 thousand," not 64,260, which implies between 64,255 and 64,264. Reporting "about 60 thousand" is not as good as 50 to 80 thousand, but a lot better than 64,260.
3. Sources that report confidence intervals. I didn't find any in this case, nor articles that mentioned any sort of uncertainty about the 64,260 figure. But even if one did, I suspect 95% of their readers would have misunderstood it, interpreting it as a Bayesian credible interval incorporating all information available to researchers, not a narrow statistical calculation about one study untethered to previous work, plausibility, or reality.

I wish I could say that was the only problem with confidence intervals, but there's another equally big one. The reported confidence interval does not incorporate all uncertainty in the authors' study. It's computed as if all assumptions the authors made—including ones known to be false but assumed for convenience—are precisely true.

To see the difference, suppose you call up 100 people at random and ask whom they're going to vote for in the next election. Suppose 60 say they'll vote for the Democratic nominee. If you selected a perfect random sample of voters, and if every respondent told you the truth about whom they intended to vote for, and all of them actually vote and vote as they indicated, then you could have a 95% confidence interval from 52.3% to 67.3% for the actual election votes for the Democratic candidate.

How did I compute that interval? If you were flipping a biased coin with a 52.3% chance of heads, the chance of getting 60 or more heads is 5%. So, with any lower probability, the chance of getting 60 or fewer heads is less than 5%. Similarly, if the coin had more than a 67.3% chance of heads, there would be less than a 5% chance of getting 60 or fewer heads.

But this massively understates the true uncertainty about the election results. We know our sample is not perfectly random; it likely included some people ineligible to vote or who will not vote, it likely overrepresented some groups and underrepresented others, and not everyone tells the truth about their intentions, and what people actually do often differs from intention. We also know that responses are sometimes misheard, misrecorded, or mistabulated. No sensible person would bet $19 to win $1 on the election result being in the range 52.3 to 67.3% without other information than this poll result.

CAPTURE–RECAPTURE ANALYSIS

At last we're at a point to consider the statistical method the authors use to inflate the Hamas figures: capture–recapture analysis. The methodology was first developed to estimate fish populations, which explains the name.

If you want to know how many trout are in a lake, you might capture, tag, and release a sample, say of size 80. You then do a second sample, say of size 100, and see how many of the recaptured fish were tagged in the first sample. If five of the recaptured fish have tags, you estimate the total trout population as 1,600. $\frac{80}{1,600} = 0.05$ tells you that you tagged 5% of the trout, which matches the $\frac{5}{100}$ or 5% of your recaptured sample that was tagged.

The formula is the product of the sample sizes divided by the number of matches: $\frac{80 \times 100}{5} = 1,600$. It's easy to derive from simple algebra.

There are important assumptions to justify this calculation. You must know that the trout in the lake remain the same—no births or deaths or trout entering or leaving the lake. The counts and tagging must be accurate. Most important, the captures in both samples must represent independent random samples of the trout population. If some trout are harder to catch than others, or once-caught trout are more shy, your estimate will be off.

Applying this method to counting deaths from traumatic injury in Gaza is problematic. The Gaza population does not stay the same. An estimated 6% of the population left since October 11, and outsiders have entered, plus there have been births and deaths not due to traumatic injury. Matching individuals is not straightforward, like looking for a tag—researchers must guess based on name, identification numbers, age, and sex, information that is often unavailable or inconsistent or manipulated. Deciding whether a death is due to traumatic injury should be straightforward, but there's little reason to think Hamas does it honestly. For deaths without a body, researchers can only guess about the cause. And none of the data sources the authors use are anything like random population samples.

A Hamas survey of the population turned up 7,581 individuals from responses given by friends or relatives, while the authors found 3,190 obituaries or notices posted on-line. Some 548 individuals were on both lists. From this, capture–recapture predicts 44,130 traumatic injury deaths. If there were 44,130 traumatic injury deaths, then Hamas "tagged" $\frac{7,581}{44,130} = 0.172$ or 17.2% of them in its survey. The obituaries found $\frac{548}{3,190} = 0.172$ or 17.2% of the deaths had been "tagged" by the on-line posters.

The authors did a more sophisticated version of this analysis, stratifying the data by age and sex. That means they did separate calculations for male and female victims who were minors, prime-age, and elderly individuals, then added them together. But that detail doesn't affect the points I'm making, nor does it make a large quantitative difference to the conclusion.

The 95% confidence interval for my basic capture–recapture analysis is 41,465 to 47,035. Remember that the true uncertainty is much larger; this is only the uncertainty if all of the assumptions made for capture–recapture analysis are exactly correct.

TWICE THE CAPTURE–RECAPTURE

How do the authors get from 44,130 to their estimate of 64,260? They do two more capture–recapture analyses using Hamas Ministry of Health counts to get estimates of 52,034 (95% interval 49,871 to 54,316) and 79,686 (95% interval 77,058 to 82,431). Note that none of these intervals include the authors' point estimate of 64,260. Again, the paper has somewhat different numbers due to stratification, but in the same ballpark and I'm interested in the logic rather than the exact figures.

What do you do when you get three different estimates of the same quantity and they are far apart—much too far to be attributed to the errors in each estimate? The authors averaged the estimates, which makes little sense, and then claimed a 95% confidence interval that excluded all three, which makes no sense. The proper response is to acknowledge your model is incorrect.

This study also introduces a new issue that I will expand upon in later chapters—how statistics often drowns out rationality and logic. Capture–recapture analysis makes a bunch of assumptions we know to be false, and switches attention from reality to abstractions. Like a skilled magician distracting the eye with one hand while manipulating with the other, misdirection with complicated formulas, Greek letters, and jargon prevents most readers from noticing the switch.

The first bit of misdirection is to treat all three data sources—the Hamas hospital identifications, the Hamas survey, and obituaries scraped from social media and obituaries—symmetrically, like three different catch-and-release samples of trout in a lake.

The most reliable data source is social media and obituary postings. There's little reason for anyone to post this about friends or family members who are actually alive, and we can trust that the posts get the identification correct.

The Hamas hospital records are the most reliable indications that the victim is actually dead from traumatic injury. There's a body in the morgue, it's hard to mistake that, and a doctor to certify cause of death. On the other hand, identifications are uncertain, with lots of missing or incorrect information.

There's also an issue of deliberate misidentification. *The Lancet* authors note about the hospital data, "Critics have raised concerns about exaggerated numbers of deaths, citing issues such as potential data manipulation, missing identifications, and inconsistencies in demographic classifications." In "see no evil" passive voice, they follow that up with "no literature search was done."

That's odd. If you cared about the truth, why wouldn't you consider the extensive work by others about errors in the official figures? Especially when the issue of fudged identification information is crucial to your study?

If the authors had bothered to check, they would have discovered that in previous conflicts, the Hamas totals have been reasonably accurate, generally within 10% or so of consensus figures estimated after the fact with additional data from Israel and censuses. However, they would have also discovered strong evidence in both past and current Hamas figures that fighting-age males were falsely classified as women, children, or elderly.

Moreover, the authors actually did note that the Hamas figures claim 40.1% of deaths were female, while the other two lists have only 28.3% female, and the Ministry of Health numbers show 29.9% under age 15, while the other two lists show only 21.1%. That suggests either Hamas is lying about the sex and age of many victims, or that the random sample assumptions necessary for capture–recapture analysis are false. Either way, it makes the paper's results meaningless.

The Hamas survey data could have the opposite problem as its hospital data. We can trust that anyone sending official death notices to Hamas would get the identification correct, but some of these might represent people who are presumed dead but are actually alive, or who died but not of traumatic injuries. There are reasons to file false death claims—to get compensation, to transfer property, to protect Hamas deserters, or people taking advantage of conflict chaos to flee marriages, debts, or warrants.

COMBINING ESTIMATES

However, we don't need to speculate on the precise nature of the errors. As long as we have three capture–recapture samples—one we trust most, and the two we trust less due to independent issues (misidentification for the hospital records, living people reported dead for the survey), we combine the three estimates by multiplying the two that include the trusted source and dividing by the estimate from the two less trusted sources. This yields an estimate of 28,813, well under the Hamas 37,877 figure and even farther under the authors' 64,260. This is using precisely the same data and methodology of the authors, just including some common sense about likely data errors.

To understand this method, let's go back to our trout capture–recapture example, but make it about cars rather than fish. We want to know how many cars are in a city, so we randomly pick 1,000 cars, record the license plates, and put electronic tags on them. We make no errors in this process.

We use traffic cameras to record the license plate numbers of passing cars, and determine if they have tags or not. These cameras usually detect tags, but often get the license plates wrong. We get 1,000 license plate numbers, 10 of which are tagged with license plate numbers that match our list. We estimate $\frac{1{,}000 \times 1{,}000}{10} = 100{,}000$ cars in the city.

We also get reports from police about tickets written. The police write 1,000 tickets and eight of the cars have tags. The police usually get the license plate numbers right, but often forget to look for the tag. Using the police numbers, we estimate $\frac{1{,}000 \times 1{,}000}{8} = 125{,}000$ cars in the city.

The trouble with both these estimates is they will be too high if we've missed any matches. If we had only the camera or only the police data, we would have to guess about the number of misses. But since we have both, we can make a better estimate.

Suppose the traffic camera and police have six tagged cars with overlapping license plate numbers. That leads to an estimate of $\frac{1{,}000 \times 1{,}000}{6} = 166{,}667$ cars in the city.

We're not going to average these numbers because we trust the initial tagging, and we have some confidence in the traffic camera tag counts but less in its license plate data, and we trust the police license plate data more than its tag-spotting. So, we multiply the two estimates that use the tagging—100,000 and 125,000—and divide by the estimate that uses the two less trustworthy sources—166,667. That gives us an estimate of 75,000 cars.

We think we tagged 1,000 out of 75,000 cars, so the 1,000 caught by traffic cameras should have matched 13.33 license plates. Since they only matched 10, we assume only 75% of license plates are recorded correctly. The police should also have matched 13.33. Since they only matched eight, we assume they notice and bother to record the tag only 60% of the time. These assumptions make all our numbers consistent.

Of course, we're not sure the numbers are correct. There are plenty of other explanations for the data. If we think the 75% correct license plates from the cameras and 60% tags spotted by police are implausible, we might look for alternative explanations. The point of the example is when capture-recapture generates three different estimates from three different samples, combining them often results in an estimate outside the range of the three. The differences in the estimates imply errors in the assumptions, and correcting those errors can lead to an overall estimate lower or higher than any of the three. In this case, we took individual estimates of 100,000, 125,000, and 166,667 and combined them to get an estimate of 75,000. This is much more logical than averaging the three inflated estimates.

BRINGING IT ALL TOGETHER

Does this approach mean I think 28,813 is the best estimate of Gaza traumatic injury deaths given the data? No, and for two reasons.

First is that the 28,813 estimate suggests that only 65% of the survey responses represented Gaza residents who actually died of traumatic injuries. It also suggests that 45% of the hospital victims were misidentified either accidentally or on purpose, or had too much missing data to match. Those fractions seem too high to me. Judging from the numbers of women and minors, it appears that Hamas miscategorized the age or sex of about 20% of identified bodies; an additional 25% due to errors or missing data seems high.

I don't know much about the topic, and perhaps my intuition on error rates is wrong. To get a better estimate, I'd talk to people familiar with these data and the situation in Gaza. I might make further adjustments to the models to make the numbers consistent. But until I got consistent numbers that seemed plausible, I wouldn't publish any estimate at all.

The second reason I wouldn't use 28,813 as an estimate is a general problem with capture–recapture analysis: it can only find deaths that have been noticed by someone. In the lake trout example, if there is a population of trout living in some inaccessible area, they will be left out of the count.

Some deaths will be noticed by lots of people: deaths of prominent people, deaths with bodies recovered, deaths captured on video, deaths of people with lots of family and friends in frequent contact. Other deaths are less likely to be noticed: obscure people without close connections, entire families killed together, people buried under rubble who were not known to be in the area, deaths of criminals, vagrants, and hermits.

Capture–recapture only estimates the number of noticed deaths. Therefore, I consider my adjusted capture–recapture figure of 28,813 to be consistent with the Hamas 37,877. I consider it plausible that the difference is unnoticed deaths. After all, Hamas totals have been reasonably accurate in the past, and Hamas has access to all the data in this study plus much more information. The UN estimated that 10,000 bodies were never recovered; many of these could be absent from all three of our lists. Moreover, there are many other problematic assumptions in this analysis, so I think it's also plausible that the figure is much higher. My 95% credible interval would be something like 30,000–60,000.

MISDIRECTION

The larger point is that in many Wrong Numbers, statistics are used to distract you from thinking about reality. I began by considering the plausibility of the authors' conclusion in terms of Hamas incentives: how many bodies could be plausibly overlooked and how accurate it's possible to be about traumatic injury deaths in wartime chaos. After reading the analysis, I thought about how plausible the authors' assumptions were, how their three estimates could be so inconsistent, and what additional information—like the accuracy of hospital identifications or survey responses—were necessary to form useful opinions. Like the authors, I used numbers, but as guides to understanding rather than ways to avoid understanding.

I learned to do things this way by betting since early childhood and keeping rigorous track of results. I've bet on horse races, poker, casino games, sporting events, news, and financial markets. This teaches many skills not found in classrooms. But I also paid attention in classrooms to some of the best statisticians and forecasters in the world.

I believe that numbers and quantitative analysis can turn up useful non-obvious truths, and lead to knowledge and success in many fields. But to get good at quantitative analysis, you need many thousands of hours making bets for personally meaningful stakes with hundreds of thousands of clear, objective, rigorously recorded events. You don't get this in academics; you might publish a few papers a year, most of which never provide clear-cut objective outcomes, and none of which are recorded rigorously. That makes it easy to cling to methods that gain approval without being right.

But you also don't get good without serious academic study. The capture–recapture concept is a clever one that few amateurs would think of—and even those amateurs who would think of it would miss hundreds of other useful ideas turned up by theoreticians, and would fall into some subtle errors that textbooks caution against.

One last minor point. The authors used extensive imputation, which you recall from Chapter 6. The authors filled in missing or inconsistent data with guesses. This is a borderline case for imputation. On the one hand, there is genuine interest in the answer, and little possibility of getting accurate data until after the conflict resolves, when it will be too late to do much good. It's impractical to gather better data until the war ends. On the other hand, the guesses significantly influence the result, a fact that the authors don't mention. It should be highlighted. While gathering fully accurate data is impractical, the authors could have picked a sample of 100 or so names to investigate further. This exercise would certainly have yielded useful detail about how many matching errors were real, and how and why they occurred.

WE'LL ALL GO TOGETHER WHEN WE GO

If this chapter wasn't depressing enough, what about predictions for 100% mortality for the entire world? I'll take that up in the next chapter.

CHAPTER TWELVE
REPENT! THE END IS NEAR

You may recall back in 2018, many officials and climate activists claiming we have only 12 years before a climate catastrophe would be irreversible. Presidential candidate (at the time) Joe Biden claimed, "science tells us that how we act or fail to act in the next 12 years will determine the very livability of our planet." *Time* magazine editor Jeffrey Kluger wrote in that periodical that the UN Intergovernmental Panel on Climate Change (IPCC) determined that "a catastrophe is nigh—that that distant future of an Earth beset by floods, droughts, wildfires and typhoons isn't distant anymore, but as little as 12 years away." Dan Zak in *The Washington Post* claimed, "we have only around 12 years to act if we want to keep the Quite Horrible from becoming the Truly Terrible." This is only a tiny sampling of the headlines, television news leads, campaign speeches, interviews, blog posts, and other repetitions of the 12-years-until-disaster claim.

EVERGREEN NUMBERS

Never one to be upstaged, Swedish teenage activist Greta Thunberg tweeted that year, "A top climate scientist is warning that climate change will wipe out humanity unless we stop using fossil fuels over the next five years."

Curiously, the 12-year figure lived on for five or six years, generally without being updated. One exception was John Kerry, the Biden administration climate envoy, who said in 2021, "Well, the scientists told us 3 years ago we had 12 years to avert the worst consequences of climate crisis. We are now 3 years gone, so we have 9 years left." But for most people, the 12 years was an ageless figure.

Where does the 12-year figure come from? A 2018 special report by the IPCC. When the report was published in September 2018, the NASA-GISS Land-Ocean Temperature Index, the measure used for most popular climate reporting, was 1.01°C. As I write this in June 2025, the index is 1.03°C. Since we're more than halfway through the 12-year period, and don't seem to be halfway to wiping out humanity, you don't hear the 2018 report quoted much. That's not to say climate change is not an issue, but probably not one that will kill everyone by 2030.

The second sentence of that document reads, "Global warming is likely to reach 1.5°C between 2030 and 2052 if it continues to increase at the current rate." The 12-year figure comes from subtracting the year of the report, 2018, from the earliest possible date of 1.5°C warming, 2030.

A minor point is nothing in the sentence mentions disaster or catastrophe, only the target 1.5°C.

NEW YORKERS CAN THROW OUT THEIR BARBEQUE GRILLS

The major point is the most important phrase in that sentence: "if it continues to increase at the current rate." This makes it a statement about the past, not a prediction about the future. The average temperature in New York City's Central Park was 28°F on December 31, 2024, and 85°F as of this writing on July 15, 2025. If temperature continues to increase at that rate, it will reach 665°F by the end of 2030. Now, 665°F is the name of a famous Singapore steakhouse which uses a special wood/charcoal oven imported from Barcelona to char its steaks perfectly at that temperature. While my statement about the past is perfectly true, I do not predict that on New Year's Eve 2030 New Yorkers will get perfectly cooked steaks by leaving their meat out in Central Park.

According to NASA-GISS, the Earth had warmed 1.01°C from 1960 to 2017, 58 years. If that rate continued, in about 29 years—2047—it would get to 1.5°C. While that's a lot more plausible than my Central Park example, the fact remains that both are statements about the past, not the future.

I don't mean to suggest this is what the authors did in their 700-page report. They didn't just look up two numbers on the NASA-GISS website and do some simple math. They didn't use 1960 as a base year, nor the NASA-GISS Land-Ocean Temperature Index.

All I'm saying is that this is what their sentence means. It's a statement about how much the Earth has warmed in the past, not a prediction of what's going to happen in the future. If you think the Earth warmed 1.24°C from 1960 to 2017, then *at that rate* it will hit 1.5°C in 12 years, by 2030. If you think it warmed 0.95°C, then *at that rate* it will hit 1.5°C in 34 years, by 2052, the authors' upper limit. So, the authors' sentence is only about how much the Earth has warmed in the past.

WHODUNIT?

There's another tricky term in the sentence, "global warming." To the authors it doesn't mean how warm the Earth is, but who's responsible. Only anthropogenic warming—warming caused by human activity—counts as global warming.

The authors think global mean temperatures have risen in the past by 0.17°C per decade, which would suggest hitting 1.5°C in 2047. They express no uncertainty about that. The range of 2030–2052 represents uncertainty about what portion of it is due to humans. The authors think it's possible that humans are warming the Earth 0.3°C per decade and some unknown factor is actually cooling the Earth 0.13°C. That's what gives the 2030 minimum date. They also think it's possible that humans are causing only about half of the observed warming, in which case they get their 2052 maximum date.

If you think the problem with global warming is hotter temperatures (melting ice, rising sea levels, and other physical effects), then you should care about future warming, not past warming or extrapolations from it. If you do focus on extrapolations from the past, 2047 is the key date.

Only if you think the problem with global warming is that humans are tampering with something pristine—and you only consider the worst possible scenario—is 2030 a relevant date. Focusing on anthropogenic warming suggests that what's happening in the world matters less than who's at fault.

Not all environmental change is bad. We hear about possible species extinctions, but not about the species that will thrive and diversify on a warmer planet (e.g., insects and sea life may be increasing in numbers and variety due to warming to date, although this is controversial). In any event, no one knows the optimal rate of speciation and extinction. We like majestic old-growth forests and exquisite biologic specializations where the climate is stable, as well as the vibrant adaptations and innovations in fast-changing environments.

Furthermore, far more of the Earth's surface is too cold for humans than too warm at the moment. Historically, warm periods are more prosperous than cold ones, and more people die in cold months than warm ones. In addition, destructive weather events are not concentrated in the warmest months or the warmest places, so there's no direct reason to expect more of them in a warmer world. Carbon dioxide is good for plants, and plants are good for both people and the environment.

SMALL CHANGE

Granted, there is reason to prefer less change to more, because more change could tip off catastrophic cascades. We know we can live with current temperatures; we can't be sure we'll be happy if things get significantly warmer. And even if a warmer world is better in some ways, the benefits could be overwhelmed by the transition costs. But these are all arguments to reduce the overall human environmental footprint rather than to reduce the temperature by any means necessary.

This is where the 12-years-until-disaster alarmism becomes toxic. Lowering 2030 temperatures significantly requires wide-scale geoengineering—for example, scattering glass beads on arctic ice or injecting sulfur into the stratosphere to reduce the temperature immediately (the IPCC report emphasizes carbon sequestration, a possibly less risky form of geoengineering, but also says that sequestration and emission reductions are not enough). Crude, dramatic rules like banning coal or outlawing air travel could slash emissions quickly, but the effects would not be fully felt in temperatures for up to a decade. Moreover, those approaches increase the human impact on the environment and introduce more uncertainty into future climate. They may bring down global temperatures, but not by 2030, and at the cost of introducing greater long-term uncertainty and possibly tripping more catastrophic cascades.

Policies like a carbon tax or building nuclear power plants take years to implement, and only begin to reduce the rate of CO_2 emissions. These work for planning horizons like limiting global warming to 2°C by 2050. But they have environmental benefits beyond temperature, their effects are more predictable than panic rules, and they're more likely to be maintained as political winds change. Also, they're much cheaper than emergency measures.

Even better would be long-term, sustainable, global agreements to leave fossil fuels in the ground permanently. These agreements could take decades to nurture. They make sense if we focus on 2100. They could serve to address all global issues, including many environmental ones, and to support world peace and prosperity. They won't cool the Earth by 2030, possibly not even by 2050, but they could deliver a better world to our grandchildren. Alarmist panic interferes with such rational consensus building.

WRITING BY COMMITTEE

Which brings us back to the IPCC special report. It contains two contradictory threads, likely as a result of being written by a committee. The 2030 date relies on huge uncertainty about how much global warming has been caused by humans—a factor of three between 0.1°C per decade and 0.3°C. But later, the report cites studies that conclude, "human-induced warming trends over the period 1905–2005" are "indistinguishable from the corresponding total observed warming." If the latter claim is true, then we know the rate of anthropogenic warming, and it will hit 1.5°C if the rate remains the same in more like 30 years than 12 years.

If we don't understand climate to the point that we have a 3:1 uncertainty band about anthropogenic contributions to warming, it's foolhardy to rush in with radical changes. When you don't understand a complex system, but you do know there are powerful offsetting forces at work, you should be cautious about fooling with it. On the one hand, if we understand climate well enough to know the amount of anthropogenic warming, the rate is not high enough to cause a crisis by 2030 if it does not accelerate. On the other hand, if we don't understand the climate well enough to be confident of the anthropogenic contribution, we should avoid massive, rushed experiments.

Even if everything the alarmists say is true, 2030 is not a feasible planning horizon. It admits only panic solutions that increase long-term uncertainty. You don't plan for the horizon you want to control, you plan for the horizon you can control. The climate in 2030 is already baked in—we should worry about dealing with it, not changing it. The climate in 2050 is in play, with many attractive policy choices to be implemented with sense, prudence, trial, and error.

NOBEL DREAMS

Do you wonder why you have so few Nobel prizes? I do, so I was interested to learn the blame lies neither with me nor the Nobel Committee, but with my father.

CHAPTER THIRTEEN

WHO STOLE MY NOBEL PRIZE?

A recent paper published by the Centre for Economic Policy Research, titled "Access to Opportunity in the Sciences: Evidence from the Nobel Laureates," found that 67% of science Nobel Prize winners have "fathers from above the 90th income percentile in their birth country." The authors, affiliated with Imperial College London, Dartmouth College, Princeton University, and the University of Pennsylvania, claim that their paper reveals extreme inequality in the science world and suggests that undiscovered geniuses from poor backgrounds never had the chance to show what they could do for humanity.

A BANDWAGON

The study received considerable press attention, including a piece in *The Guardian* claiming that it showed "a lot of talent wasted ... and breakthroughs lost."

"The Nobel prizes highlight that we have a biased system in science and little is being done to even out the playing field," wrote scientist Kate Shaw in *Physics World*. "We should not accept that such a tiny demographic are born 'better' at science than anyone else."

This study contains several statistical and conceptual errors, making its findings meaningless. It provides no evidence that unequal opportunity in science limits human progress.

For starters, how did the authors determine who was "born better" and thus had a better chance of winning a Nobel Prize? The study examined what winners' fathers did for a living. It found that since 1901, people with scientists for fathers had 150 times the chance of winning a science Nobel versus the average person.

Scientists earn more than the population average, which allegedly shows that coming from a wealthier family gave them a boost. But it's common sense that money is at most a small part of the advantage children of scientists have in winning Nobel prizes. Children of successful people often excel in the same fields as their parents. Look at movie stars, top athletes, political leaders, military commanders, or some of the most successful people in pretty much any field.

THE BELL CURVE STRIKES AGAIN

The size of the advantage may seem surprising, but this is typical when you look at the extremes of the bell curve. Even small initial advantages can result in extreme differences in outcome.

Suppose instead of Nobel prizes in science we were talking about an Olympic gold medal for the 100-meter dash. Suppose everyone in the world got to participate. There would be thousands of people a step or two behind the winner.

Now, suppose that 10% of the population—say, anyone with a left-handed mother—started the race with a two-step-head start. The average runner with a left-handed mother would only be two steps ahead of the pack, but we can almost guarantee that the winner would be one of them.

But the authors don't treat winning a Nobel Prize like a race, they suggest it's like winning a coin-flipping contest in which innate talent, culture, and hard work don't matter.

"If talent and opportunity were equally distributed," they write, "the average winner's parent would be at the 50th percentile."

Let's say everyone in the world participates in a coin-flipping contest to get 24 heads in a row, which has similar probability to winning a science Nobel Prize. The 1% with scientist fathers get two free heads, giving them a modest 8% advantage—that is, they get two more heads, 8% of 25, than people without scientist fathers. They will have 300 times the chance of winning the contest than children of non-scientists.

The same mathematics applies to children of scientist fathers, who have 150 times the chance of winning a Nobel Prize. That could result from a modest 8% advantage in scientific talent and opportunity. The bell curve strikes again.

PATERNAL HEAD STARTS

So, why would having a scientist father put someone eight percentile points ahead of the pack? The study authors say it's their families' higher income or education, but those are not the first factors I would point to.

One key factor is genetics. Though we haven't identified a Nobel Prize gene, some helpful qualities for scientific accomplishment—like IQ, lack of major congenital disabilities, conscientiousness, and curiosity—are partly influenced by DNA. Another factor is culture, and having a scientist father makes it more likely you were born into a family, place, and culture that values science.

Of course, children of scientists are also likely to have more opportunities. According to the study's authors, that's the problem we need to fix. When writing about the paper's findings on X, co-author Paul Novosad quoted Stephan Jay Gould: "I am, somehow, less interested in the weight and convolutions of Einstein's brain than in the near certainty that people of equal talent have lived and died in cotton fields and sweatshops."

The paper's authors write, "Our evidence suggests that there is a large number of 'missing scientists'—individuals who could have produced important scientific discoveries, but did not receive the complementary inputs required over their lives to do so."

Of course, improving education and opportunities for workers in cotton fields and sweatshops is a worthwhile goal (and eliminating that sort of unpleasant low-wage labor is even more worthwhile). However, the paper misunderstands how scientific discovery works. Just because the children of non-scientists aren't getting their share of Nobel prizes doesn't mean they aren't making valuable contributions to science or other fields.

Scientific progress is based on the contributions and discoveries of thousands of people whose names we never hear. Geniuses are important, but innovation doesn't depend on one individual. We'd have Newton's laws without Isaac Newton, we'd understand radioactivity without Marie Curie, and we'd have found the Higgs boson without Peter Higgs. Literature is different: we wouldn't have Shakespeare's plays and sonnets without Shakespeare.

REDIRECTION

Redirecting all children into science to help equalize Nobel prizes won't mean more Nobel prizes, only perhaps different winners. It would likely mean more scientists, but perhaps more than we can fund. It could deprive the world of top contributors in other fields like literature, politics, arts, and entertainment—fields where, unlike science, top contributions cannot be duplicated by others. And it won't necessarily equalize outcomes, because children of high socioeconomic status will still have advantages over children of low socioeconomic status, whatever fields people choose.

Nobel Prize winners also aren't always the most productive scientists. Some recipients win for a single insight or a fortuitous observation. Often the winners seem to be nearly random selections from several people who published similar findings around the same time. Some Nobel prizes were awarded for work that turned out to be wrong.

The paper did show that children of engineers, doctors, business owners, lawyers, and judges were also more likely to win Nobel prizes, although they had a smaller advantage than the children of scientists.

Again, that advantage probably had more to do with genetics, interests, and culture than family wealth.

ERRORS IN VARIABLES

The paper also has another significant problem: the authors use the father's occupation to guess childhood income and education, which in turn are used to guess socioeconomic status. However, these are not perfect correlations.

The authors are applying group characteristics to individuals, which, as we discussed in Chapter 6, is the ecological fallacy. There are plenty of Nobel winners whose childhood socioeconomic status was typical of their fathers' professions. But there are also plenty who don't fit the mold.

Ada Yonath, who won the 2009 Nobel Prize in chemistry, had a father who was a business owner and rabbi, which the authors coded as the 98th education percentile. However, Yonath's father was actually an impoverished grocer who died when she was young, meaning she had to take on multiple jobs to support her family.

Harold Urey, who won the 1934 Nobel Prize in chemistry, was the son of a minister, placing him in the 98th education percentile. However, his father died when he was six, and he spent his childhood in poverty.

Linus Pauling won the 1954 Nobel Prize in chemistry. His father owned a business, and Linus was coded at the 97th wealth percentile. However, the business was a drug store, and Pauling's father got sick when he was five and died when he was nine. Pauling's practical-minded mother thought going to college was a waste of time.

BAD IS GOOD!

The authors acknowledged this issue but claimed that the Nobel Prize winners in their study were, if anything, more likely to be born to fathers at the high socioeconomic status ranks of their fields, and, therefore, the imperfect correlations strengthened their results.

This is circular reasoning. The authors want you to start by assuming their finding is true—that socioeconomic status is a causal factor in winning science Nobel prizes. Good scientific inquiry doesn't start by assuming what the author is trying to prove. This bias leads researchers to make false assumptions about evidence. It's like a detective who assumes someone is guilty and considers having an alibi as additional evidence against her. Innocent people don't need alibis.

If you don't assume family socioeconomic status is the main factor in winning science Nobel prizes, there's no reason to think the winners' fathers had higher-than-average socioeconomic status for their fields. And, therefore, the errors in guessing wealth and education from profession weaken the authors' case rather than strengthen it.

By the way, this is a common error I find in academic papers. Authors acknowledge their data problems and false assumptions, but claim these actually strengthen their results, using the same circular logic.

Suppose you want to prove women are smarter than men. You give a test to 100 men and 100 women, and find that 55 of the top 100 scorers are women. Your p-value is 0.14, above the conventional threshold of 0.05, so typically considered not statistically significant by journal editors.

You argue that there are lots of errors in your data—miscategorized sex, non-binary individuals, mistakes in test scoring, tests not perfectly measuring intelligence. If you assume women are smarter than men, the errors are more likely to reduce the measured number of women in the top 100 than to increase it. So, you want your findings published despite the high p-value. But if you instead begin by assuming equal intelligence between the sexes, the errors are equally likely to increase or decrease your measurement, they only increase your p-value to something even larger than 0.14.

The authors of this study fail to realize that their data actually show that science Nobel prizes seem to be more meritocratic than anyone would have guessed. There is certainly more advantage to having the right parents for winning Oscars, top political offices, and sports awards. But good news doesn't make for sensational headlines or viral social media posts.

MY STORY

I was not truthful when I wrote in the last chapter that my father is to blame for my small number (zero) of science Nobel prizes. In fact, he was a scientist. I was not an exception, I probably got about as much head start as is possible. He had a PhD in physics from the University of Chicago, and my mother had a Master's in chemistry from the same school. We lived near the University of Washington, where I attended some of the best public schools in the country. I clearly was in a top education percentile, with a family, culture, and environment that valued science.

Economically we were in what I consider the sweet spot—enough income not to have to worry about necessities, but with five kids, not enough extra to get into trouble. My mother had to work as a registered nurse to make ends meet and I had to work my way through college, but we were certainly above median if not in the upper-middle class.

Socially it's even harder to say. We were Jewish in Seattle, where there were few Jews. The city at the time had a strong northern European antisemitic strain, which was felt even in the university district. My father had been tagged by anti-communists during the McCarthy era, and we were in considerable legal and social jeopardy until the mid-1960s. He had been the editor of the *Chicago Maroon* as an undergraduate and written some leftist editorials, but his main sin was accepting an invitation from the Soviet Union to college newspaper editors to visit the country (the State Department blocked the trip). On the other hand, he was a full professor and a scientist—keeping his job thanks to the only lawyer in Seattle willing to defend an accused communist—which carried a lot of social weight in those days.

I was definitely raised in a culture of science and exploration. My parents' friends included many scientists and also professors of other subjects. My father actively participated in my attempts to find patterns in the numbers I found in the back of the newspaper—agricultural data, stock prices, sports boxscores—which I found far more interesting than the ephemeral nonsense on the front page.

He had mixed feelings about my determination to profit from the patterns. As a semi-communist he had contempt for taking money without doing useful work. But as a curious investigator himself he was interested in the subject, and proud that I could "beat the dealer," as Ed Thorp put it, in horse racing, poker, and stock options. Ed's books were a major inspiration to me, although I did not meet him until later in life. Also, my father was grateful that I would have little trouble paying my way through college.

To mollify his misgivings about gambling, my father got me many opportunities to work on scientific research projects, starting in middle school. I did my share of test-tube washing and making coffee for the team, but I was also the computer programmer and statistician on projects. It amazed me that even by the late 1960s, most scientists could not use computers and had only a B-student/introductory-course knowledge of statistics. This was a formative experience in my willingness to believe my own calculations over the opinions of people who knew far more about the subject than I did.

The project I remember best never led to a publication. The Air Force had given $2 million to a guy without anyone understanding exactly what he was going to do with it—only that he had an awesome IQ. This was at the height of Sputnik-reaction science spending. The scientist built an elaborate machine and then killed himself, burning all his notes. He had no collaborators or assistants. The Air Force offered the machine to anyone willing to figure out what it did.

My father volunteered out of curiosity, and the two of us spent many hours tracing its components and wiring. It obviously had a design; it wasn't random junk like you might see in the background of a Hollywood movie lab. It was intriguing; it gave you the feeling you were very close to some essential insight, but it couldn't quite come into focus. It was easy to imagine that with a minor tweak we'd have a working teleporter or universal translator or anti-gravity machine. After a few months, my mother made us give it back to the Air Force. But as Bluma Zeigarnik noticed a century ago observing waiters, it is the uncompleted tasks that remain in our memories.

I judge I had about the best early-life edge to win a science Nobel as anyone. I've continued to work on science investigations in many fields my entire life—generally as a data analyst and programmer, but also mixing chemicals, taking surveys, running lab equipment, and other hands-on science. I've also served as a methodology peer reviewer for hundreds of papers in major journals.

While I've never come close to doing anything that might merit a science Nobel Prize, I have worked with winners, and also with people who went on to work with winners. The majority, but only a small majority, had backgrounds that gave them legs up in science, and some others had backgrounds you might have thought would disqualify them. I did not observe any great difference in ability between the winners and dozens of similar near-winners—although both winners and near-winners could be easily distinguished from merely competent scientists.

PROFESSORS VERSUS WISE GUYS

In the next chapter we'll see how an ESPN documentary tried to answer the eternal question of whether the house always wins.

CHAPTER FOURTEEN

WHY ARE THERE POOR QUANTS?

I have led you here, midway through the book, under false pretenses. I have tried to give the impression that there are a few egregious statistical studies out there, and some common tendencies that undercut the reliability of most others. My position is far more radical.

YOU OUGHT TO HAVE DONE A BETTER EXPERIMENT

The great physicist Ernest Rutherford was quoted as saying, "If your experiment needs statistics, you ought to have done a better experiment." This aligns with my dictum to ignore odds ratios below 3—a 3-to-1 difference is obvious without careful statistical computation. You should still check for statistical significance—three treatment successes and one control success could be random chance, but you have the kind of result that suggests you have zeroed in on a causal mechanism.

Consider a double-blind, controlled drug trial. You recruit 100 pairs of patients with each pair as similar as possible in terms of symptom severity, age, general health conditions, medical history, sex, race, etc. One patient in each pair is selected at random to test your new drug, the other to get the best existing treatment. An experimenter evaluates the result in each patient. Neither patient nor experimenter know which drug was given.

Suppose the new drug gives a better result for 80 of the 100 pairs—an odds ratio of 4. We don't need a statistician to tell us the new drug is an improvement on average.

On the other hand, suppose in 51 pairs the patient who got the new drug did better. Once again, no statistician is needed to tell us the improvement from the new drug, if any, is small on average, and that we'll need a larger sample size or more precise identification of patients to be confident about whether there is any improvement at all.

But what if the treatment does better in 60 pairs? The new drug seems promising with a 50% higher success rate, an odds ratio of 1.5. But if the treatment and control are equally good, there is a 5.7% chance (the p-value) that either the treatment or control will have 60 or more successes. So, this result does not meet the conventional threshold of a p-value below 5%. Incidentally, there are other methods for computing the p-value that can give somewhat different answers, including some that would categorize this result as significant at the 5% level.

But what you really need in this case is not a statistician but subject matter experts. You need to talk to the patients and caregivers to get details, and study lab tests and other data. Which patients got better, and when? How much better were the successes? What side effects, good or bad, were there? Why did the treatment and the control work when they did, and why didn't they when they didn't. Your goal should not be to rush to publication or drug approval as soon as you can manufacture a p-value below

5%, but to gain understanding and prediction accuracy such that there is no need for statistics to make your case.

CONTROLLING PEOPLE, NOT SEEKING TRUTH

That said, journals do have to decide what to publish, and regulators have to decide which drugs to approve. Some kind of rational but arbitrary criterion is a reasonable basis. For reasons given in Chapter 9, p-values are not the right metric, you should incorporate prior probability and power as well. But when used in this way, statistics are used to control humans, not to uncover truth.

Let's compare the double-blind controlled study described above—considered the gold standard of scientific research—with a Bayesian doctor. Dr. Betty Bayes has a reason for trying a new treatment, and that reason suggests to her which patients are most likely to benefit from it relative to the conventional treatment. She tries it on one and pays close attention to all aspects of the case. This might lead her to adjust doses or ancillary factors, or to look for somewhat different patients. She reads other case histories and publishes hers. Eventually the Bayes doctors arrive at a consensus use for the new treatment. This is, in somewhat idealized form, how medical treatments are actually selected by real healthcare workers.

Betty's approach has many advantages. Each patient is given the treatment his doctor thinks is best for him, given current knowledge, whereas double-blind controlled trials assign treatments randomly, meaning half the patients get a treatment believed to be second-best for them. Double-blind controlled trials only really work for single-ingredient drug treatments—combinations of ingredients or doses or other factors require impractical sample sizes and most non-drug treatments cannot be concealed from patients and experimenters. Bayesian methods can work with every type of therapy. We don't need to score patient results along a single dimension—better or worse; we can note tradeoffs that may make different treatments appropriate for different patients. Bayesian knowledge is applied as soon as it is accumulated; no long delay as sufficient amounts of evidence are collected, analyzed, and put into operation. The wisdom of crowds is harnessed with many doctors and types of patients with different perspectives.

The double-blind controlled trial has only one offsetting advantage—it eliminates experimenter bias and prejudice. Unfortunately, that's only in theory. In practice, it's easier to put a thumb on the scales in double-blind controlled trials than in Bayesian investigations.

There is also a sneaky double switch in the double-blind controlled trials, which is present in all classical hypothesis testing. We want to know which patients will do better with the new treatment. This is not a matter of random chance; there are reasons why the new treatment will work for some patients but not others, and be worse than the old treatment for some patients but not others. Seeking out these reasons should be the goal of investigators. Pretending the effects of the treatments are random allows statistical victory—p-value under 0.05! Hurrah!—to be declared before the goal is reached. We pretend what we're investigating is some kind of dice roll, absolving us of the necessity to explain anything.

That's one switch. The second is that the classical statistician is unable to make any statement about the frequency that the new treatment will be better than the old for future patients. Instead, he introduces his own randomness by the assignment of treatment or control to patients. The p-value tells us nothing about the probability that the new treatment will be better for the average patient in the future; it's a statement about the probability that a random assignment will result in 60 or more pairs favoring either the treatment or control. The statistician manufactured randomness to make a statement about that randomness, and hopes you will be misled into thinking it is a statement about reality.

THE RENO CONFERENCE

In 1974, an economist at the University of Nevada, Reno, Bill Eadington, called a National (later "International") Conference on Gambling and Risk-Taking. Unlike most academic conferences that attract specialists, Bill's conference appealed to advantage gamblers, casino executives, gambling regulators, psychologists treating problem gamblers, and mathematicians and economists interested in the subject.

In the 1970s and 1980s, and to a lesser extent later, this was the place to find the world's great advantage gamblers gathered together. Its only competition was the Blackjack Ball, held annually in great secrecy—Bill's conference was the only venue open to anyone.

Advantage gamblers play casino games and make bets that are designed to have a built-in edge for the house, but in ways that switch the advantage to the player. They are not cheaters—advantage gamblers are the people who most hate cheating, moreover they're often victims of casinos and bookies who cheat them. The point of advantage gambling is to read the rules and find ways to win because you're smarter than the house. As patron saint (and good friend) Ed Thorp put it, the point is to "beat the dealer," rather than to win money.

Most casino executives and regulators took a different view. They were businesspeople, not gamblers. They thought the deal was players paid the house edge as a kind of tax that went to pay for the glitzy surroundings, free drinks and shows, dealers' salaries, and heavy taxes levied on gambling. Anyone who refused to pay the tax, whether by illegal cheating or clever exploitation of loopholes, was morally a thief.

The conference was the only place where both groups got in a room and argued it out. Another perennial debate was between psychologists (who usually thought their patients' problem was gambling, and the treatment was behavior modification or psychoanalysis) and advantage gamblers (who thought the patients' problem was losing, and the treatment was to teach them to win).

Both of those are understandable differences of opinion you might expect. A less obvious one was between advantage gamblers who made their livings with regular betting, and mathematicians and economists who lived on salaries and did little or no gambling for personally significant stakes.

The academics would show up at advantage gambler presentations and make great efforts to debunk any claimed positive results. They might attack the theoretical basis for the method, or claim the edge was too small to be practical, or assert that it relied on a temporary inefficiency that had been corrected, or object to the calculations of statistical significance. They tended to dismiss the actual financial results, either by disbelieving them or claiming they were cherry picked or otherwise unrepresentative.

Advantage gamblers would return the favor by showing up at academic presentations and asking, "How much did you personally bet on this system, and what were your results?" Most academics considered the question both rude and irrelevant. But advantage gamblers wanted proof in the form of actual realized profits, not paper calculations of how much the professor could have made. Moreover, anyone with the claimed results—and most academic presentations claimed edges greater than advantage gamblers deemed possible—who did not take some personal advantage, couldn't really believe the system worked.

"THEN WHY ARE YOU POOR?"

The most famous example of this oft-repeated debate was when an advantage gambler, exasperated by a long back-and-forth, asked an academic: "Then why are you poor?" These five words crystallized the difference in perspective. To advantage gamblers, the question was as obvious as asking a fortune teller why she didn't win the lottery, or a faith healer why he was sick. If you have this great and useful power, why not use it for yourself? But to most of the academics at the conference, the pursuit of scientific truth was a great and noble calling, and using it to make money—especially in as morally dubious and sordid activity as betting—was beneath their dignity.

This is a specific example of a broader phenomenon. If you want to be accepted among gamblers, you have to be prepared to back any opinion you express with a bet. As economist Alex Tabarrok (a professor) said when defending Nate Silver (a bettor), betting is a tax on bullshit.

If a gambler says, "Wanna bet?" it's not a rhetorical question. You are expected to be able to formulate a clear betting proposition. If you can't do it, gamblers think you didn't really know what you meant, or hadn't thought it through. If you come up with something so qualified that no one would take the other side, then you weren't offering a useful opinion in the first place. If you have a clear bet but refuse to put a personally meaningful amount on it, you're no gambler.

While there are many unpleasant things about the society of gamblers, I've always liked this aspect. You find it to a lesser extent among financial traders as well. It makes most civilian conversation seem like blather, people pontificating with unreasonable certainty about things they wouldn't bet a nickel on.

Academic presentations nearly always involved highly complex applications of tools found in statistics textbooks and journal articles. Often, they involved difficult data to obtain. The implied message was that very smart people with a lot of work could get massive advantages. Advantage gamblers, on the other hand, relied on much simpler methods seldom found in textbooks and not accepted by most journals to gain smaller advantages that required patience, careful bet sizing, and discipline to exploit.

Neither side thought it was impossible to beat the house. The debate was over whether advantages were large but difficult to find, or moderate but easy to find. In the former case, academics could argue they didn't seek profit from gambling because the money wasn't worth the effort. In the latter case, the academics did not act indifferently enough to money to refuse profits of several thousand dollars for a couple of hours' effort.

An offshoot of this debate was whether anyone could claim to be a statistician without long experience making successful predictions in many thousands of independent trials. If you win in a casino, it's not because you are a clever writer or successful schmoozer at faculty meetings. People are trying as hard as they can not to give you money; no one is giving you credit for credentials, demeanor, ancestry, skin color, or anything else. Each bet is an independent trial. Academics can go entire careers without making even one clear-cut, objectively verified prediction measured against the best efforts of all other predictors. How can you know whether a statistical method works without trying it under controlled conditions with a large independent sample? Isn't the entire idea of statistics founded on empirical testing?

Advantage gamblers used their methods for all life decisions, because they trusted them. Few academics seemed inclined to do the same, suggesting they didn't trust their methods. Advantage gamblers borrowed freely from academic work; academics never seem to pay attention to tools with long track records of betting success.

"THEN WHY AREN'T YOU RICH?"

The academic comeback was, "Then why aren't you rich?" This is a valid question. Successful advantage gamblers made nice livings, but only a few were billionaires, and those all had partners and organizations. The really wealthy advantage gamblers were more entrepreneurs than independent bettors.

One answer is scale. The fact you can make $10,000 with two hours' effort doesn't mean you could make $10 million in a 2,000-hour working year. Financial trading, which involves similar skills, can be expanded far more easily than casino gambling and sports betting, and many advantage gamblers moved into finance or other fields.

Another answer is lifestyle. There is an undeniable appeal of earning money without a boss, working when and where you choose, living solely by your wits, surrounded by people who have no clue what you're doing. But for most people, those attractions fade, while the disadvantages get more irritating—the company of gamblers, social disapproval, needing to be constantly at the top of your game, boredom. When you're learning, the thrill of discovery makes the activity seem worthwhile, but going through the motions of long-established strategies feels unproductive compared to activities like teaching, scientific research, building businesses, or raising a family.

I gave the keynote speech at the 2006 conference at Harrah's Lake Tahoe Casino in Reno. Afterward, Bill Eadington introduced me to Bob Beiner, a producer for ESPN. He wanted to do a documentary, tentatively titled "Wise Guys Versus Professors." He'd heard some of the debates in the sessions and thought it would be instructive and entertaining to see whether the advantage sports bettors were more accurate than the academic mathematicians, statisticians, and economists. Incidentally, Beiner had me incorrectly categorized as a professor, since I had academic degrees and published in academic journals. I was firmly in the wise-guy camp.

I was enthusiastic about the idea because it was the one way to end the debate that was acceptable to both sides. After 32 years of fruitless arguing that changed few minds, we could settle the issue. Both sides had to accept a test under controlled conditions. Or so I thought.

Beiner's idea was that a select group of successful National Football League (NFL) sports bettors and academics who had made presentations on NFL betting would submit weekly picks to ESPN during football season for three years to see which group did better. The documentary was to be supplemented with interviews to explain approaches as well as NFL officials, gambling regulators, ordinary retail bettors, and others.

AN NFL ADVENTURE

The rest of this chapter is a moderately detailed description of a simple NFL betting system I developed for the documentary. If your interest is how to be a successful sports bettor, the methods I describe still work, but they're 1990 vintage, old-fashioned even in 2006, and ancient in 2025. The state of the art has improved dramatically since, especially with the incorporation of data science and machine learning. In the 20th century, sports bettors concentrated on the imperfections of the betting market, and spent little energy predicting game outcomes. Today, there have been major advances in game prediction. You might find my system contains some useful general background, but you should seek out more up-to-date sources before you risk your money.

But I did not include the story for aspiring sports bettors. Rather, it's intended to make clear what real quantitative prediction is, and highlight how far short most academic studies using statistics fall.

I expect most readers will skim the material. If you do, I hope you come away with the following points of comparison between truth-seeking and publication-generation.

I Built My System in a Couple of Hours One Afternoon

I read many academic papers in top journals that describe even less work—downloading some data someone else collected for other purposes, running it through canned statistical software, manufacturing a p-value below 0.05 (or sometimes failing), and claiming a publishable result. These papers usually have multiple authors, sometimes more than a dozen, yet nevertheless appear to represent no more than a few hours work by one person.

Granted some papers describe work of gathering and cleaning data. But even many of these are minimal efforts and low-quality data—polling undergraduate psychology classes, collecting self-selected, anonymous Internet responses, using unpaid and untrained students to run toy experiments. And in a depressing number of cases, when data fraud is discovered, none of the named authors take responsibility—it seems no one can remember the name of the wandering graduate student who gathered or managed the data, there was zero data security so anyone could have changed the numbers or mixed up versions, and no one can produce the raw data files.

I also grant that there's a lot of work to writing a paper, beyond the essential analysis. But this is also often of very low quality. The "previous work" sections are often slanted toward making the current paper seem both important and surprising—and in any case, are usually a year or more out of date by the time of publication. You can find much better background easily. The descriptions of the work done are rarely complete and accurate; when I try to replicate the results I usually find that authors misstated details or left things out. The abstracts and conclusions often diverge considerably from the actual findings. It's not uncommon that they seem to have been written by the lead author before the study was done, with the data and analysis appended afterward.

All of this contributes to the fiction that this stuff is hard, and that the authors have invested substantial expertise and work in the paper. Many academic papers I read that rely upon statistics could be done better and described more honestly and clearly by a single researcher without exceptional expertise or talent, in a few days.

I Set a Reasonable Goal, and Achieved It

I boasted I would get a 55% success rate, and hoped to do better than all other competitors selected by ESPN, and of course better than the bookies. Most statistical studies want 95% confidence, or equivalently, 5% significance. To get this, they measure against "null hypotheses" that are easy to beat. For example, the standard null hypothesis is that the treatment has no effect of any sort, not just that the treatment is unhelpful for its intended goal. That's virtually impossible, thus easy to disprove.

To make it even easier to get 5% significance, researchers choose statistical methods that add additional assumptions, such as that variables have Gaussian (usually called "normal," but there's nothing normal about them) or some other distribution, or that observations are independent. There are almost no real examples of Gaussian distributions. Many things are roughly bell-shaped, but most have either limits or fat tails or some other deviations from the Gaussian shape. Many things are close to uncorrelated, but very few are independent. Null hypotheses can be rejected at the 5% or even lower significance levels because these and other assumptions are false, not because the hypothesis the authors claim is true.

Adding to the woven web of guesses mainly requires small improvements to the best existing work, not 95% upendings measured against invented, easy-to-beat, null hypotheses. And if those 95% confidence/5% significance results are false, as they are more often than not, their value is negative.

I Didn't Start or Stop with Publication

I announced my intention and methodology ahead of time, then built and published my model. I monitored performance afterward, not just how much money it made, but whether its assumptions remained valid. I made all data and code available and up-to-date, with thorough expositions on my website. I discussed results with anyone who asked. I helped people implement the model on their own, and make improvements.

Contrast this with the hit-and-run procedure of some academics. Work is done with knowledge limited to a small group. After the numbers are in, people decide what the hypothesis was. A journal article is written and submitted for publication. The actual procedures are cloaked in jargon and ambiguity; the data is kept secret. No follow-up is done to see if the results hold up, and no help is offered to people trying to replicate the results.

I Started with Causal Effects, and Only Claimed Prediction

In many Wrong Numbers, authors begin with observed correlations, and end by claiming—or at least implying—causation. If you start with variables for which you have solid causal cases, and find that they are correlated with the variable of interest, you have some kind of a case. Correlation does not prove causation, but if you already have good reason to suspect causation, correlation can strengthen your case.

Or you can start with observed correlations, even without much reason to think the relations are causal. This cannot make a causal case, it can only reveal correlations, which can be used (with caution) for prediction. And it can provide guidance in the search for causes.

I did the most conservative thing: I used causal variables but only claimed prediction. Many Wrong Numbers do the completely unsupported thing and use observed correlation to claim proof of causation.

ENDING THE DEBATE

I had an ambitious goal. I wanted a bulletproof demonstration that it was easy to make money in sports betting, that it did not require an exceptional IQ, knowledge about the sport, or significant work. After decades of witnessing academic dismissal of all evidence, I hoped to lay the debate to rest. Therefore, I went beyond the ESPN requirements.

One common academic objection is that the advantage gambler did not have one simple system, but was constantly changing it to gain advantage. Related to this was the charge that the system was entirely ad hoc, with no justification, and therefore could not support any general conclusions about sports betting.

I used a single system that I published and never modified, and detailed exactly how I picked it based on long-established general principles. It used only simple, easily available public inputs, no inside information or complicated or obscure data. I posted my picks immediately after betting on my website, www.eRaider.com, which got reasonably heavy traffic, including many people who used my picks or methodology. I corresponded with a few dozen users, but based on traffic immediately after I posted my weekly picks, there could have been over a thousand. The picks were covered in both academic and popular publications. I even had both an app and a spreadsheet so people could do the calculations themselves. I disclosed the actual spread at which I got my money down. I never changed anything about the bets after my initial posting, nor the system ever.

I actually placed $100 bets on each game at the same time each week (early Tuesday morning when the major lines came out). This was to get around the automatic academic comment that advantage gambler results were based on listed odds and spreads, but that real bets could not be placed on those terms all the time—that odds and spreads changed and bookies cut off customers who made money.

ESPN allowed the picks to be submitted up to game time, and calculated the results based on the consensus line at kickoff. But that's not always possible to achieve. Also, ESPN ignored the vigorish—the fact that bookies don't offer even-money bets, they charge more for losers than they pay for winners. Full retail vigorish is usually 10% on losing bets—you either lose $110 or win $100. It's usually possible to get lower vigorish, but I computed all results based on full retail vigorish.

ESPN had already answered several other usual objections. I didn't have 50 different predictions ("locks," "big money plays," "sure winners," etc.) and afterward picked one to promote. There was only one set of picks. I didn't cherry pick starting and ending points to make things look good.

TRACK RECORD

The table below shows the system results. I did have one problem: 2007 was a terrible year, 2006 was mediocre, and 2008 only average. As a result, I was up only 13 wins, 136–123, and 0.7 profit units ($70 if I had paid full retail vigorish), which was not going to convince anyone. My 52.51% win percentage was barely above the 52.38% breakeven with full retail vigorish. That was far short of my boast of 55% over three years.

Season	Wins	No bets	Losses	Net wins	Profit
2006	50	176	41	9	4.9
2007	37	184	46	–9	–13.6
2008	49	182	36	13	9.4
2009	58	180	29	29	26.1
2010	45	187	35	10	6.5
2011	49	178	40	9	5.0
2012	49	175	43	6	1.7
2013	43	190	34	9	5.6
2014	50	186	31	19	15.9
2015	49	178	40	9	5.0
2016	43	185	39	4	0.1
2017	61	166	40	21	17.0
2018	51	190	26	25	22.4
2019	41	194	32	9	5.8
Total	675	2,551	512	163	111.8

I elected to keep the system going, which is a technical violation. See, if I had started with three great years, like 2009, 2017, and 2018, I would have been up 170 to 95, a 64% win percentage, with $6,650 profit and a clear statistical proof that the system was profitable. If you keep a system running until it works, you might eventually get lucky.

I didn't want to compound the problem by choosing to stop after a good season. Fortunately for me—but not for the world—the 2020 COVID season gave me a great excuse. I did not trust the system under the dramatically changed conditions of 2020, so it was a natural stopping point. Even better, 2019 was a below-average year, so I wasn't stopping after a big win.

Under full retail vigorish, you need to win 11 games for every 10 you lose to break even. The system had 675 wins versus 512 losses, a 57% win percentage. The wins brought in $67,500 and the losses cost $56,320 for a net profit of $11,180. The p-value for the null hypothesis that the system's true long-term win rate was 52.38% (the breakeven win rate) or lower was 0.01%, far below the conventional 5% level.

Now I hope you remember that p-values alone aren't meaningful. We need to ask the prior probability for the result and the power of the test. If the null hypothesis is that the system was actually breakeven or money-losing, that is it had a 52.38% win rate or worse, it would take 651 wins out of the 1,187 bets to reject the null at the 5% level. If the true win rate were 55%, as I had boasted, there was a 55.49% chance of getting 651 or more wins. So, the power of the test was 55.49%.

If you start by granting me a 50% prior probability that my system had a 55% win rate, with a 50% probability that it was merely breakeven at 52.38% win rate, then 1,000 good systems would produce 555 that rejected breakeven at the 5% level, and 47 breakeven systems that also rejected at the 5% level. That means the experimental result that the system worked has 92% posterior probability.

Now you might start out more skeptical, in which case your posterior probability would be lower. Or you might want to take into account that the system had 675 wins, something a breakeven system would accomplish only one time in 1,000. Anyway, as Jean Rasczak said to Johnny Rico in the movie version of Robert Heinlein's *Starship Troopers*, "Figuring things out for yourself is the only freedom anyone really has. Use that freedom. Make up your own mind, Rico."

BINARY FACTOR MODELS

The basic go-to model of professional sports bettors from the 1960s to the mid-1990s was the binary factor model. It still works fine, but advances in data science have introduced more competition. Of course, many other models were used as well, but binary factor was the workhorse. One way to tell an ivory tower statistician without any extensive experience in having to make accurate predictions versus meaningful benchmarks is she never considers using binary factor models.

My model used three binary factors. Each team got +1 if it had a losing record against the spread in the season to date, −1 for a winning record, and 0 if it was even (technically, "binary" means only two values, but coding some inputs as ties retains the binary spirit; anyway, that's what everyone calls these models). Each team got +1 if it had more giveaways (fumbles lost and interceptions) than takeaways in its last game, −1 if it had more takeaways, and 0 if they were even. Finally, a team got +1 if the spread had moved against it since before the previous week's games had been played, and 0 for both teams if the spread had not moved.

You added the three factors for each team, getting a score from −2 to +3. You then took the home team's points and subtracted the visiting team's points. A result of +3 or higher meant bet on the home team, −3 or lower meant bet on the visitor, totals from −2 to +2 meant no bet.

Why these factors? One of the biggest problems with predicting football games, and many other outcomes, is it's easy to find complex models that predict every past game perfectly, as long as you have enough inputs relative to the number of past games or make your model complicated enough. Traditionally, these "overfit" models were considered worthless in predicting future outcomes, although recent advances in data science have led to some sophisticated machine learning algorithms that do employ perfect fits. But I had not seen these in 2006, and in any case that type of model would have been too complex for my purpose.

Binary factor models protect against overfitting by using only a few (typically three to seven) inputs, and only allowing two (or three with zeros) possible values for each. Moreover, developers insist on factors that have been shown to work in unrelated applications, and have causal explanations that can be validated. That last is important so you can tell if your system is failing without the expensive indication of losing money. The factors are added rather than combined in more complex ways.

An important advantage of binary factor models is maintenance. Professionals can monitor many factors, 20 or 30, and seamlessly slide factors in and out like an NFL defensive coordinator shifting players and alignments. I did not take advantage of this for my demonstration, but it would have improved performance considerably.

MODEL DESIGN

For three-factor NFL prediction, I wanted to get about 52% performance out of each factor. If those were independent, I'd get a 62.5% chance of winning, but I hoped for 55%, and got 57%.

The normal academic assumption was that bookies set betting lines efficiently, so that almost all factors—home versus visitor, favorite versus underdog, team coming off a win versus team coming off a loss, etc.—would be close to 50% and give no edge to gamblers trying to exploit them. But that's the view from 30,000 feet. Up close—and advantage sports bettors spend more energy analyzing the bookmaking business than the games they bet on—it's clear that few factors will be near 50%; most will pile up around 48% or 52%.

The reason is bookmakers are businesspeople, not gamblers. They set spreads to maximize their return-to-risk ratio, not to offer exactly 50/50 propositions to their customers. For almost every game there will be reasons to move the spread away from the exactly fair point. But bookmakers cannot afford to move the spread so far that there are single-factor bets with more than 52.38%—or less than 47.62%—probabilities, because these would allow profitable single-factor bets to customers.

Thus, a bookmaker has to balance competing considerations when setting a spread: risk reduction by getting close to even action on both sides of the bet, positive edge by having any excess on the favorable side for the bookmaker, making sure no single factor allows a profitable edge and helping each customer lose a little over the season (the bookmaker's revenue is limited by how much its customers are willing to lose, season-winning bettors cost revenue, excessive losses only speed revenue without increasing the season total, but cost customers and can lead to other problems).

Another issue is bookmakers have only a crude adjustment—a half point of spread (they can reduce vigorish to even things out but only by small amounts and this costs revenue). On average this allows them to move probabilities in about 2% increments—so they might have to choose between 49% or 51%. And that's on average: if the favored team has around a 60% or 75% chance of winning, the increment is much greater because the spread will be near three or seven points and those are very common win margins. A bookmaker may have to move things in increments of 4% or more. Finally, bookmakers do not like whole-number point spreads if they can be avoided, since if that is the winning margin, the bookmaker returns all bets and collects no vigorish.

In practice, this means most factors run up against the 47.62% or 52.38% barriers rather than settle in near 50%. Everyone in the business—but few academics it seems—is well aware that combining factors can lead to profitable betting, but not many bettors do this, and most retail bookmakers will refuse the action if customers try this. Some bookmaking operations for professional bettors will take action, but only from known customers, and will only quote spreads and vigorish after hearing which way the customer wants to bet. The hard part of making money in sports betting is getting profit-maximizing businesspeople to consistently send you money, not making picks that win 55% of the time against published spreads.

IT'S NOT JUST FOR SPORTS BETTING

Incidentally, something similar is true in financial markets as well. They are very close to random from the point of view of people far from the market. But on a big trading floor, or with sophisticated computers and data, many profitable patterns are easy to see. Exploiting them is trickier than finding them.

There's no magical wisdom of crowds to make prices accurate, and no smooth forces pushing prices toward a fixed equilibrium. Rather, there are sophisticated mechanisms that evolve to keep all arbitrage opportunities below a level that would allow unacceptable profits extracted. With lots of independent mechanisms of this type you don't expect to find prices perfectly balanced; rather, most of them are likely to be pushed up against one of their thresholds.

To see this, suppose you measure the heights of 1,000 people. You will have two people at the extremes—ignoring ties—one tallest and one shortest. But suppose you also measure people's incomes and plot height and income on a two-dimensional graph. Now, if you draw the border to surround all the points, you will find many people on the border—not just the tallest, shortest, richest, and poorest, but someone who is taller than everyone who makes more money, and richer than anyone who is taller, and so on. As you add more measurements, everyone is on the outer border. I call this "the unbearable emptiness of high-dimensional space." Similarly, if you have mechanisms to enforce thousands of potential arbitrage relations, nearly every security price will be on the outer border, at the limits of many of its enforced relations.

One major example is financial prices have natural tendencies to trend—that is, for yesterday's winners to go up again today—and also to mean-revert—yesterday's winners to go down today. If you pick a day at random, the next day's price move is very close to equally likely to be above or below the average move for the security. But if you parse data carefully, you can find trends and mean reversions at different time scales. They balance on average in the long run, but in the short run they can work in the same direction. Or if you work on a global trading floor seeing all the flow and interest, you can discern trends or reversals from counterparty actions.

The same phenomenon exists in many systems: lots of easy-to-find small edges that must be carefully balanced in order to gain useful advantage, few parameters that are set individually to great precision, variables that tend to form clouds at fixed distances from the equilibrium—like electrons around an atomic nucleus—rather than everything collapsing to the ideal equilibrium. This was one of the great insights I developed working with Fischer Black; he famously called it "noise."

THREEFOLD WAY

Why limit yourself to three sports-betting factors? Most professionals would use more, five to seven, but I used three because I wanted the model to run three years without maintenance. More factors means more chance that some will lose value and require replacement.

But why not 20 or 50 factors so you could win nearly every time? The problem is correlation. If factors have positive correlation, they give you much of the same information, and don't add much to your overall win rate. If they have zero or negative correlation, they offset to the point that you rarely have a combined signal strong enough to bet on. Moreover, too many factors lead to overfitting. Long experience, in sports betting anyway, has led most professionals to use five to seven factors, with a bench of around 20 or so potential replacements.

There have always been people who used more factors, and more complex systems than binary factors. Data science has encouraged this approach. But remember, I was trying to make the point that it's easy to make money sports betting, and these alternatives are not easy. For that matter, running a professional binary factor model is not easy—sports betting will not allow you to live on a beach somewhere sipping tropical drinks under a palm tree while your laptop makes automated bets and the money rolls in. But making a few thousand dollars per year with a few hours' work is easy.

Back to my three factors. Why bet on the team that has net lost to the spread over the season? Remember the bookmaker's goal to help all customers lose a little. That means helping people who bet their favorite team every week to end up with small losses. Also, the public tends to prefer teams with winning records against the spread. These are general tendencies seen in many betting markets.

How about turnovers? Turnovers are mostly random, or result from losing teams rationally taking excessive risk. They have a large effect on the score, and spreads systematically overreact to the score. Again, overreaction to recent noise is found in many applications in both sports betting and other fields.

Another form of overreaction is betting on the team the spread has moved against since before its most recent game. There's a lot of noise in game outcomes even beyond turnovers, and overreactions are common in many fields.

MAINTENANCE AND VALIDATION

I built my model to run without maintenance in order to strengthen my case that it was easy to pick winners against the spread with 55% accuracy. But monitoring for maintenance is a major advantage of binary factor models. I tracked each week that each of the factors was performing at around the 52% level. I also measured each factor's marginal contribution—the outcome of bets that were only made due to this factor, and the outcome of bets that would have been made except for this factor.

These checks can provide early warnings of changing circumstances before the model starts losing money. More often, they provide reassurance that a run of losses is just bad luck, that the model is fine. This information can help you consider replacing factors or otherwise adjusting the model. Without them, you learn of problems the expensive way by losing money, and you likely adjust too much for random noise.

In addition to the statistical checks above, it's important to have causal checks. That is, we don't just check that each factor is working about 52% of the time and making a sufficiently positive marginal contribution, we monitor the causal theory underlying it using data that does not overlap with the model inputs.

For example, to check that lines are overreacting, we track teams that play each other two or more times in a season. Suppose the Seahawks were favored by 6.5 points in their first meeting with the 49ers, but by only 3.5 points in their second. If this is an overreaction, the Seahawks should beat the spread more than half the time.

One nuance is we have to adjust for home-field advantage. The traditional bookmaker assumption was that home field is worth 3 points in spread. If the Seahawks had been favored by 6.5 points in Seattle over the 49ers, that suggests they would be favored by 3.5 points at a neutral site, and 0.5 points in San Francisco. So, if they were in fact favored by 3.5 points in a second game in San Francisco, that would mean the spread had actually moved in their favor, and if it was an overreaction, the 49ers are a better bet.

Three points is more like the maximum home-field advantage; for some pairs of teams it's near zero. Also, in many cases it depends on the weather. I used a simple historical regression model to adjust for home-field advantage for the purpose of this check.

The point is, the check does not overlap with the system since it's comparing games weeks apart, using a measure that is not included in the factors. That's what makes it valuable. It's a way to verify that bookies are still overreacting in a way that wouldn't show up directly in system performance. Moreover, it's a more direct test of overreaction since it involves the same two teams.

To validate the turnover factor, we do two logistic regressions. In the first we regress game outcome (1 for home team win, 0 for home team loss) on four variables for the entire season, excluding the game in question: home team win percentage, visiting team win percentage, home team net turnovers, and visiting team net turnovers. If turnovers are mostly random, then a home team with more turnovers than takeaways will have a win percentage less than its underlying ability, and therefore will be more likely to win than its season-excluding-this-game win percentage would indicate. So, we expect a significant positive coefficient on home team net turnovers and a significant negative coefficient on visiting team net turnovers.

Then we regress game outcome against the spread (1 for home team covers the spread, 0 for home team fails to cover) on the same variables as above, but using only games up to the week prior to the game in question. That is, for week eight games, we use win percentages and turnover margins only through week six. This avoids using the week seven data used in the system. This is measuring the same phenomenon we use in the system, but with non-overlapping data.

You'll recall I object to multivariable logistic regression for causal studies. I have hardened my attitude against this over the years, and would not have done things this way today. Although the ultimate goal of the system is only prediction, for which multivariable logistic regression is fine, the validation check is supposed to be a causal analysis.

To validate the tendency to keep teams even against the spread, we look at the record against the spread according to net wins season to date. We expect not just that teams with net losses against the spread will beat the spread more than half the time, but the more losses, the greater the advantage, and the more net wins, the greater the disadvantage. This is called a "dose–response" check and it's a standard way to get evidence for causality.

THE HARD PART

All of the above is the easy part, picking winners against the spread 55% of the time. The hard part is getting people running businesses to consistently send you money.

I got my start in sports betting with horse racing, making picks for the salesman father of a friend of mine, who rewarded me with 10% of his winnings. This was pari-mutuel betting. The track took a fixed percentage (15% at the time, usually more today) and didn't care who won or lost. In that case, picking winners was enough.

But most sports betting in the 1960s and 1970s was controlled by organized crime, after University of Chicago mathematician William McNeil invented the point spread which allowed nationwide consolidation of betting. I earned my living as a poker player at the time, but I dabbled in casino gambling and sports betting as well. If you won consistently at casino gambling, you were banned or worse. If you won consistently at poker, you gained respect and moved to a higher level of competition. If you won consistently at sports betting, you were embraced by the organization.

One day in the mid-1970s, a guy came up to me and told me that all my NFL betting had to be done early Monday morning, at $2,500 per game. In return, all my bets were taken, I didn't have to put up cash, and my winnings were paid promptly in cash late Sunday night.

In those days, Las Vegas employees set the pre-pre-opening line after the last Sunday-night game (there were Monday-night games at the time, but they were treated as an afterthought and had not yet been fully integrated into the organization system). This line was offered to people—all mob connected—who took the bets from insiders: players, coaches, referees, and other staff. They were allowed to bet $25,000 per game, and based on their bets, the line was adjusted to the pre-opening line.

Bettors like me, mostly quants, were offered that line at $2,500 per game, and our action led to further adjustments and the opening line announced midday on Monday (except for the two games featuring the teams to play that Monday night, whose opening lines would be set on Tuesday).

People sometimes accuse organized crime of fixing games, but the opposite was the case. The mob took 5% of all betting action, and that's what it wanted. If it had wanted more, it would have charged more vigorish, but it calculated that would cost it more action than it would gain in more revenue per bet. Its revenue was limited by what bettors were willing to lose; it was in no hurry to get that money. It wanted bettors to seem to have a run for their money. Incidentally, contrary to normal economic intuition, the mob used its monopoly on bookmaking to reduce the price to customers over what independent bookies had charged.

The mob had a strong interest—stronger than regulators or league executives—in avoiding scandal that might harm its business. The reason all insider betting was funneled through mob bookies was partly to get that information for the Las Vegas line setters, and partly to keep it from spreading too widely, but mainly to keep track of insider betting. The organization tried to make sure that insider bettors did not get into financial trouble, and strongly discouraged any obvious actions to favor the insider's bet.

While this picture seems clear today, it was less obvious when living through it. I finally got the message when my system ran into a losing streak and I stopped betting for a few weeks while I worked on it. The guy who told me how to bet my $2,500 showed up and told me my accumulated losses over the past few weeks were forgiven; they wanted my continuing action. That's when I realized I wasn't beating the house, I was working for the mob. So I quit and only got back into sports betting when the organization monopoly was broken in the early 1980s.

THE SITUATION TODAY

Although there is now a diverse and competitive marketplace for sports betting, and most operations quickly cut off or limit consistent winners, it's possible to make a steady income if you do it right. There are a number of strategies; the one I chose was to put in my bets as soon as the opening lines were available, at sophisticated sites known to cater to professionals.

By betting only $100 per game, my wins didn't cost the sites much, and they gave useful information about how smart money was likely to flow net during the week. Smart money tends to come in early or late, and the late smart money is what worries bookies. If I had placed my bets just before kickoff, I would have been quickly blocked. The same thing is true if I had tried to use less sophisticated sites.

I could have made more money placing somewhat larger bets at multiple sites until I figured out how much I could get away with, or using other tactics, but I wanted to keep the experiment simple. The professional operations I know—and sometimes fund and mentor—use higher-quality models and make many more bets, including over/under, prop bets, and other sports and non-sport markets.

The point to take away is that quant prediction against the spread is easy, even in the largest and most efficient betting markets. A couple of hours' work is sufficient for a 55% win rate. But making even a modest living is a lot of work—developing and maintaining many models, getting bets placed and paid off. Quant methods really work, and not just in sports betting, but they're not secrets to infinite effortless wealth.

REPLACING THE MASK

We now return to our regularly scheduled programming. No more rants against people who wouldn't bet a nickel of their own money on their research claims. We briefly explore the history of statistics for what it has to say about Wrong Numbers.

CHAPTER FIFTEEN

STATE-ISTICS

Have you ever wondered why we use the same word for the applied science of mathematical probability and aggregate numbers compiled by governments? The answer goes back nearly three centuries, and explains many Wrong Numbers today.

THE THREE FACES OF STATISTICS

In 1749, Prussian professor Gottfried Achenwall introduced the noun "statistik," which you can understand best by parsing it as "state-istics." He meant the systematic collection of both quantitative and qualitative data about states.

German-speaking Europe at the time was divided into many principalities whose overlords changed frequently due to death, marriage, war, and other transactions. Many princes were completely unfamiliar with their possessions, so they sent inspectors to compile data to be used to extract maximum resources—money, goods, services, soldiers, etc.—from the population.

This was by no means a new idea, rulers had been doing something similar for thousands of years. Achenwall and his successors developed methods to make the process more systematic, accurate, and useful.

An entirely different tradition developed, mainly in England. The Prussian system was run by the prince for his personal advantage, with data kept secret, and was purely descriptive; English work was done by amateurs outside the government. The government returned the favor by ignoring the work, which was published openly. It went beyond description to explanation and inference.

Revolutionary France attempted a synthesis. After the revolution, a bunch of Paris lawyers found themselves in charge of a country with over 40 languages (only a minority of the population spoke anything recognizable as Parisian French), much of which none of them had visited. It was a bit like the Prussian princes. As Charles de Gaulle would lament 170 years later, "How can you govern a country which has 246 varieties of cheese?"

The answer, as you've probably guessed, was "statistiques." Like the Prussian version, it was a top-down centralized effort organized by top officials. Drawing on English ideas, it enlisted local amateurs—generally schoolteachers or judges—to fill out detailed questionnaires. In a compromise between the two versions, the data were shared among a class of elite civil servants, not restricted to top officials like the Prussian system, nor available to everyone like the English.

In a mix of description and analysis, the compilers averaged all the measurements, under the assumption this would describe the perfect French community and citizen. This is the attitude that gave "abnormal" and "deviant" their negative connotations.

The Wrong Numbers in the rest of my book are statistics in the English sense—the poor inferences—or the French—the bad math used to count things like deaths. This chapter is devoted to the Prussian Wrong Numbers that come from misuse of official statistics.

BLACK AND QUINE

An important mentor in my life is the logician and philosopher Willard Van Orman Quine, who taught at Harvard. I pestered him with so many questions after class that he finally sent me to speak to a former student of his, teaching at MIT at the time. "He asked the same questions you do," Quine told me, "maybe he's found better answers than I can give you."

That turned out to be another important mentor, Fischer Black. Black is famous today for the Black–Scholes option pricing model and other contributions to mathematical finance, but I knew nothing of that at the time. Black spoke with me for hours, and I returned many times. Although I never took any of his classes, I ended up being the closest thing to a student he ever had.

As far as I know, I'm the only person who took everything he said seriously, and also who believed most of it. Most people treated him like an eccentric genius, mixing great insights with total nonsense. His "quirky" (to be kind) demeanor and personality put off many people. I got a reputation as the only person who understood him, mainly by saying, "Yes, Fischer really said that, and yes, he meant it."

The topic that first sent me to see Fischer was the logic behind the economic aggregates like the unemployment rate and inflation rate that were given such weight in my economics classes. It seemed to me that they were too aggregated to be meaningful. There are many different employment conditions, for example: employed in a job you like and expect to keep, employed in a job you hate, employed but expecting to be laid off, unemployed but with excellent prospects of getting a good job, unemployed with few good prospects, working part-time but not getting enough hours, and so on. Dividing everyone into employed, unemployed and looking for work, and unemployed and not looking for work obscured more than it revealed. Granted, economists looked at a number of different employment indicators, but all seemed far too crude to be useful.

Or take gross domestic product (GDP), the total value of all goods and services produced in a geographic region and sold to end users in a period. Some of those products were defective or toxic; many were unused or wasted in failed efforts. Many goods and services were not bought and sold, such as someone cleaning his own house or volunteering at a homeless shelter. Bad (e.g., environmental damage) and good (e.g., discoveries and inventions) production that is not measured may have value as great or greater than things bought and sold. A large part of the economy was government, whose services are not priced in market sales. Money spent in wars is counted as production, even though it only destroys.

NOT WRONG NUMBERS

I don't deny that these and other economic aggregates carry useful information, especially when you look at a lot of them that capture different aspects of the economy in different ways. When unemployment is high, labor market conditions are difficult for many workers. When GDP is growing rapidly, times are good for most people. But it seemed to me that much of the field of macroeconomics consisted of elaborate efforts to create numbers that could support more elaborate efforts to relate them statistically without having much contact with reality.

On top of the definitional issues, all these statistics were hard to measure. Since 1947, US real GDP has grown at a compound annual growth rate of 3.1%, according to the official figures from the Bureau of Economic Analysis (BEA). The BEA first estimates the real GDP growth rate around one month after the end of each quarter, then makes a second estimate about a month later, and a third estimate about a month after that—three months after quarter end. The average difference between the first and third estimates is 1.3%, so if the first estimate was 3.1%, the third could be 1.8% or 4.4% if the amount of the revision is average. And that's not the difference between the measurement and reality, it's the difference between the same people using the same methodology, just with slightly more information.

Let's try to tie that to something objectively measurable, the price of the S&P500 stock market index. My economics professors were in agreement that the stock market was too volatile, overreacting to events and dependent on irrational bubbles and panics.

The simplest reasonable model for stock market valuation, known as the Gordon model, said the index should equal $\frac{D}{r-g}$, where D is the dividends expected in the next year, r is the rate of return investors demand to take the risk of stocks, and g is the expected growth rate of dividends. As I write this, the S&P500 is 6,664.36 and dividend futures predict $79.90 in dividends in 2026. That makes the Gordon model denominator 1.20%, suggesting investors demand 1.20% above the expected growth rate.

That's the expected growth rate over the long-term future. Fifty percent of the present value investors pay for the S&P500 today consists of cash flows expected 60 or more years in the future. Economists couldn't measure the growth rate in the quarter just past with error less than 1.3% (and again, that's not the error in their measurement, just the difference in opinion of the same people using information one month against three months after quarter end). If stock market investors reduced their expectation of growth by 1.3%, the stock market would fall 52%. If they increased their expectation of growth by 1.3%, stock prices would be infinite.

And that's just the growth rate. Economic models of what stock market investors should demand were even farther from observation (this is known as the "equity risk premium puzzle"). I thought measurement error alone made these economic aggregates useless for practical purposes, even if they had been theoretically sound. And, of course, the measurements were about the past and often months out of date, when decisions depended on the future.

RUNNING ON EMPTY

Fischer had been thinking along similar lines for a decade, and had much more sophisticated views, with evidence to back them up. We began a productive collaboration (I was most definitely the very junior partner in it) that would lead to his famous "Noise" speech and his book, *Exploring General Equilibrium*.

Fischer did arrange for me to get a summer job on the National Standby Gas Rationing Project. The slot was supposed to go to a senior graduate student—I was a freshman undergraduate. After the Arab Oil Embargo of 1973–1974, which had Americans waiting in long lines for gasoline and often unable to get it, the federal government wanted the ability to impose gas rationing if necessary in the future.

I was assigned to the group working on fuel supplies for agriculture. One of the highest priorities was to assure adequate gasoline to produce and distribute food. I'm a city boy and had no idea if tractors used gasoline or diesel fuel. I called the Department of Agriculture and got passed around until we located the guy who knew about such things. He was out. I did know that Ford made most of the tractors in the country at the time. So, I tried there.

I reached the right guy, who told me I was in luck, he had just finished a comprehensive economic model of tractor distribution and could confidently state that 75% of the tractors in the country were diesel.

That afternoon, the Department of Agriculture guy called me back. I listened to him out of politeness as he told me that he too had just completed a model: "75% of the tractors in the country run on gasoline," he said. I replied, "You mean diesel, right?" No, he meant gasoline. I told him what the Ford guy had said and he replied that Ford's figure was for new tractor sales (not true, I had considerable detail about the Ford estimate and how it was derived). Later, the Ford guy claimed the Department of Agriculture guy counted tractors rusting in barns and sold to Mexico years ago (also not true).

I did manage to narrow the gap considerably by working through the details of the two models. Much of it was different definitions, but there were also significant disagreements on basic facts that should have been fairly easy to verify objectively. What really struck me is, neither expert seemed interested. Both were more than willing to teach me, neither showed the slightest interest in learning from me or the other expert.

THE RUSSIANS ARE COMING

Even more disheartening was the reaction of others working on the project. When I told my story, people laughed and topped it with even more egregious examples of misinformation from and disagreement among sources that ought to be reliable and authoritative. Let me emphasize that these economists were all very smart and sincerely interested in producing a workable plan for the good of the country. All were far more experienced than me. Yet, none of them shared my view that the entire project was futile due to working at far too high a level of aggregation with unreliable data. The plan was full of Wrong Numbers.

I proposed that we should look to the experience of Soviet Union economic planners. At the time, Russians were two generations ahead of the West in applied mathematics, and had five decades of experience with the kind of central economic planning we were attempting. The Soviets put people who would be mathematics professors in the United States into factories to manage operations.

My suggestion went nowhere, as my co-workers were convinced communist central planners were idiots. I couldn't even get support for seeking counsel from living American managers who had worked on World War II rationing and planning.

Incidentally, after the breakup of the Soviet Union I had the opportunity to meet Gosplan workers who fled to Wall Street. We had detailed discussions of the National Standby Gas Rationing Plan, and they pointed out the rookie mistakes we had made. They were very far from idiots, and they appreciated the actual difficulties of central planning. They had much lower expectations, based on 50 years of experience, but did know how to meet those expectations. They thought it would be possible to avoid a complete economic breakdown, but assumed there would be massive drops in productivity and many disasters. The actual plan had impossibly high expectations and vanishingly low chances of meeting even the low Soviet expectations.

Fischer, in my opinion, made the opposite error of the project economists, but at the time I didn't have the support to convince him. He thought the entire project was completely doomed. He did not think it was possible to meet even the low expectations the Soviets told me about years later.

BIGGER PROBLEMS

The National Standby Gas Rationing Plan was never activated, so it did little harm. It did lead to a lot of publications by economists on the project, which in my opinion were more useful than average because the work had at least some contact with reality and purpose.

Much more damage was done by a major research area from the 1920s to the 1970s relating prices to industry concentration, with the basic idea that fewer firms in a sector, and greater market share for the largest firms, led to inflated prices and profits. This is not entirely false, but the truth is much more nuanced than the broad aggregate generalization. However, it was supported for half a century by bad aggregate data that formed an important pillar of Keynesian economics—a pillar since discredited—and justification for harmful government anti-trust and other regulation. It bears some responsibility for the terrible economic malaise of 1970s "stagflation."

A lot of papers used monthly data collected by the government on prices in various industries. This appeared to show a U-shaped distribution, with lots of prices that changed every month, and lots that rarely changed. This led to the false "kinky demand curve" theory. It held that firms expected a big loss in sales from small price increases—since competitors would keep prices the same and customers would quickly switch—but little gain in sales from price cuts—since competitors would quickly match the cuts.

Eventually, people figured out that the U-shape was an artifact of the data. Some goods changed price daily or even more often, but they were lumped together with goods that changed prices up to once per month. On the other side, goods that failed to change price over a study period were lumped together, whether they changed price every two years or every 20 years. When corrected for these aggregations, the U-shape disappeared, replaced by a unimodal distribution more like a bell curve.

Another hazard of working with aggregate data was illustrated by a major finding that more firms in a sector meant more frequent price changes, which were taken as a sign of competitive prices. Eventually, people figured out that the more firms in a sector, the more firms that were polled, and if any one of them changed prices, the average changed. After correction, there was no correlation between number of firms and frequency of price changes.

The point is not that people made mistakes. That happens all the time. Error is an essential part of trial-and-error. As civil engineer Henry Petroski put it: "No one wants to learn by mistakes, but we cannot learn enough from successes to go beyond the state of the art."

The point is that the field of macroeconomics was content to forget the discredited research and continue using the same techniques that had led it astray in the past. There were mistakes, but insufficient learning from mistakes.

FRED

I have been using the Internet since DARPAnet in the 1970s. Before that, interlaboratory data were mainly communicated on reels of magnetic tapes. A typical 1960s-era tape might hold up to 50 megabytes. While that will sound tiny compared to your one-terabyte iPhone (20,000 times as much), it could be around 200 times the memory capacity of a 256-kilobyte computer we might be using.

Because the tape capacity was fixed and seldom filled with data, labs would stick in some files for fun with the unused space. The most common types in my experience were line-printer text files that produced soft-core pornographic images from the typed characters. Another popular item was text-based multiplayer games based on science fiction or fantasy works. Labs would include original productions as well as improved versions of files they had received. This acted as a kind of proto-Internet.

Last year I was giving a talk at Bloomberg about that bygone era when I was asked, "What did we think the Internet was going to evolve into?" I had to think for a bit before answering, "We thought it would be FRED."

In case you don't know, "FRED" is Federal Reserve Economic Data, an extremely useful website for a huge variety of data. I don't think many people in the 1960s and 1970s imagined social media, smartphones, on-line shopping, and banking—we did expect pornography and games, of course. But the main use of computer tape exchange and DARPAnet was transmitting data. I think most people imagined in the future you could download any kind of data on any topic.

Unfortunately, too few of us realized that much of the data would be wrong, and that many of the users wouldn't understand the data that wasn't wrong.

GREEDNOMICS

In 2024, dictionary.com added the word "greedflation" to its list of actual words, which it defines as "a rise in prices, rents, or the like, that is not due to market pressure or any other factor organic to the economy, but is caused by corporate executives or boards of directors, property owners, etc., solely to increase profits that are already healthy or excessive."

I find that "greed" is rarely a useful concept in economics. It usually means people did things in their interest instead of yours. People who act to increase their profits are generally acting in their own interest. We may wish that interest were different, or that they lacked the power to raise prices, or that they would transfer those additional profits to us by lowering prices, but where does greed come into the equation? Why are they greedy for increasing their profits, but we're not greedy for wanting the money instead?

Dispensing with the idea of greed allows us to approach the issue rationally. If we think the problem is the interest capital owners have in increasing profit, we might support a progressive profit tax (often called a "windfall" profit tax), or caps on investment profit. There are economic arguments on both sides about whether these would increase or decrease inflation, as well as whether their overall economic effects are good or bad. These are debates that can be resolved by theoretical and empirical work.

MEASURING GREED

A non-profit called Groundwork Collaborative, with the mission of driving "policy change with credibility, expertise, and impact," claimed credit for helping push "greedflation" into the common political parlance. They might be right. The group authored a widely cited study that purports to show how outsized corporate profits have caused rising prices. This study was co-authored by Liz Pancotti and Groundwork Collaborative's Executive Director Lindsay Owens.

The report exploited the usual tricks of partisan data analysis. Rather than showing data for the entire period under discussion, it selected short intervals that supported their claims. For example, "prices for consumers have risen by 3.4% over the past year" while "input costs for producers have risen by just 1%." Their evidence was that, in 2023, the Consumer Price Index grew faster than the Producer Price Index. As you may remember, from the start of the pandemic to June 2022, producer prices soared 51% due to supply-chain problems and lockdown. Consumer prices rose only 15% due to weaker-than-normal demand, due to lockdown, layoffs, and economic uncertainty. As the economy reopened in the second half of 2022 and 2023, supply-chain issues eased and producer prices actually fell 11%, while consumer prices rose 5% as people began spending again. Over the entire period, producer prices were up 35%, while consumer prices only 20%. But by ignoring everything before and after 2023—when consumer prices were catching up to producer prices—the report made its misleading claim.

But that's not what made this report a Wrong Number. Cherry picking is too common to highlight in this book. Moreover, while it's a tactic for misleading careless readers, cherry-picked numbers are literally true. It's up to readers to ask, "Why give numbers for 2023, when consumer inflation was falling? You're blaming greedflation for price increases in 2021 and 2022, a time when producer prices were rising much faster than consumer prices."

The Wrong Number this study illustrates is misunderstanding official government economic statistics. Many researchers are careless about this. The Producer Price Index does not measure "input prices to producers," as the report claims. It measures the prices at which producers sell their products to wholesalers. It's a price index, not a cost index. So, comparing it to the Consumer Price Index tells us nothing about corporate profit or "greedflation." At best it tells us which corporations—producers—are squeezing which other corporations—wholesalers, distributors, and retailers—for whatever profits are available. And while there are temporary ups and downs in the relation due to major disruptions like the pandemic, in the long run, producer and consumer prices have to synchronize.

PRICES AND PROFITS

Senator Bob Casey (D–Pa) has been particularly outspoken about greedflation. He published his own flawed economic research on the topic, claiming in one report that "from July 2020 through July 2022, inflation rose by 14%, but corporate profits rose by 75%, five times as fast as inflation."

The problem is that Casey chose to use a different measure of corporate profit than the BEA. Unlike the BEA, he didn't adjust his top-line figures for what's known as inventory valuation and capital consumption adjustments, which distort the data if you don't correct for them.

Consider a company that makes its product for $0.93 and sells it for $1.00, about the average profit margin for US businesses. Now, 14% inflation comes along and the selling price goes up to $1.14. Since the $0.93 costs have already been incurred, the paper profit goes up to $0.21, or from 7.5 to 22.6%. But the purchasing power of the $1.14 the company gets is the same as the $1.00 it would have received had there been no inflation. Its real profits have not increased but its corporate taxes probably will.

If we look at things in economic terms rather than simple accounting, we have to acknowledge that the nominal value of the inventory went up 14% from $0.93 to $1.06. The company spent $0.93 making it, but that was $0.93 in dollars with 14% more purchasing power than current dollars. Moreover, its capital investments in factories, trucks, farmland, or other assets were also made in old, uninflated dollars, so the depreciation expense for those assets should be increased by 14% for consistency. This is why inventory valuation and capital consumption adjustments are particularly important in times of high inflation.

Corporate profits have been rising since 2016, with a brief interruption and some volatility during the pandemic. They've been growing because the US economy has been growing—corporations sold more goods and services, workers earned more money, and the economy was running faster.

That's why it makes sense to look at corporate profits as a fraction of domestic income. If we make that adjustment, most of the effect that Casey trumpeted has disappeared.

During his speech at the Democratic National Convention, Casey said: "We're fighting for honesty … will you fight for it?" Casey should take a look at his own data as part of that fight. Greedflation may be an effective political talking point, but there's nothing honest about it.

MORE INFLATION

It's not just money that inflates, journalists inflate numbers from studies as well. The next chapter illustrates that, and asks what it means to save a statistical life.

CHAPTER SIXTEEN

DID MEDICAID EXPANSION SAVE 100,000 LIVES?

"More Americans will die—at least 100,000 more over the course of the next decade," wrote Yale law professor Natasha Sarin in a *Washington Post* column about the Medicaid cuts in President Donald Trump's One Big Beautiful Bill.

CAN YOU TRUST THE EXPERT?

"That isn't hyperbolic," Sarin added. "It is fact."

The average reader might be inclined to believe Sarin, who holds a Harvard PhD in economics as well as a Harvard law degree, and served in the Treasury Department during the Biden administration. But contrary to her characterization, her claim is hyperbolic, not "fact."

I promise this is the last chapter putting numbers on deaths. Death will appear in some chapters, but we won't be counting bodies. Sarin's assertion merits a chapter because it reflects a fundamental misunderstanding of the concept of "statistical lives saved" that underlies many Wrong Numbers.

Sarin and prominent journalists misinterpreted a recent working paper published by the National Bureau of Economic Research (NBER). As a semi-professional debunker of bad research, I can say with some authority that the authors of that study, Dartmouth economist Angela Wyse and University of Chicago economist Bruce D. Meyer, wrote an excellent paper—a rarity among academic studies these days. Moreover, the authors were generous with their time in helping me to replicate their results. But the University of Chicago's press office trumpeted the paper's findings, declaring: "Medicaid expansion under the Affordable Care Act saved about 27,400 lives between 2010–22," which is highly misleading.

That take was echoed in coverage of the study by major news outlets. "The expansion of Medicaid has saved more than 27,000 lives since 2010, according to the most definitive study yet on the program's health effects," reported Sarah Kliff and Margot Sanger-Katz in *The New York Times*. Their article was headlined "As Congress Debates Cutting Medicaid, a Major Study Shows It Saves Lives."

The story was also picked up by *Time* ("Medicaid Expansions Saved Tens of Thousands of Lives, Study Finds"), *NPR* ("New Studies Show What's at Stake If Medicaid Is Scaled Back"), *NBC News* ("Proposed Medicaid Cuts Could Lead to Thousands of Deaths, Study Finds"), and several other news outlets. These journalists either didn't read the study, didn't understand it, or willfully misrepresented its findings for partisan reasons.

EQUAL-OPPORTUNITY MISREPRESENTATION

In the past, conservative opponents of Medicaid have been equally guilty of misconstruing academic research to support their policy views. That is what happened with the most famous study on the subject, "The Oregon Experiment—Effects of Medicaid on Clinical Outcomes," which *The New England Journal of Medicine* (NEJM) published in 2013. The NBER and NEJM papers offer similar accounts of Medicaid's impact on health, but both have been misinterpreted to suggest opposite conclusions.

Let's start with the claim that the expansion of Medicaid during the Obama administration "saved about 27,400 lives" between 2010 and 2022. Where did that figure come from? Wyse and Meyer's paper estimated that the Medicaid expansion reduced mortality among eligible adults between 0.40% and 4.52%, compared to similar populations in states that refused the Medicaid expansion.

How did Sarin conclude that "over 100,000 and likely closer to 200,000" preventable deaths will be caused by the One Big Beautiful Bill Act and the expiration of the premium tax credits? She cited evidence that those things would cause 16 million Americans to lose health insurance. Using the numbers from Wyse and Meyer's paper, which Sarin relied upon, suggests that it could actually cost between about 3,000 deaths (0.4% decline in 10-year mortality) and 37,000 deaths (4.52%). So, there is a major math error, in addition to the heroic assumption of using Medicaid expansion data from 2010 to 2022 to project effects of reduced insurance coverage in 2026 to 2035.

The University of Chicago press release and the journalists who picked it up at least multiplied correctly: 27,400 is indeed the midpoint of the Wyse and Meyer estimate of lives saved by the Affordable Care Act's Medicaid expansion. But this is misleading for a more fundamental reason. The sum of statistical lives saved vastly exceeds the number of actual lives.

Think of all the things that have saved your life. Every breath you take, every heartbeat, every car and lightning bolt that didn't hit you. Yet, you're only alive once. Even if we restrict ourselves to the effects of government programs, the total statistical lives saved by all programs is far greater than the population.

So why isn't the mortality rate negative? With bodies coming out of graveyards like *Night of the Living Dead*? Because these same government programs also take many statistical lives. Wyse and Meyer only show one side of the ledger—the reduction in mortality among people who gain Medicare eligibility. On the other side are the statistical lives lost from the people the money is taken from, or the programs cut.

"Cowards die many times before their deaths," said Shakespeare's Julius Caesar. "The valiant never taste of death but once." But coward or valiant, you will die many statistical times before your death. Fortunately, you will be saved the same number of times ... minus one.

Counting statistical lives saved or lost is a debased currency, because it counts each actual life multiple times. And citing only the good side of the ledger makes it impossible to evaluate.

When *New York Times* readers are told that "the expansion of Medicaid has saved more than 27,000 lives since 2010," they are misled into imagining 27,000 people who would be dead if it weren't for the Medicaid expansion—27,000 actual lives saved. Misinterpreting statistical lives saved in this manner is a common partisan tactic that turns rational policy debates into moral finger pointing.

UNCERTAINTY

Then there's the crucial issue of uncertainty. The 95% "confidence interval" reported by Myer and Wyse ranged from 4,500 to 50,000 statistical lives saved. That 95% is a *pro forma* calculation required by journal editors with little relation to actual uncertainty, as we discussed in Chapter 11. It assumes all approximations and models the authors used were errorless and that there were no data errors, and it ignores all information other than the specific numbers used in the paper.

For example, the authors lost track of over 400,000 people in their sample, 14% of the total, and had to guess whether they lived or died. The uncertainty from that guess is not reflected in the width of the 95% interval. They assumed that no one moved to another state or moved out of the income range for expanded Medicaid eligibility. They had to estimate from historical trends what the mortality rate would have been without Medicaid expansion.

None of this is meant as criticism. This type of economic analysis is challenging, and approximations and models are often necessary. But the point is that you cannot take the *pro forma* confidence interval at face value, treating it like a Bayesian credible interval someone might use to make bets. Far more than 5% of papers claiming 95% confidence turn out to be false. It's plausible that Medicaid expansion saved no statistical lives—even looking only at the positive side of the ledger—and it's plausible it saved over 50,000 statistical lives.

TURN THE OTHER CHEEK

Turning attention to the negative side of the ledger, after the Medicaid expansion, total expenditures increased by more than $1 trillion. That spending also costs statistical lives, because the same money could have been allocated to other potentially lifesaving programs, such as vaccinations, suicide prevention, mental health services, drug treatment facilities, screening for cardiovascular risk factors, and replacing old cars with newer, less polluting and safer models.

Alternatively, the money could have remained in taxpayers' bank accounts, which also could promote good health. Mortality declines with income. Even if the Medicaid expansion were a cost-effective way to improve mortality, you'd still have to consider the other side of the ledger to decide if it were a net benefit. I won't address the moral question of whether it's just to take money that will kill one person who earned it, to give to save two lives of other people who didn't earn it.

Medicaid expansion may not have been a cost-effective way to reduce mortality, because a large share of healthcare spending is not targeted toward saving lives. Think of all your medical bills, including the ones insurance paid, and ask how many were for matters of life or death. Most likely, you purchased healthcare for symptom relief, a speedier recovery, an improved quality of life, reassurance things weren't serious, routine and preventative care. Collectively these things increase life expectancy, but that was not their main purpose. You gained some statistical years of life, but the measures didn't reduce the number of times you will die.

The lifesaving medical measures with the biggest impact—such as vaccinations, bandages, and antibiotics—are relatively cheap. The main justification for Medicaid expansion is to relieve financial stress and make beneficiaries more physically comfortable, not to save lives.

THE OREGON TRAIL

Now consider the 2013 NEJM study trumpeted by many conservatives, which examined various health measures. It found that Medicaid enrollment resulted in large and statistically significant improvements in patients' subjective estimates of their health and quality of life, as well as significant reductions in their financial stress. But it did not find a statistically significant impact on mortality or health.

One typical health finding concerned the impact of Medicaid access on average Framingham risk scores—which predict the risk of strokes, heart attacks, and other cardiovascular events over 10 years. The Oregon study was unable to determine if Medicaid coverage led to a moderate increase or a moderate decrease in the score. Conservative commentator Avik Roy, writing about the study in *Forbes*, opined that the Oregon study "showed no difference in health outcomes" at the one-year mark. This is using absence of evidence as evidence of absence. The Oregon study left plenty of room for Medicaid coverage to cause significant improvements in health, including a 19% reduction in Framingham risk scores. It's true that it was also possible that Medicaid coverage did no good or even harmed health measures.

The Oregon study did not find a statistically significant cardiovascular benefit from Medicaid access. But that does not necessarily mean there was no benefit; it just means this study failed to find one. The basic message of the NEJM study is the same as the upshot of the NBER paper: we don't know much about the health benefits of getting Medicaid coverage, other than they can't be large enough to show up in overall mortality statistics without painstaking analysis of gigantic samples that depend on approximations and assumptions—and sometimes not even then.

WHY DO GOOD STUDIES LEAD TO BAD REPORTING?

Both studies were well designed, with clear descriptions of the data and methodology, and provided valuable insights. In both cases, the researchers pre-registered their hypotheses, an essential procedure to make statistical results credible. Both sets of authors devoted more energy to trying to falsify their conclusions than to building them up.

The two studies are more valuable in combination than individually. The NEJM study had the advantage of random assignment and detailed individual data. The NBER paper had a much larger sample size and time interval, but assignments were non-random and data limited mainly to whether people lived or died, with 14% of the sample completely unknown.

Both found significant benefits to Medicaid recipients, although they did not establish that these benefits were any greater than could have been obtained by simply giving each recipient several thousand dollars per year. Neither study convincingly answered whether Medicaid improved health or saved statistical lives.

Both studies examined a range of issues and provided important insights to people interested in healthcare policy. They just didn't lead to a simple conclusion like "Medicaid is worthless" or "Medicaid is a cost-effective way to save real lives." Unfortunately, their nuanced findings were misrepresented by partisan journalists looking to score cheap political points.

LOVE STORY

We now turn attention to a positive topic: love and reconciliation. And guns.

CHAPTER SEVENTEEN

A GUN CONTROL LOVE STORY

The *New York Times* published an 11-minute documentary by Brian Dawson titled "'It Was Really a Love Story.' How an N.R.A. Ally Became a Gun Safety Advocate." It tells a heartwarming story of how friendship transcended political differences and convinced a right-wing partisan to come to terms with the truth about firearms.

THE ODD COUPLE

The film stars a couple of improbable friends: Dr. Mark Rosenberg, who for many years oversaw research on gun violence at the Centers for Disease Control and Prevention (CDC) as the director of its National Center for Injury Prevention and Control, and "NRA Pointman" Republican Jay Dickey (R–Ark.), who was the author of an amendment inserted into a 1996 spending bill that prohibited the CDC from using federal funds to advocate or lobby for gun control.

The story is also framed by the findings of a famous (or infamous) 1993 CDC-funded study, which was "the first piece that we funded by external scientists," Rosenberg recounts. It allegedly showed that owning guns made Americans overwhelmingly less safe. According to the film, the National Rifle Association (NRA) lobbied for the Dickey amendment due to the 1993 study's damning results. The organization "didn't think it would be good for business," Rosenberg says, "and they went to Congress, and they said, 'You have got to stop this research because it's going to result in all Americans losing their right to have a gun in their homes.'"

In classic "meet cute" romcom style, Dickey and Rosenberg started out as "mortal enemies," but after making small talk about their kids during a chance conversation, they developed "an incredible friendship," as Rosenberg recounts. Years later, they were habitually ending their conversations by telling each other "I love you," and "we really meant it," Rosenberg says. Through the power of this human connection, Dickey ends up seeing reason and changing his mind. He comes to believe that the amendment bearing his name was a mistake.

IN THE EYE OF THE BEHOLDER

I want to be careful about this next part. When I watched the documentary, there was no doubt in my mind from the words and images that it suggested an erotic dimension to the relationship—not necessarily a physically consummated homosexual affair but a significant sexual attraction. Some people I have discussed it with agree, but others say we are projecting our own prurience on entirely asexual material. If you care about this, you can watch it for yourself and make up your own mind.

Either way, the video is a story of redemption through friendship that's well tuned to our own hyperpolarized times. The lesson is that if blind partisans aren't swayed by empirical evidence, human connection might just do the trick. "Underneath what people think are such opposing forces are some very important shared values," Rosenberg says.

Although the moral of the documentary is undoubtedly true, every other detail is wrong. The takeaway from the story of Dickey, Rosenberg, and the 1993 gun study at the center of the piece is that the congressman was correct to begin with. The CDC shouldn't be doing gun control advocacy and lobbying with public health funds, and it shouldn't be financing shoddy research on any topic. Moreover, treating guns as a public health issue is a deeply misguided approach.

THE EXPLOSIVE STUDY

The study in question was "Gun Ownership as a Risk Factor for Homicide in the Home," published in *The New England Journal of Medicine*. It looked at 388 people who had been killed in their homes and matched them to 388 neighbors of similar age, sex, and race. Some 174 of the victims lived in houses where at least one gun was present versus only 139 of the matched controls.

With scary music and breathless claims, the video tells viewers that if you had a gun in your house, you were "200% more likely to be shot and killed with a gun" and 400% more likely to kill yourself.

These are both exaggerations and misstatements of the study results. It didn't address suicide risk at all, nor gun homicides. It found households in which a resident had been murdered at home by any means had a 25% greater frequency of having a gun, not 200%. But this doesn't mean owning a gun increases your risk of being killed by 25%.

In the first place, the relevant statistic to the chance of being killed is not the frequency of guns in the houses of murder victims, but the rate of murder in houses with guns. In this case, the 313 gun-owning households in their study had 174 murders (56%) versus 463 households without guns with 214 murders (46%).

But this ignores the base rate. In the entire United States over the study period, the chance of being killed on purpose at home in a year was about 0.001%. If the study's results extrapolate to all households, the households with guns will have 0.0002% more residents killed on purpose at home than households without guns.

PICK AND CHOOSE

It's our old friend multivariable logistic regression again, used to assert cause. And, as usual with these studies, the finding that owning a gun made study subjects less safe was selected from among much stronger statistical results that didn't fit the authors' political views and, thus, weren't mentioned in the study. Yes, 25% more victims' homes had guns than control homes, but 38% more victims had controlled security access to their property. Why not lobby against gates as a public health matter? Twenty times as many victims had gotten in trouble at work because of drinking, so why worry about guns when drinking at work is two orders of magnitude more dangerous? Renting and living alone were far more dangerous than having a gun. Victims were less likely than controls to own a rifle or a shotgun, so why not a government program to distribute long guns as a public health measure?

This echoes a point I made earlier about ignoring odds ratios of less than 3-to-1. The result in this study (56% vs. 46%) is a 1.2 odds ratio. These are easy to find in any data set. The authors studied 31 different factors that might influence the chance of being murdered in your home. They didn't pick out the largest factors with the strongest statistical evidence to emphasize or put in their paper title, they picked the one they wanted for political reasons.

Consider instead the 20-to-1 odds ratio for people who had gotten in trouble at work for drinking. This is the kind of result that seems likely to be causal, and can give some insight into reasons. We might learn a lot by looking into the individual cases. Did people who get in trouble for drinking at work tend to shoot their spouses, while the ones without guns batter their spouses but don't kill them? Do the people lose their jobs, turn to drug dealing, buy guns, and get murdered in the normal course of business, while the ones who don't turn to crime, don't buy guns? If you really want to understand the relation between gun ownership and home homicides, focus on the high odds ratios, not the marginal ones.

Another issue is the study design. Comparing victims to non-victims can make sense in medicine. When a new disease appears, for example, researchers compare victims to outwardly similar non-victims to get clues about the cause. In the early days of AIDS, the CDC identified a "4H club" of Haitians, homosexuals, hemophiliacs, and heroin addicts. Most of the sick fell under one of those four categories, whereas non-4H members were seldom infected. While the first H turned out to be a false clue, the last three suggested correctly a blood-to-blood or blood-to-mucous membrane transmission.

With a new disease, we don't know much about transmission so we look at all victims versus all non-victims. But with gun ownership, we can identify obvious mechanisms, such as the gun owner shooting a spouse, or an attacker stealing the gun and shooting the gun owner. If the resident's gun was not the murder weapon, as was true in most of the cases (in fact, most of the homicides were not committed with guns, and most of the ones that were did not use the resident's gun), it's not clear the case should be included at all.

In any event, for guns, it's silly to lump all deaths together. It makes sense to consider gun suicides, gun killings of home invaders, killings while the resident was attempting gun self-defense, killings unrelated to the resident's gun, and other cases individually.

Another difference between guns and medicine is we also don't care equally about all deaths. If a woman kills a violent attacker threatening her family, that's a bad thing only to a tunnel-vision public health researcher adding up total deaths. Some gun deaths are good, some are bad, some—like a suicide of a terminally ill person in great pain—are debatable. A doctor treating AIDS patients doesn't ask whether the patient is a good or a bad person, but courts adjudicating gun deaths care a lot about justifiable versus accidental versus criminal homicides.

A more technical criticism is that the study uses flawed statistical methodology. Most journals require research to demonstrate the results are unlikely to result from random chance. Overall, 40.6% of subjects and controls had guns in the house. If gun ownership has no effect on homicide rates, there's a 4% chance that 174 or more of the subjects would own guns. That's less than the arbitrary 5% threshold many journals use, so the results are deemed statistically significant. The researchers did a more complex statistical analysis to arrive at the same 4% significance.

The issue with both my simple calculation and the researchers' more complex one is they are only accurate if there are no errors in the data, the precise effects of all controls is known, and all relevant controls are included. We know there are significant errors in this kind of data, we have little idea about the effects of controls, and we know there are many relevant factors that were not measured.

For example, 32 of the deaths were associated with drug dealing, and 92 with other felonies. Since the control households were not matched for criminality, it's highly unlikely they contained similar numbers of criminals. If we exclude those 124 deaths as probably not due to having a gun in the house, the home-homicide rate for gun-owning households drops to

37%, less than the 46% for gun-free households. Four of the victims were shot by police, and 11 were cases of self-defense; there seems little reason to lump these in with victims shot by intruders or domestic murders.

DRILL DOWN

A serious study would drill down to find differences between households with murders and those without, to see if there were some subgroup of gun owners with three times the risk of being killed at home than gun non-owners in the same subgroup. This would be the kind of evidence that would make it plausible gun ownership had a causal link to getting murdered.

Another technical criticism is the 1993 study ignores the vast literature by psychologists, sociologists, criminologists, and statisticians on crime and violence. It cites only public health studies and general references. This is a common problem with public health literature. It exists in a closed world that does not learn from other fields, nor do researchers in other fields build on it. There is no attempt to weave webs of conjecture.

Despite the study's problems, which have been widely reported, Rosenberg attributes all of the criticism to gun manufacturers concerned about potential loss of sales. Though the Dickey amendment prohibited the CDC's Injury Center from spending money on gun control promotion and advocacy, Rosenberg blames it for shutting off all research into gun violence.

Rosenberg sums up the Dickey amendment as follows: "If you do research in this area, we will harass you." An example of the harassment Rosenberg gives is "the threat of congressional inquiries" that can "wreak havoc with your research."

Why does Rosenberg think that taxpayer-funded research shouldn't be subject to congressional inquiry? Rather than stating that he was willing to answer sensible and relevant questions, Rosenberg wanted to be shielded from congressional Republicans like Dickey, whom he deemed ignorant and evil. He specifically cited Rosenberg's question about whether he favored a complete ban on civilian gun ownership, claiming it proved "Worse than not understanding, he [Dickey] doesn't care." It's hard to see how asking for a senior official's policy views proves the questioner doesn't care about homicide victims.

The Dickey amendment didn't prevent the CDC from gathering and analyzing data on gun injuries and deaths, only advocacy and lobbying. Many gun control researchers rely on CDC data. But gun control is part of a much larger issue of crime, violence, rights, and policy effects; it's not something that can be studied usefully with infectious disease models, methods, and data.

SCARE TACTICS

Much of the screen time of the video is devoted to entirely irrelevant scary scenes of shooting and shells with threatening graphics. It ends with text on screen noting that the $25 million restored to the CDC for gun control research is only a fraction of a percent of its budget. It doesn't mention that gun homicides are also a fraction of a percent of total US deaths, or that guns are not a disease.

Dickey, who died of Parkinson's disease in 2017, may have come to regret pushing for the amendment that bears his name, but he remained concerned about the 1993 study, which would have complicated *The New York Times*' narrative and which the film left out. It uses a clip from CNN in which Dickey says he had a "change of heart" because of "the weight of all of the incidents that have occurred … The kids and the innocent people who are being killed deserve our attention."

What's not included is a moment from that same clip in which Dickey states his ongoing concerns about the 1993 study and how it was carried out. "We wanted research done for gun violence, and that's what the money was paid for," he says. "But we found out that as we went along, that not only was the research being done just to support gun control, but we weren't even given access to what the collected data was. So it was clear that we needed to do something and to stop what was being done."

Dickey was right. Guns are not a pathogen and violence is not a disease to be controlled. What is needed is not propagandistic films or sloppy research. We need cross-disciplinary research on what drives human beings to violence, whether with a gun or without one.

BE WARY OF PUBLIC HEALTH

There is a more general point here. How often have you heard someone say that some issue or another is a "public health matter"? The only support they offer is the issue has some effect on someone's health. But they're actually making a very serious claim.

There are some true public health issues: sanitation, pandemic control, vaccinations. What these have in common is one person's actions can have more effect on the population than the individual. For that reason, we often override the most fundamental human rights. We may insist a healthy person be quarantined—infringing on her right to liberty—in circumstances very likely to kill her—infringing on her right to life and the pursuit of happiness—to protect the public. We may force people to be vaccinated, infringing on their right to control their bodies. Only in wartime and natural disasters do we act similarly.

Another unusual feature of public health issues is we count the number of deaths, without asking whether they resulted from individual choices or forces beyond individual control, or whether the deaths were bad (innocent person murdered by a criminal), neutral (terminally ill person in great pain committing suicide), or good (mass shooter killed to save innocent lives).

Public health seems to attract authoritarians and elitists. The field often consists of experts making decisions for everyone else, and having them enforced in violation of human rights. Some of these people reluctantly accept vast powers in the hopes of doing vast good on the few issues that can justify authoritarian rule. But others seem just to like authoritarianism, and to want to apply it to any issue that affects anyone's health—meaning any issue.

CALL THE POLICE

Our next chapter drills down on fatal police shootings, which make up 1% of the ones studied above. Most chapters deal with studies that should be refuted, or even retracted. There's a flip side to that. Retracting a right number is a form of Wrong Number.

CHAPTER EIGHTEEN

DO YOU FEEL LUCKY? WELL, DO YA PUNK?

When I was in college in the 1970s, a classic example that appeared in nearly all introductory statistics courses was the fact that although White workers at every level of education earned more on average than Black workers, at every level of income, White workers had more education than Black workers. The first observation suggested that Blacks were discriminated against by being paid less for the same skills, and the second that White workers were being discriminated against by needing more education to get the same level of income. Statistics professors tell me this observation is no longer safe to make, even in a statistics course.

NOT SO FAST!

Let me hasten to say that the data do not refute the claim that Blacks are discriminated against economically. Nor do they support the claim that Whites are discriminated against economically. The example was taught to make a mathematical point, not one of social justice, one way or the other.

It is very common to find data that suggest different conclusions depending on your direction of inference. A teacher might observe that her Black students go on to earn less money than her White students of equal ability and insist labor markets discriminate against Blacks. A worker might notice that his White co-workers have more education than his Black co-workers of equal rank and income and allege reverse racism. It's a mistake for both the teacher and the worker to reason from their observation without considering the perspective of the other.

To understand the effect, consider a simplified example. Suppose there are only two levels of education, low and high, and two levels of income, low and high. There are 100 White workers, 30 of whom have low education and low income, another 30 have high education and high income, with 20 each with low education and high income or high education and low income. There are 15 Black workers, 7 with low education and low income, 2 with high education and high income, and 3 each with low education and high income or high education and low income.

		Education					
		White workers			Black workers		
		Low	High	Percent high education	Low	High	Percent high education
Income	Low	30	20	40%	7	3	30%
	High	20	30	60%	3	2	40%
	Percent high income	40%	60%		30%	40%	

Among workers with low education, 40% of Whites but only 30% of Blacks earn high income. Among workers with high education, 60% of Whites but only 40% of Blacks earn high income. So, at both education levels, Whites earn more than Blacks on average.

Among workers with low income, 40% of Whites but only 30% of Blacks have high education. Among workers with high income, 60% of Whites but only 40% of Blacks have high education. So, at both income levels, Whites need more education on average to attain it.

PILOTS VERSUS STEWARDESSES

I first encountered this issue outside a classroom when working on a sex discrimination suit against United Airlines in the early 1980s. Our side offered a standard regression showing that if you adjusted for qualifications like education, experience, special skills, and so forth, women were paid something like $10,000 per year less than equally qualified men. The other side responded using exactly the same data to show that at every level of income, men had higher qualifications than women making the same amount of money.

Our side won the case but I don't think the statistical wrangle mattered much one way or the other. And neither regression was very meaningful since in those days men had entirely different airline jobs (pilot, mechanic, baggage handler, executive) than women (stewardess, middle manager, secretary). How do you compare the qualifications of a male pilot with a high-school education who learned to fly in the military, with a female college graduate with 10 years' experience managing the airport operations coordinating passengers, baggage, security, ticketing, and dozens of other matters?

Why is this situation so common? Consider the generic table below for two different groups. One question is whether the ratio of C to A and D to B is higher for one group. The reverse question is whether the ratio of B to

A and D to C is higher. The two questions are unrelated. In a simple case of discrimination, one group will earn more money at all levels of education, and have less education at all levels of income. But in many practical cases, discrimination is more complicated.

	Low	High
Low	A	B
High	C	D

How might this come about? Consider the first example above. There's clearly discrimination. For both White and Black workers, 20% have low education and high income, and 20% have high education and low income. But 47% of Blacks and only 30% of Whites have low education and low income, and 13% of Blacks versus 30% of Whites have high education and high income.

		Education					
		White workers			Black workers		
		Low	High	Percent high education	Low	High	Percent high education
Income	Low	30	20	40%	7	3	30%
	High	20	30	60%	3	2	40%
	Percent high income	40%	60%		30%	40%	

Imagine that before the civil rights era, the large majority of Black workers were in the low-education, low-income box. As laws and social attitudes changed, some low-income Black workers got raises and other Black workers got more education. So, there was progress. But it takes time to acquire education and then rise to high income. Moreover, the obstacles for the most elite jobs were removed more slowly than for less exalted positions. So, there was some remaining discrimination.

Of course, this is just a simplified textbook example, real labor market statistics paint a far more complicated picture and the history of civil rights advances has many twists and turns. My only point is you should consider comparisons like this from both perspectives—income levels by race for people with similar educational and other qualifications, and qualification levels by race for people with similar incomes.

FATAL POLICE SHOOTINGS

A recent example is an academic paper about police shootings: "Officer Characteristics and Racial Disparities in Fatal Officer-Involved Shootings." The journal, *Proceedings of the National Academy of Sciences*, requires a non-technical "significance" section. The authors included the phrase, "white officers are not more likely to shoot minority civilians than nonwhite officers."

The next thing that happened was conservative pro-police commentator Heather Mac Donald relied on the study to tell Congress, "There was no evidence that officer race (i.e., Whiteness) predicted the race of the shooting victim." That's precisely what the study found.

There are two questions we could ask, and as discussed above, they are logically unrelated.

1. Given that a White officer shoots and kills a civilian, is the victim more likely to be Black than if a Black officer did the shooting?
2. Given that a Black civilian is shot and killed by a police officer, is the officer more likely to be White than if a White civilian is shot?

If we're wedded to a simple racism explanation, then we'd assume there are some color-blind situations in which police officers of any race would fatally shoot a victim regardless of race, but there are also some evil White officers who kill Black civilians without justification. Those extra killings would make both (1) and (2) true. But as we know from the income/

education example, it's possible for one of the two statements to be true, but not the other.

Do we care about the difference? Yes. While neither statement by itself tells us what we should do, (1) makes us think about police officer selection and training. We want White and Black officers to be making the same decisions and not to let the victim's race influence them. Since (1) tells us that's not happening, it focuses our attention on officers.

On the other hand, if (1) is false but (2) is true, it suggests Black civilians resist White officers more than Black officers, perhaps from fear of being beaten or killed without justification. Changing civilian behavior requires increasing Black civilian trust in White police and (2) focuses our attention on victim attitudes.

Unfortunately, it's very difficult to measure these questions. Officers and victims do not come in only two races, there are Hispanics, Asians, Native Americans, mixed race, and other categories. Shooting statistics are heavily influenced by factors like areas with a lot of Black people have more Black officers and more Black civilians, so more chance of a Black officer shooting a Black civilian. Most police officers have a negligible probability of ever drawing a gun on duty in their careers, while a few police officers—those in the most violent places or with violent specializations—do most of the killing. Most civilians have a negligible probability of being shot and killed by police, while a few civilians—the violent criminals—are most likely to be killed. Most police shootings involve multiple officers, and some involve multiple civilians, including innocent bystanders or hostages.

THE STUDY

This particular study was by no means perfect. There are issues with the data and objections to some of the statistical techniques. It used multinomial regression, which is similar to the multivariable logistic regression I criticized in Chapter 5, but in this case it's justified because the authors are using it for prediction rather than causal analysis. Unfortunately, critics assumed the predictions the paper and Heather Mac Donald mentioned were causal claims.

The appropriate response for people wanting to challenge Mac Donald's testimony would be to do their own studies to demonstrate officer race predicted the race of the shooting victim. Perhaps larger sample sizes or better analysis could predict victim race from officer race. Another alternative would be to concede there's no evidence White officers are more likely to kill Black civilians than Black officers are, and to rely on other evidence for racism in police killings.

Instead, critics mounted a successful campaign to have the study retracted. They claimed "White officers are not more likely to shoot minority civilians than nonwhite officers" meant the race of the victim did not predict the race of the officer—claim (2) above—and since the paper did not investigate that hypothesis, it should be retracted.

It's barely possible to support the critics' reading of the phrase out-of-context, because English is not precise about logical relations. But the meaning is clear—claim (1) above—if you read the entire sentence: "We find no evidence of anti-Black or anti-Hispanic disparities across shootings, and White officers are not more likely to shoot minority civilians than non-White officers." The phrase refers to disparities across shootings (Heather Mac Donald's point) not officers (what the critics claimed the phrase meant). You could also look to the title of the paper: "*Officer Characteristics* and Racial Disparities in Fatal Officer-Involved Shootings" (my emphasis). No one who read even the non-technical "interpretation" summary section, or the abstract, could be confused about the meaning, much less anyone who read the paper.

Nothing in the study denied there was racism in police shootings. The value of the study was to point likely paths for solutions. It was people who insist on racism of individual White officers who took exception to the paper. Unable to find evidence against its conclusions, or to make technical objections to the methodology stick, they grabbed a partial sentence out of context from the non-technical summary and misunderstood it, or pretended to. These people misrepresented the paper, not to support a false narrative, but to discredit the paper.

WHAT SHOULD HAVE HAPPENED

The proper response by the authors would be to tell critics, "Read the whole sentence you're criticizing, or look at the title of the paper." They could issue a public statement: "Heather Mac Donald's use of our paper is accurate, and her critics are misrepresenting the paper to discredit it."

A neutral action would have been to rewrite the non-technical summary of the paper. There's no way to avoid any possible ambiguity of any partial sentence taken out of context. The authors could have explicitly disavowed this particular one. But it's legal contracts that are written to prevent any possible misunderstanding, and they are unreadable to most people. The whole point of non-technical summaries is to make the work accessible to intelligent non-specialists.

Compare the clear original, "We find no evidence of anti-Black or anti-Hispanic disparities across shootings, and White officers are not more likely to shoot minority civilians than non-White officers," to the authors' proposed rewrite, "We find no evidence of anti-Black or anti-Hispanic disparities across shootings, and as the proportion of White officers in a fatal officer-involved shooting increased, a person fatally shot was not more likely to be of a racial minority." I'm pretty sure anyone confused by the original would be more confused by the rewrite, and many people who understood the original perfectly would misunderstand the replacement.

I think the authors violated academic integrity when they placed the clarification of the non-technical summary in a correction to the paper itself. They claimed the paper's results were correct and that they had been "clear about the quantity we estimated." To correct things already correct and clear is not honest.

The groveling apology one author sent to the *Wall Street Journal* for having "overstepped" and failed to "uphold the high standard"—without conceding that anything in the paper was false or misleading—is merely unseemly, and blaming Heather Mac Donald for his problems rather than the people who actually did misrepresent his work (not to mention his own spinelessness) is pathetic.

The major academic crime is retracting the paper. Retracting a result you know to be true and clearly stated should carry the same academic consequences as knowingly publishing a false one. When the Soviet Union outlawed Darwin, or Maoist China Einstein, or Nazi Germany imposed racial and eugenic theories—the problem wasn't that serious researchers began publishing false results, but that they retracted true ones and switched to other fields. The Catholic Church did not demand Galileo publish Ptolemaic astronomy essays, merely that he retract his heliocentric ones. When the US government imposes gentler coercion by restricting funding and access to information in fields like gun violence, nuclear testing, recreational drugs, abortion, fetal cells, nuclear winter, etc., the problem again is not false publications in these fields, but lack of true ones.

These researchers have less excuse than scientists threatened by totalitarian horror regimes. They did not risk gulags, farm labor, concentration camps, or burning at the stake. I don't know if they feared losses of jobs or grants, or perhaps that law enforcement agencies would no longer share the data they needed for their work, but such things do happen. Anyway, I don't like to criticize individuals without knowing the full circumstances in which they made their decisions. I'm not especially heroic myself, so I'm not going to claim I would have stood up to whatever pressures they may have felt.

But the scientific community should reject the retraction. Like publication, retraction demands justification. The one given by the authors, that Heather Mac Donald misrepresented their work, is both false and inadequate.

PUT ME IN COACH, I'M READY TO PLAY, CENTERFIELD

I don't want to give the impression that quantitative analysis is a minefield of Wrong Numbers. Let's take a Field of Dreams trip.

CHAPTER NINETEEN

SEVENTH-INNING STRETCH

Let's switch gears so *Wrong Number* is not relentlessly negative. I'm a big believer in quantitative methods and I use them all the time for life decisions, to make money, and to form opinions.

EXPLORATORY DATA ANALYSIS

The first professional statisticians I worked with were John Tukey and Frederick Mosteller. At the time (1974, my freshman year in college) I was pretty oblivious and didn't wonder why they singled me out. Reflecting on it later, after experience selecting and mentoring younger people myself, I think it was because I had done lots of statistical analyses and acted—bet—on the results, or formed my opinions from them. I doubt they were impressed by my technical skills in statistics as I was entirely self-taught and had made errors. I think they wanted to nurture a student who would apply the skills they could teach to make choices and change his mind, rather than to pass tests or get publications.

Tukey wrote the classic text *Exploratory Data Analysis* and Mosteller titled his autobiography *The Pleasures of Statistics*. These convey their attitudes. When I took Mosteller's course as a freshman, I had already been doing data analysis and statistics for science journal articles for five years (of course, under supervision of professional researchers and often checking by professional statisticians and peer reviewers). I was also making money betting on baseball, among other things. Poker was my main source of income, but I liked to keep my hand in other forms of advantage gambling.

Mosteller hired me for a project analyzing baseball—specifically the prospects of the Boston Red Sox. Tukey was involved in the project, although he had more interest in physical characteristics—player heights, field dimensions, pitch speed—than in winning or losing games.

What I took away from both men was not just a rigorous academic education in formal statistical theory, but a love of applying the techniques for all sorts of prediction and explanation—elections, sporting events, authorship of the Federalist papers, varieties of sexual behavior—all by exploration with a strong spirit of play animating the serious mathematics. Both men were obsessive about testing statistical methods against objective reality as rigorously as possible.

In homage to these men, and many other like-minded women and men, I include this chapter.

TAKE ME OUT TO THE BALL GAME

I'm a lifelong baseball fan. One argument I've heard since childhood is how the great baseball players of the past—the Josh Gibsons and Babe Ruths, the Cy Youngs and Rube Fosters—would fare in the modern game.

One camp holds that athletes have progressed enormously. The gold-medal times of the *Chariots of Fire* runners in the 1924 Olympics wouldn't win a high-school state championship today. Competition draws from a far larger pool of competitors today compared to the past, and nutrition, training, and medicine are far superior. Ty Cobb, transported by time machine as an 18-year-old rookie in 1905, would struggle to make a 2025 high-school team—or so some baseball fans argue.

The other camp holds that old-time players were far more focused on baseball and steeped in its culture than any modern players can be. They had no television and spent much less time in school. Other sports didn't have the cultural appeal and economic opportunities of baseball. Sandlots and vacant fields were available everywhere. When kids weren't playing baseball, they were probably doing manual labor rather than playing video games or doing homework or working their phones. And players were not as distracted by agents, endorsements, and media as they are today. Semi-professional teams in every town and company nurtured talent. Moreover, with only 16 White major-league teams plus perhaps 6 top-quality Negro major-league teams, and smaller rosters, talent was less diluted.

I believe in getting a quantitative answer to questions like these. Not because they're automatically right, but because they narrow the range of plausible disagreement. You can't get definitive answers to questions like these, but you can rule a lot of popular answers out. Moreover, careful analysis focuses attention on the true unknowns by stripping away the things we can demonstrate objectively.

I don't claim I have approached this question in the only or best way. This chapter is not supposed to be an exemplar of perfect analysis, just an account of something that is not a Wrong Number.

I WEAR THE CHAIN I FORGED IN LIFE, REPLIED THE GHOST

Without a *Field of Dreams*, we can't see Walter Johnson pitching to Aaron Judge, but we can compare 2023 players to 2024. Consider all the pitchers who pitched in both 2023 and 2024. They allowed 0.14 fewer runs per nine-innings pitched in 2024 versus 2023. Since the pitchers were the same, we can take this as evidence that 2024 offense was 0.14 runs per nine innings worse than 2023.

But maybe the difference was not caused by worse offense but by rule changes, or different interpretations or other factors like equipment or parks. We're going to apply this logic over all baseball history, and we know runs-per-game goes up and down quite a bit over time. Sometimes we have reasons to explain it, but most of the time we have only conjecture.

So, let's get a second estimate by looking at hitters who played in both 2023 and 2024. Keeping hitters constant, we find pitchers held them to 0.31 fewer runs per nine innings. So that suggests 2024 defense was 0.31 runs per nine innings better than 2023.

The beauty of these two estimates is they contain the change in the balance between defense and offense in opposite directions. So, when we average the two, we automatically adjust for factors that favor or disfavor scoring. The average of 0.31 and negative 0.14 is positive 0.09, so we think baseball teams got 0.09 runs per nine innings better in 2024 versus 2023.

Now I know there are some issues with this method, but suspend consideration of them for a moment to make sure you understand the logic. We measure the change in average hitting quality from 2023 to 2024 by looking at what the 2024 hitters did against a constant population of pitchers, compared with what the 2023 hitters did against the same pitchers. We measure the change in average pitching quality by keeping the hitters constant and comparing the success of 2024 pitchers to 2023 pitchers. Then we average the two to get an estimate of the overall change in team quality from 2024 versus 2023. I'm going to chain the estimates together to compare 2024 teams to teams from the distant past.

PATCH IT UP

Some issues are easy to address. We might not want to use runs per nine innings as our measure of quality. We could use measures that adjust for defensive quality, or base running, or other factors other than pitching and hitting. We could try to make explicit adjustments for new parks, rule changes, and expansion. I won't go into these other than saying I've run lots of alternative specifications and get pretty similar results.

The thorniest issue is age. We're not really keeping the pitchers and hitters constant, because they're both one year older in 2024 versus 2023. We could hope that improvements among the younger players offset declines among the older players, but it doesn't. I know that because I tried it and got results that don't make sense (I'll explain that a bit later).

You might try subtracting from each pitcher's 2024 numbers the average one-year improvement or decline based on his age—adding to a

21-year-old pitcher for the average improvement from 21 to 22, subtracting from a 38-year-old pitcher for the average decline from 38 to 39. The problem is you'll be subtracting the average improvement or decline in overall baseball quality as part of your adjustment, getting rid of the signal you want to measure along with the noise of age.

So, I split the analysis by age. Instead of averaging the overall pitching estimate with the overall hitting estimate, I took all the pitchers who were, say, 27 years old in 2023 and averaged their improvement estimate with all the hitters who were 27 years old in 2023. The assumption is that hitters and pitchers get better and worse with age in about the same pattern. That's not exactly true, but it does account for most age-related effects. Then I took an average of all the age-specific estimates, weighted by the product of outs in both seasons by both pitchers and hitters. This dramatically reduced the volatility in the change estimates.

THE BOTTOM LINE

The result was that baseball teams have been getting better at a pretty steady rate of 0.04 runs per nine innings since 1871. That means they add one run per game every 25 years. A 1960 baseball team playing a 1935 baseball team would average one more run per game than its opponent in the game.

We have some natural experiments to see if this method makes sense. We know the quality of play dropped during World War II as many players went into military service and some marginal players took their places. The numbers show team quality dropping by 0.06 runs per nine innings from 1940 to 1941, and another 0.04 from 1941 to 1942—those numbers are 0.10 and 0.08 runs below the long-term average 0.04 increase. There was a 0.01 increase from 1942 to 1943—still below the 0.04 average—and a 0.04 decline from 1943 to 1944.

Things came back a little from 1944 to 1945, 0.04, an average increase. But 1945 to 1946 saw a huge 0.22 jump, with another 0.15 from 1945 to 1946.

The other time we know baseball quality declines is when the leagues expand. Adding new teams brings in players who would not have been major leaguers in prior seasons. In the 1961–1962 expansion from 16 to 20 teams, overall quality declined 0.13 runs per nine innings. In 1969 the majors went from 20 to 24 teams, and quality dropped 0.07 runs per nine innings. In 1977 quality dropped 0.10 runs per nine innings as two more teams were added. Two more teams in 1993 resulted in a 0.07-runs-per-nine-innings decline. The final two-team addition in 1998 to 30 teams is the only exception, a 0.01 increase in quality. But this was proportionately the smallest expansion, and the increase was still less than the long-term average.

When I wrote earlier that skipping the age-adjustment step led to results that didn't make sense, this is what I meant. It did not show consistent declines in quality in years when I knew they had occurred.

TEAMS FOR THE AGES

The table below shows how the quality of major-league baseball play increased over the traditional baseball eras. The fastest improvement was from 1901 to 1939. World War II slowed the increase. One surprise is the integration era, in which Black players were allowed into the game and representation of Latin players increased in tandem, had only an average improvement, given that many of the greatest stars of all time were Black and Latin players during these seasons. One explanation is integration was slow. Another is the Korean War pulled many players into military service. While baseball was still "America's game," college and Olympic sports, and professional basketball, football, and hockey, were gaining attention, drawing athletes and money away from baseball. Urbanization and development meant fewer kids had easy access to fields, and increased emphasis on education took time away from baseball and manual labor.

Era	Seasons	Average yearly improvement
Pre-modern	1871–1900	0.03
Dead Ball	1901–1919	0.05
Live Ball	1920–1939	0.06
WWII	1940–1946	0.02
Integration	1947–1960	0.04
Expansion	1961–1976	0.02
Free Agency	1977–1993	0.04
Steroid	1994–2005	0.03
Post-steroid	2006–2024	0.04

The expansion era naturally slowed improvement, but things have been pretty steady since. The steroid era was known for spectacular increases in home runs, but those only favor offense over defense, they don't cause a net increase in quality (and performance-enhancing drugs helped pitchers as well). Anyway, the era shows up with slightly below average overall quality improvements.

The next table shows the top 20 major-league baseball teams of all time, ranked by *Baseball Reference* wins-above-replacement (we discussed WAR in Chapter 6). I show the team's actual regular season record, and what my analysis projects the team would have done in a 162-game season in which all major-league baseball teams since 1871 (excepting the Negro major leagues for which I don't have comparable statistics) participated.

Team	Record	Projected record
2001 Seattle Mariners	116–46	131–31
1927 New York Yankees	110–44	92–70
1931 New York Yankees	94–59	90–72
2019 Houston Astros	107–55	139–23
1969 Baltimore Orioles	109–53	118–44
1976 Cincinnati Reds	102–60	115–47
1939 New York Yankees	106–45	112–50
1973 Baltimore Orioles	97–65	113–49
1906 Cleveland Naps	89–64	49–113
1976 New York Yankees	97–62	111–51
1953 Brooklyn Dodgers	105–49	105–57
2023 Atlanta Braves	104–58	135–27
1962 San Francisco Giants	103–62	102–60
1975 Cincinnati Reds	108–54	118–44
1971 Baltimore Orioles	101–57	115–47
1930 New York Yankees	86–68	75–87
1983 Detroit Tigers	92–70	107–55
1912 Philadelphia Athletics	90–62	53–109
2017 Houston Astros	101–61	131–31
1955 Brooklyn Dodgers	98–55	101–61

The 2001 Seattle Mariners are tied with the 1906 Chicago Cubs for the most wins in a season, although the Cubs did it in 155 games (with three ties) instead of 162. Nevertheless, the Mariners are statistically the best team in history compared to other teams in the same season, at least by the *Baseball Reference* metric. 2001 was Ichiro Suzuki's rookie year, in which he won Rookie-of-the-Year, Most Valuable Player, plus a gold glove, silver slugger, and All-Star berth. The team had other stars as well, but its real excellence was having at least very good players at all positions with more-than-adequate backups.

Non-quantitative baseball fans are apt to name the best team ever as the 1927 Yankees with Babe Ruth, Lou Gehrig, and other greats. My analysis says they would be a good team in 2024, but not a top one. The 2019 Houston Astros show up as the best team ever (the 2017 Astros in 19th place were aided by illegal sign stealing, but the 2019 Astros were innocent).

The dead-ball-era Cleveland Naps are projected to win only 49 games in my hypothetical all-time season. That's about what a team of replacement players selected among minor-leaguers or waived players would do. The other dead-ball-era team in the top 20, the 1912 Athletics, do not fare much better. The 1930 Yankees are better than those two, but still project out to a losing record in the all-time league.

But the other great teams of the past still look great, if significantly below the great teams of the 21st century.

PLAY TIME

If you have fond memories of Remy from *Ratatouille*, you should enjoy the next chapter, but I have to issue a trigger warning if you couldn't sleep after watching *Willard* or *Ben*.

CHAPTER TWENTY
RATPOCALYPSE!

As the earth gets warmer, there's one species that supposedly will really benefit. "Climate change is amazing," reported *National Geographic*. "If you're a rat."

"WILLARD! THERE ARE RATS IN THE BASEMENT!"

The horrific prospect of these pizza-dragging, toilet-bathing, plague-spreading, baby-eating, cannibalistic beasts swarming the sweltering streets of our major cities helps to explain why a recent study allegedly demonstrating a global warming-induced increase in the urban rat population received such widespread media coverage. As is often the case, journalists were not sufficiently skeptical, nor did they take the time to read the study closely.

Published in *Science Advances*, one of the top science journals in the world, with 19 co-authors, the paper claimed to link rat populations to global warming. If the study results were true, it would be great news. Rats thrive in exactly the same temperature ranges as people, so if global warming is helping rats, it must also be helping people. If we don't like the extra rats, there are far cheaper ways to control them than cooling the entire planet—like not leaving garbage out.

How did the study authors measure the growth in rat populations? By counting rat complaints reported by residents.

It uses these complaints to compare rat populations in different cities, which is the study's first major problem. The data don't allow for an apples-to-apples comparison. In San Francisco, for example, the authors examined the trend in all pest complaints, including those involving rodents and insects, from 2010 to 2022. In Boston, only actual dead rats or rat bites were included. In Dallas, the trend was estimated from 2013 to 2019. Some cities changed categorizations and added or eliminated categories over time.

The city of Cincinnati keeps a record of the entire complaint, and many of the incidents included in the study had nothing to do with rats. There were calls about roaches, bedbugs, cats, dogs, raccoons, and mice. One complaint was about a pregnant tenant. Yet these were all counted as rat complaints.

If your data mixes apples and oranges, you'll get meaningless results.

"TEAR HIM UP!"

The problems with the underlying data alone would render the study's findings invalid. But we're just getting started.

The next problem is that rat complaints aren't a good measure of rat populations. While the authors acknowledged the limitations of their approach, they also cited three studies to support the claim that rat complaints accurately measure the growth of the rat population.

However, these three papers actually say—as one did explicitly—that "citizen complaints for rats ... were bad predictors of measured rat activity." They point out that there were more rat complaints in areas with fewer rats because one rat can cause alarm but when rats are common, people don't bother notifying the city. They also found that in places with more people, there could be fewer rats and more complaints; after all, it's people who complain, not rats. Also, people in wealthier areas complained more frequently than those in poorer areas.

An important but more technical criticism is all three papers discussed only differences among neighborhoods in the same city at one time, which does not logically tell us anything about comparing trends over time in different cities.

This is another example of authors misrepresenting support for a key point their entire paper depends on. And the peer reviewers for this major science journal apparently didn't bother to check.

"AND HEAR THEM! DON'T YOU HEAR THEM DOWN THERE?" "IT'S JUST THE WIND"

Next, the authors took all this unreliable data and compared it to changes in temperature in 16 cities. That showed growth in rate populations was negatively correlated to warming over the study period. In three cities, temperatures rose and rat complaints fell. And in the eight cities that cooled, there were more rat complaints. The only city with a clear association between rising temperatures and increased rat complaints was San Francisco.

The authors did acknowledge this in the paper, finding "no correlation between monthly mean temperature" and increasing rat populations, and that "the trends in rat numbers were not linked to ... mean minimum temperature in each city."

Yet, the journalists who trumpeted the study in articles and on local TV news reported the opposite. Why did they get it backward? Most of the fault lies with the journalists, who didn't bother reading the study. However, the authors made a different claim in the study that was easily misunderstood.

There is a bit of good news here. University of Richmond biologist Jonathan Richardson, a co-author of the study, was gracious with his time while I was trying to understand his paper. He responded to my email and was very helpful in resolving some issues I had in replicating the study results, which is unfortunately rare among researchers. However, his careful wording when talking to the media helps explain why the study was widely misinterpreted.

In a video interview about the study, Richardson said: "What we found is that cities that are experiencing warmer climate trends, so temperatures that are increasing over time, also are experiencing the fastest increases in rat population growth." Isn't that the opposite of the data and the statements in the paper?

Not quite. Note the phrases "climate trends" and "over time."

What he means is he's correlating city rat population growth over the past decade or two with regional temperature increases since 1901. But if he had put it that way, journalists might start to question what this finding has to do with current temperatures.

Consider Tokyo, one of the 16 cities included in the study. The authors tabulated rat complaints from 2008 to 2021 and then compared that data to rising temperatures in the entire country of Japan since the year 1901. They found a correlation. So what?

"OUR TIME WILL COME"

Were the rats smart enough to measure country-wide average temperatures and remember them for over a century when deciding, in 2008, to start causing enough of a ruckus that Tokyo residents would file more rat complaints with the city? Are the rats secretly climate change activists?

Temperatures in Japan did increase from 13.7°C in 1901 to 17.0°C in 2007. However, by 2008, when rats began their 13-year campaign to scare humans into filing more complaints with the city, the warming had started reversing. During the study period, from 2008 to 2021, Tokyo's mean temperatures fell from 17 to 16.6°C.

Global warming will not bring a rat apocalypse, and these disease-carrying pests will not be swarming the sweltering streets of our major cities anytime soon. Any more than they already are, at least.

Linking rats and global warming yields sensational headlines for advocacy journalists who want to sound the alarm about climate change. But this study used shoddy data, was presented in a deeply misleading way, and the media should have paid it no attention whatsoever.

CHALLENGING THE CRITICS

Next, we'll consider another aspect of global warming: how partisans use wrong Wrong Numbers as offensive weapons.

CHAPTER TWENTY-ONE

UNSETTLING TREATMENT OF *UNSETTLED*

This chapter is a bit of a reversal. The points I've made about Wrong Numbers are sometimes used maliciously by people to criticize valid work. No statistical work is perfect, and robust criticism is necessary to thrash out truth. But useful criticism must be supported by reasoned argument, not catch phrases.

THE BOOK

In 2021, the physicist and New York University professor Steven Koonin, who served as undersecretary for science in the Obama administration's Energy Department, published the best-selling *Unsettled: What Climate Science Tells Us, What It Doesn't, and Why It Matters*.

The book attracted extremely negative reviews, filled with *ad hominem* attacks, such as a short statement appearing in *Scientific American* and signed by 12 academics that, instead of substantively rebutting Koonin's arguments, calls him "a crank who's only taken seriously by far-right disinformation peddlers hungry for anything they can use to score political points" and "just another denier trying to sell a book." Even if those claims were true, which they are not, they wouldn't speak to the claims in Koonin's book.

I couldn't find a single negative review of *Unsettled* that disputed its claims directly or even described them accurately. Many of the reviewers seem to have stopped reading after the first few pages. Others were forced to concede that many of Koonin's facts were correct but objected that they were used in the service of challenging official dogma. True statements were downplayed as trivial or as things everyone knows, despite the extensive parts of *Unsettled* that document precisely the opposite: that the facts were widely denied in major media coverage and misrepresentations were cited as the basis for major policy initiatives.

When dissenting scientists are implicitly compared to Holocaust deniers, or their ideas are considered too dangerous to be carefully considered, it undermines public respect for the field and can lead to catastrophic policy mistakes. It's human nature to favor evidence that confirms our biases and leads to simple conclusions. But for science to advance, it's essential that moral certainty does not override objective discussion and that personal attacks do not replace rational consideration of empirical evidence.

GARY YOHE

In a review of *Unsettled* in *Scientific American*, Gary Yohe, an emeritus professor at Wesleyan University, gives the impression that he didn't read past the first few pages. The book has nine chapters filled with examples of exaggerations and outright falsehoods in both scientific and popular accounts. Yohe mentions just four claims taken from the first two pages, plus one from a chapter subtitle, and manages to refute none of them. He seizes on the assertion, which appears on page 2, that "the warmest temperatures in the US have not risen in the past fifty years."

"According to what measure?" Yohe asks. "Highest annual global averages? Absolutely not." If he had kept reading, Yohe would have found a detailed account of precisely what measure Koonin was using and the evidence that record high temperatures in the United States are no more common than they were in the 1970s. And if he hadn't missed the words "warmest" and "US" in the sentence he did read, he would have been reminded that Koonin is talking about the highest summer temperatures in the United States, not annual global average temperatures.

Yohe attacks Koonin's assertion that "heat waves in the US are now no more common than they were in 1900," claiming that "this is a questionable statement depending on the definition of 'heat wave,' and so it is really uninformative. Heat waves are poor indicators of heat stress."

If Yohe had read the book, he would have found the official heat wave index used and why it matters. He offers no evidence that "heat stress"—something even less well defined and, hence, less informative than "heat wave"—is greater now than in 1900.

Yohe also focuses on the book's title, *Unsettled*. He claims that "Koonin deploys that highly misleading label to falsely suggest that we don't understand the risks well enough to take action." Actually, Koonin's argument is that claims of harm from human climate impacts have been exaggerated and are misrepresented in the press and that we should undertake more sensible and longer-term policies than many activists and politicians currently advocate. He thinks we should take different action, not no action.

In another article published on the website of the Union of Concerned Scientists, Yohe writes that although Koonin is "a very skilled and well-respected physicist," he should follow the approach of those who "are on the front lines," who "know what they are doing [because they] ... have been doing this for 15 years."

PERMISSION TO SPEAK

Koonin has been attacked by others for not being a climate scientist by trade. In most dogmatic religions, only the anointed are granted the authority to speak. But science is supposed to be a discipline that's open to anyone who can interpret relevant material.

Moreover, Koonin is not doing original climate science, he's relying on the same climate scientists Yohe and others use. He's adding his long experience as a top science policymaker and scientific knowledge as a top physicist to discuss policy responses to the findings of climate science. He's acting like a doctor reviewing the data generated by lab technicians to recommend treatment options to a patient. A doctor doesn't have to draw the blood and run the MRI machine to have an opinion on therapies—and the people who draw blood and run MRI machines are usually not qualified to be doctors.

On top of that, Koonin has in fact published important climate science work. And the arguments in *Unsettled* require insights from physics, economics, politics, diplomacy, engineering, and other fields. Climate science alone cannot tell us what we should do.

"*Unsettled* is a book you can accurately judge by its cover," wrote Mark Boslough, a fellow of the Committee for Skeptical Inquiry, in *Yale Climate Review Connections*, and it seems as if he did just that, despite the popular advice against it. Boslough denies that anyone in the media, politics, or otherwise of prominence has claimed that climate science is settled. Counterexamples to that claim are extremely easy to find. Boslough ignores all of the book's substantive points because the cover was the only part worth reading.

Koonin is accused of having "cherrypicked and carelessly misrepresented many of his sources" by Bob Ward, the policy and communications director of the Grantham Research Institute on Climate Change and the Environment at the London School of Economics and Political Science.

Though his refutations are weak, at least Ward does seem to have read the book. In one chapter, Koonin takes the media to task for its overheated account of the link between human CO_2 emissions and hurricane frequency, such as a *USA Today* article headlined: "Global warming is making hurricanes stronger, study says." That article states unequivocally that "Human-caused global warming has strengthened the wind speeds of hurricanes, typhoons and cyclones around the globe." Koonin points out that the study on which that article is based doesn't make that claim with such certainty.

ERROR TYPES

Koonin quotes directly from the study, but Ward accuses him of having omitted another excerpt from the same paper, which reads: "From a storyline, balance-of-evidence, or Type-II error avoidance perspective, the consistency of the trends identified here with expectations based on physical understanding and greenhouse warming simulations increases confidence that TCs have become substantially stronger, and that there is a likely human fingerprint on this increase."

Ward must be confused about what that sentence means because it doesn't support the *USA Today* article nor undermine Koonin's point. It's a classic example of using jargon to sneak a personal opinion into a work that is supposed to be scientific.

A Type-II error means failing to reject a false null hypothesis. In this case, the null hypothesis is that human actions are not making tropical cyclones stronger. So, from a Type-II error avoidance perspective—that is, if you want to be sure you don't make a Type-II error—you should assert that human actions are making tropical cyclones stronger, whatever the evidence says. But science and statistics are not about avoiding Type-II errors only, they're about balancing Type-I (rejecting a true null hypothesis) and Type-II errors.

In the scientific part of the paper, the authors were unable to reject the null hypothesis, meaning they were unable to find strong evidence that human actions were making tropical cyclones stronger. Of course, absence of evidence is not evidence of absence. It's certainly possible that human actions are making tropical cyclones stronger, but this paper found only mild evidence suggestive that tropical cyclones are getting stronger, and no evidence of a human cause.

By "storyline" and "balance of evidence," the authors mean consistent with what other people think—in this case, computer simulations of physical interactions, or models. So even though this study did not find human actions were making tropical cyclones stronger, we should dismiss that finding because other people say human actions are making tropical cyclones stronger. Once again, the authors have departed from science to give opinions.

Stripping out the jargon, the paper's authors are saying, despite the scientific findings—suggestive evidence that tropical cyclones have gotten stronger, not enough for statistical significance, with no evidence of a human cause—we're better off assuming that humans are causing stronger tropical cyclones.

That's not unreasonable, as it does little harm to assume it if it's false and it could do a lot of harm to overlook it if it's true. Koonin likely agrees with that. But he's certainly correct and Ward is wrong, that the jargony opinion inserted into the science doesn't justify unambiguous headlines like "Global warming is making hurricanes stronger, study says." And Yohe is wrong that omitting that personal aside and reporting only the science in the paper is cherry picking.

GREENLAND

After Koonin wrote a *Wall Street Journal* op-ed entitled "Greenland's Melting Ice Is No Cause for Climate-Change Panic" in February 2022, a publication called *Climate Feedback*, which calls itself "a worldwide network of scientists sorting fact from fiction in climate change media coverage," published a response. It labeled Koonin's article "Cherry-picking, Flawed reasoning, Lack of context, Misleading."

The point of Koonin's op-ed was straightforward and illustrated by a graph showing Greenland ice loss every year from 1900 to 2022. It shows Greenland losing ice, but at a rate that goes up and down over time, both before and after global warming which is thought to have begun around 1960. The main driver cannot be anthropogenic climate change, or we would see more ice loss in the climate-change era than in the previous era, and ice loss increasing with Greenland temperature or global atmospheric CO_2 concentrations. Carbon dioxide emissions and warming may be important, but other factors were clearly more important in the past.

Koonin acknowledged that "the United Nations' Intergovernmental Panel on Climate Change projects that for the most likely course of greenhouse-gas emissions in the 21st century, the average annual ice loss would be somewhat larger than the peak values shown in the graph."

How is it "cherry-picking" to show all the data? Columbia University's Marco Tedesco claims that "the article picks only the last 10 years, excluding the remaining time series for the context." And yet, the graph published in the op-ed clearly shows the data since 1900 and addresses all of it.

Ironically, the *Climate Feedback* review is guilty of cherry picking. It claims to rebut Koonin by stating that a 2015 article in *Nature* "found that ice loss between 2003 and 2010 'not only more than doubled relative to the 1983–2003 period, but also relative to the net mass loss rate throughout the twentieth century.'"

In other words, *Climate Feedback* picked the fastest eight-year increase over the 121-year span shown on the chart and compared it to the lowest 21 years. That's the definition of cherry picking. It's also irrelevant to the climate change debate because both periods occurred in the time period of rapid global warming.

REHASHING HEATWAVES

Eric Rignot of the University of California, Irvine, who contributed to *Climate Feedback*'s attempt to rebut Koonin, dismisses the op-ed by claiming that it's rehashing "the old argument that the 30s were warmer than present [which] is false," when in fact that's not the argument and has nothing to do with Koonin's point.

In another *Climate Feedback* article—this one is a review of a video that Koonin made to summarize his book—Southern Illinois University's Justin Schoof disputes Koonin's claim that US heatwaves are no more common today than in 1900: "The 2018 U.S. National Climate Assessment shows that the heat wave season in the United States has increased in length since the 1960s," he writes. This is doubly irrelevant, since it refers to a different metric and a different time period than Koonin referred to. To make matters worse, Schoof is citing precisely the data that Koonin explains are misleading in his book.

Why does it matter that Koonin's critics don't want to bother responding to his arguments? Substantive debate is how science advances. If climate science is just an echo chamber, we may make perverse short-term overreactions to the data that have large costs and possibly even negative environmental effects. Many historical policy disasters have been caused by people claiming they shouldn't have to engage with informed critics.

Unsettled is about more than just climate policy—it seeks to free science from the shackles of organized dogma, the sole domain of an anointed elite, who feel justified calling their critics "cranks," "deniers," and "disinformation peddlers." Why engage with a heretic when he can be banished from the church altogether?

THREE LITTLE WORDS

No one disputes that diversity, equity, and inclusion are all good things. To some people, abbreviating them to DEI is a handy way to save seven syllables, and perhaps emphasize how the three work together. To other people, however, DEI has unmoored from its underlying words and become a euphemism for identity politics, quotas, shaming, and stereotyping. I take no position on that dispute. I only point out some Wrong Numbers enlisted in its service.

CHAPTER TWENTY-TWO

DIVERSITY + EQUITY + INCLUSION = BETTER PERFORMANCE?

A germ of conventional wisdom that has emerged in the last decade is the claim that diversity in corporate boards and senior executives has been proven to improve company performance. *The New York Times* claims, "A growing body of research shows that more diverse teams outperform their peers." The Nasdaq market justified diversity disclosure rules with the statement, which the SEC accepted: "There is a compelling body of credible research on the association between company performance and board diversity."

YES, VIRGINIA, THERE IS A STUDY

Unlike most "studies prove" bandwagons, this one actually has an underlying study. The consulting firm McKinsey & Company addressed this question in 2015. The study has been updated three times—each time the claimed improvement is larger.

Among scientific researchers, finding that something is bigger each time you measure it is a sign you might not understand what's going on. Only among non-scientific ideologues is continuing escalation of claims proof of their validity.

The BBC used the third incarnation, "A 2020 McKinsey & Company analysis of 1,000 US firms showed companies with more gender diversity within their leadership teams were 25% more likely to have higher profits than their peers who did not." The 2015 original was cited in California Assembly Bill No. 979 (overturned on May 15, 2023 for being "a race-based quota"), which mandated diversity in corporate boards: "According to a report by McKinsey and Company, for every 10 percent increase in racial and ethnic diversity on the senior-executive team, earnings before interest and taxes rise 0.8 percent."

The McKinsey tetralogy, and a similar study by one of their competitors, Boston Consulting Group, continue to be the main sources because they make the most straightforward claims. That's possible because they do not conform to academic publication standards. There is an extensive academic literature, but none of it bears directly on the question and, in any event, the weight of it suggests diversity is either unrelated to or bad for corporate performance.

After opening by asserting they already know "intuitively" that diversity improves corporate performance, McKinsey leads with this blatant contradiction: "While correlation does not equal causation (greater gender and ethnic diversity in corporate leadership doesn't automatically translate into more profit), the correlation does indicate that when companies commit themselves to diverse leadership, they are more successful."

The first phrase and the parenthetical are correct, the last phrase contradicts it and is wrong. All observational studies like the McKinsey one can show is that two things are associated. Companies with greater diversity tend to be more profitable. They cannot show that when companies commit to diversity, profits increase. It could equally well be true that when companies earn higher profits they increase diversity, or that some other factor—such as having brand names, or operating internationally—leads to both diversity and profits.

HELMER AND HECTOR

Another issue is McKinsey chose a perverse measure of diversity, the Herfindahl–Hirschman (H&H) index. There's a real diversity story about another H&H, the bagel makers. By 1972, it had become increasingly difficult to find authentic Jewish bagels in New York, even on the Jew-heavy Upper West Side where I lived most of my life. Two Puerto Rican brothers-in-law, Helmer Toro and Hector Hernandez, founded H&H Bagels on Broadway and 80th Street and revived the cultural tradition for three generations of Jewish food lovers. But too often today stories like that are counted as cultural appropriation rather than genuine diversity.

Most people think a diverse board should reflect population percentages of individuals. But the H&H index mandates that boards and executive suites be composed of the same number of people in each category. McKinsey chose as categories: Blacks, Non-Hispanic Whites, Hispanics, Near Easterners, East Asians, South Asians, Native Americans, and Other.

To see what this means, imagine a company identified 200 candidates who were a perfect cross-section of the US population for eight board seats. Since it's a perfect cross-section, and Native Americans are 0.5% of the US population, there would be one Native American. The company would be required to take her, regardless of qualifications. The company could choose one each among two Near Easterners, three South Asians, eight East Asians, and eight Others (mostly mixed race). They could pick one each from 23 Blacks, 38 Hispanics, and 117 Whites.

This is the widely despised strategy of "tokenism," not most people's idea of diversity. And as you increase the number of groups to represent by incorporating sex, sexual identity, religion, immigration status, economic class, education, and other factors, you end up with every individual unique, and every board equally diverse because it has no two identical members.

H&H JURIES

Although this is not at all what most people mean by "diversity," it's not completely crazy. I first used the H&H index back in the 1980s when I was working to promote more diverse juries. Other people had demonstrated that all-White juries could deliver shockingly racist verdicts, even in places supposed to be liberal and tolerant. What we then discovered is the presence of even a single Black person on a jury completely changed the outcomes for Black defendants, plaintiffs, and victims. Adding additional Black jurors beyond one did not always help Black defendants (it did help Black victims and plaintiffs). This meant focusing on the overall proportion of Black jurors was not the best way to analyze jury composition fairness, at least from the defendant's view. A more important statistic was the number of all-White or all-Black juries.

I personally came to the conclusion that a perfect "jury of your peers" would have at least one member that matched all your characteristics that could matter to the deliberations. A lesbian middle-aged Asian woman

PhD working as a chemist should have a lesbian, a middle-aged person, an Asian, a PhD, and a chemist on her jury. That way there would be one person who was her peer in one respect. Without such a representative, juries can credit misconceptions, and jurors feel free to exhibit negative stereotypes about groups. A single representative makes a big difference.

I failed to convince many other people of my view.

I could support a big company having a Human Committee with H&H diversification to ensure the company was not misunderstanding groups of employees, customers, or communities. I wouldn't want to turn the business over to them. Juries have to be unanimous, while boards of directors often have to act on majority votes, because shutting a company down for a "hung board" is foolish. Juries are supposed to be unbiased and to make decisions only on the evidence provided in court. Jurors are not supposed to be experts. Boards of directors are supposed to have expertise and to use all their knowledge.

My personal views aside, the H&H index is not what most people think DEI means, so even if the McKinsey research were sound, it wouldn't justify the proposals made in its name.

HARRISON WHITE

I was recommended to the jury project by the mathematical sociologist Harrison White, whose teaching influenced my approach to the issue—an approach that made no impact on legal minds. Harrison wrote a book, *Anatomy of Kinship*, that used network theory to analyze societies. The book enthralled me as a teenager because it showed fairly advanced mathematics could not just predict social outcomes, but actually explain them.

Like many science-fiction fans of my generation, I was intrigued by the concept of "psychohistory" in Isaac Asimov's classic *Foundation* series. It compared individuals to atoms of a gas whose individual actions were unpredictable, but whose macrolevel effects could be projected with precision. This allowed Streeling University mathematics professor Hari Seldon to track the fall of the Galactic Empire (modeled on the fall of the Roman Empire) and shape the millennia of chaos (modeled on the Dark Ages) to speed transition to a better society (modeled on the Enlightenment).

While *Anatomy of Kinship* was less epochal than psychohistory, it was real, and psychohistory was fiction. It demonstrated the mathematics underlying kinship, one of the deepest emotional and cultural forces. It was an early step toward a scientific understanding of culture.

White, along with Quine and Mosteller, whom I mentioned earlier, were important reasons I chose to go to Harvard. For my first semester I chose six classes, including the ones taught by these three. My appointed advisor refused to sign my card because four courses was the maximum load recommended for freshmen, and four of my six selections were graduate courses.

I went to the rulebook and discovered I did not need my advisor's signature, any faculty member could approve my card. So, I went to see Harrison, who was bemused, telling me no undergraduate had ever asked him to sign a card before. When I explained the situation, he said: "Of course you should take the courses you want to take," and signed.

Over the next four years, I took his seminar every semester. The three-hour weekly course consisted of participants presenting the work they were doing or contemplating, and the group offered comments, criticisms, and suggestions. This experience, both defending my own work and learning from many brilliant, creative minds, shapes my approach to DEI even today. Many participants in those seminars went on to impressive careers in science or other fields.

To describe the McKinsey approach in structural terms, every group—Blacks, Non-Hispanic Whites, Hispanics, Near Easterners, East Asians, South Asians, Native Americans, and Other—is a node, a circle if you draw things on paper. There are only eight circles, and every individual is in exactly one. All are the same size with no particular arrangement.

The corporate board is another node, which is ideally connected to each of the people nodes, and equidistant from all of them. Less diverse boards have no links to some nodes, or stronger links to some nodes than others.

Such a model would have been thoroughly shot down in Harrison's seminar. There are far more than eight groups, and each individual is a member of more than one. There are many useful ways to think of diversity, equity, and inclusion, but equidistant from all groups is not one of them. Most important, McKinsey offered no objective way to verify that this model either described important real-world dynamics or corresponded to what people meant by DEI.

PERFORMANCE MEASUREMENT

The McKinsey definition of corporate performance is also misleading. They use the fraction of corporate revenue left after operating and overhead expenses, which is used to pay the government and investors, and to reinvest in the business. The high-profit companies that in other contexts are denounced as "price gougers" and "employee abusers," since they take much more from customers than they pay in wages.

It's true that value investors, such as Warren Buffett, like profitable companies. But most investors prefer growth companies that keep prices down to get more customers, and that spend big on new products and continuous improvements—resulting in lower profit margins but higher revenue and faster profit growth. Profit margin is a strategic choice, not a metric of business success.

Some companies compete on good quality for a low price, while others charge more but maintain name brands customers are willing to pay more for. In the beverage sector, it's hard to charge more than competitors for generic water, so Primo Water has a 3.60% profit margin, while Coca-Cola enjoys 23.39%—not because it is run better than Primo, but because people will pay more for its name-brand formulations than similar generic products. Ford chugs along on 2.46% margins, Tesla buyers are willing to cough up 15.47%. Hyatt offers a clean, affordable room for 3.30% profit margin, Intercontinental Hotels promises luxury and earns 16.22%. Levi Strauss jeans command 4.04% profit, LVMH luxury clothing delivers 18.52%. TripAdvisor's generic services earn 0.56%, Meta gets 29.41%.

This suggests a plausible reason for the relation McKinsey claims to have found. Luxury companies protecting brand names may choose to burnish their corporate reputations with popular board appointments, while companies focused on minimizing costs to keep customer prices low are worrying about other things.

BACK TO p-VALUES

The final problem with the McKinsey study is statistical significance. McKinsey observed that 47 of 91 companies with the lowest gender-diversity scores had higher profitability than their national industry average, while 54 of the 91 companies with the highest gender-diversity scores did.

The first thing to note is that the lowest gender-diversity-score companies had slightly more than the expected 45.5 companies with above-median profit, so both diversity and lack of diversity seem to be good for profits. The second point is the result could easily be the result of random chance if diversity and profitability are unrelated. There were a total of 101 companies in the two groups that were above median. If we flipped a fair coin to assign them randomly to the bottom and top diversity groups, there's a 28% chance that one or the other group would get 47 or fewer of the high-profit firms. By convention, you need a chance below 5% (the p-value analyzed in Chapter 9) to claim a result is statistically significant.

Another problem is the McKinsey test has very low power. If the actual probability of above-median profit companies having high gender-diversity scores were $\frac{54}{101}$, there is only a 10% chance that the study would show a significant result at the 5% significance level. If you assume the hypothesis had a 50% prior probability of being true, then 100 similar studies would turn up 14 false results and only 5 true ones. So, based on the evidence, the hypothesis is more likely false than true.

McKinsey claims its results are statistically significant but does not disclose the methodology nor the significance level used. In subsequent reports it refers to the 2015 results as significant at the 10% level—double the usual threshold—but the results fail to meet that as well.

The result for what McKinsey calls "ethnic" diversity—which is based on ancestry rather than sex—is slightly better. Some 43 of 101 above-median profits were from the low-ethnic-diversity group, 58 from the high-ethnic-diversity group. This gives a p-value of 8%, so not statistically significant at the conventional level, but under the 10% claim made in the future publications. Now the power rises to 30%, so we expect 4 false results and 15 true ones. If we ignore all the other issues, this conclusion is more likely to be true than false. If we thought it had a 50% chance of being true before looking at the data, we might give it a 79% chance after seeing the results.

BEYOND IS WHERE WE BEGIN

The Boston Consulting Group (BCG) study was better in some ways, worse in others. It used a small (98 companies) and narrow (only Swiss, German, and Austrian companies) sample. On the other hand, it defined diversity not merely by sex or ethnic identification but across six dimensions: sex, country of parents, age, education, work for other companies, and work for other sectors, but it used the same flawed methodology in which "diverse" means having the same number of board members in each category. That's reasonable for sex, if you think sex is binary, but not for age, education, or country.

BCG defined corporate performance as the fraction of revenue generated from new or enhanced products across the last three years. Like profit margin, this is a strategic choice, not a measure of company performance. Some companies constantly introduce "new and improved" products; others focus on developing long-lasting designs. Some sectors have change forced by technology or fashion; other sectors have stable product lines.

Like most areas of academic research, especially for politicized questions in the social sciences, most published results are wrong. There are good papers relating diversity and performance, but none that I can find address the question in the sense it is generally understood in the popular media stories and legislative debates, and certainly none provide clear support that diversity improves corporate performance.

DO THE RIGHT THING

It would not be hard to do a good study—or more accurately, two good studies—on this question. One interpretation of "diversity is associated with improved corporate performance" is that investors should look for diverse companies and avoid non-diverse ones. With decades of high-quality data on many thousands of stocks, it's not hard to determine whether investors on average do better with stocks in diverse or otherwise-similar non-diverse companies.

This question does not require establishing causality. It doesn't matter whether diversity causes outperformance, or outperformance causes diversity, or both are caused by some third factor. Investing in diverse companies either wins, loses, or makes no difference. This is what investors care about.

Another advantage is you don't have to start out with some narrow definition of diversity. You can test lots of diversity metrics to see which ones work best.

The other relevant diversity/performance question is if companies are forced to diversify their boards, will their performance improve? This is the question relevant for California lawmakers, Nasdaq, the SEC, and other bodies pushing diversity as a social goal.

The easy way to study this is to look at the effect of laws or campaigns to increase corporate diversity. Here causality does matter, which is why the studies are natural experiments rather than pure observation.

These studies do require pre-selected definitions of diversity, whichever ones are pushed by the laws or campaigns. But they allow study of many aspects of corporate performance, not just return to shareholders. Presumably the campaigns are not primarily done for shareholder benefit—after all, if shareholders want diversity, they can vote for it directly.

We could study each campaign for the effect on things like discrimination lawsuits, surveys of employee satisfaction by diversity group, job growth, wage growth, price changes, environmental policies, customer service—any metrics we think are important.

Both diversity and corporate performance are complex concepts with multiple aspects. How aspects of one interact with aspects of the other, and also with exogenous factors, is certainly going to be complex. Teasing out the more important and stable interactions would be valuable, but no one seems interested in doing it. The results would no doubt be complex and unsatisfying to political partisans. Ideologues, legislators, regulators, and popular media are looking for clear, simple answers—and McKinsey and BCG are happy to supply them.

The rest of us, for now anyway, should be content to think about diversity and corporate performance separately, on their own terms, without insisting that we know one causes the other.

GOOD STORIES

Most of the Wrong Numbers in this book are embedded in badly written, jargon-filled, misleading articles. In the next chapter we'll look at a few Wrong Numbers that mar a well-written, popular, insightful book.

CHAPTER TWENTY-THREE

21ST-CENTURY MUCKRAKING

Matthew Desmond is a Princeton University professor and the recipient of a MacArthur Fellowship, a Pulitzer Prize, a PEN/John Kenneth Galbraith Award, and a National Book Critics Circle award. His recent book, *Poverty, by America*—a *New York Times* bestseller that was ecstatically well reviewed in many mainstream outlets—attempts to reframe the national policy debate around poverty.

THE FIRST INVESTIGATIVE JOURNALISTS

Two generations before Woodward and Bernstein helped expose Watergate and other Nixon administration scandals, reporters like Nellie Bly, Henry Demarest Lloyd, Ida B. Wells, Upton Sinclair, Ida Tarbell, and others exposed corruption and wrongdoing in meticulously researched riveting prose, frequently immersing themselves in their stories, often at considerable personal risk. Desmond is a worthy heir to their legacy. He is a master storyteller who gathers firsthand anecdotal material to illuminate social problems. But his novelist's eye for detail can cause readers to overlook the absence of big-picture analysis or useful solutions.

What causes poverty in America, according to Desmond? He answers with bland, awkwardly worded slogans, such as: "Poverty persists because some wish and will it to." He says we need "policies that refuse to partner with poverty, policies that threaten its very survival."

Desmond gets more specific about what doesn't cause poverty. He dismisses cultural explanations, such as single-parent households and declining marriage rates. He quickly dismisses the idea that the welfare state traps people in cycles of dependency, claiming that these arguments rely on anecdotal evidence, even though there's a vast systematic literature on the subject. Desmond doesn't take up political scientist Charles Murray's basic challenge to explain why it is that between 1949 and 1964 the American poverty rate dropped by 22 percentage points before the government did anything significant to help. After President Lyndon Johnson launched his war on poverty, the decline leveled considerably.

IT'S THE CAPITALISTS, STUPID

Desmond approaches his firsthand investigations with the preconception that poverty is a byproduct of capitalist exploitation. Prices aren't set in a competitive marketplace, in his view; they're just a projection of greed. It's "tempting," he writes, "to blame rising housing costs on anything other than the fact that more than a few of us have a god-awful amount of money and are driving prices higher and higher through bidding wars."

I could accept that people with too much money are driving up the prices of art, rare wines, political campaigns, and other things that are in limited supply and rich people like. But why would billionaires get into bidding wars to own low-cost housing? And if they did, the competition wouldn't kick out the current residents, it would just change the owners of the buildings. And if low-cost housing values did rise, more would be built, making things better not worse. Desmond's book is full of similar nonsense pronouncements.

A chapter on the real estate market titled "How We Force the Poor to Pay More" argues that it's twice as profitable to be a landlord in the inner city. His evidence for this claim is a 2019 paper he co-authored in the *American Journal of Sociology* that uses data so crude that it really tells us nothing. It omits important costs—like return on equity capital—and benefits—like real estate appreciation—that strongly bias the results in the direction Desmond wants. It ignores how landlords in poor areas are shamed, sued, occasionally jailed, forced to go to court to evict families, and must routinely travel to dangerous areas. Those headaches scare away most investors, which means that those who stick it out can charge more.

The way to reduce costs in poor areas is to do the opposite of what Desmond advocates and make it easier for landlords to do business, such as streamlining the process of evicting tenants who don't pay rent and celebrating people who provide safe, affordable housing to poor people.

WELFARE FOR THE RICH

Another chapter attacks government welfare for the rich and middle class, and though he makes some valid points, again Desmond is sloppy with numbers. In 2020, he writes "the federal government spent more than $193 billion on homeowner subsidies," mostly benefiting "White" people "with six figure incomes" as compared to "$53 billion" for "direct housing assistance for low-income families."

By limiting his tally of what low-income families get to "direct housing assistance," he leaves out the entire $260 billion budget of the Department of Housing and Urban Development. And by limiting it to "federal," he excludes roughly $70 billion in state and local housing subsidies. He also excludes tax breaks, tax credits, and other indirect federal low-income housing subsidies.

The largest share of the $193 billion figure that Desmond counts as "homeowner subsidies" is an income tax that doesn't exist—an estimate of what people who own their homes would pay if they were taxed on the imputed rental value of their real estate. The logic is that if you buy a house and rent it out, the rent you receive is taxable income, so if you live in the house yourself instead of renting it, you should pay tax on the rental value.

As a general matter of tax logic, Desmond has a point, although it's hard to know how far to take it. Should everyone pay income tax on the rental value of their cars, appliances, and clothing? And their college degrees? If we legalize selling organs for donation, would we tax everyone on the value of their kidneys?

In any event, taxing imputed rental value of owner-occupied housing would do nothing to reduce poverty. If the government started taxing homeowners on imputed rental value, homeowning a primary residence would be less attractive, and home prices would fall. This would reduce construction jobs and housing supply. Existing homeowners who switched to renting under the new tax regime would not stop occupying homes, so the reduced supply would mean more homeless poor.

GREED IS BAD

Desmond has a tendency to juxtapose the hardship of the poor and the resources of the rich. But he also concedes that there's "no evidence that the United States has become stingier over time" and, in fact, "federal relief [for the poor] has surged" even under Republican administrations. He seems to want homeowners to pay more taxes simply because he thinks homeowners are rich and White, so punishing them with higher taxes is a good in itself.

Desmond's initial celebrity came from his best-selling 2016 book, *Evicted: Poverty and Profit in the American City*, which was excerpted in *The New Yorker*. The book argues that eviction is a major cause and exacerbator of misery for poor people.

The evidence Desmond assembled actually shows that eviction is one thread in a skein of causes—and one of the less tractable ones to address.

Evicted concludes with an epilogue that pushes strident policy views completely at odds with the detailed stories about poor families forced out of their homes which fill the rest of the book. Desmond is an engaging storyteller who manages to convey the experience of his extensive personal interviews and observations—he just doesn't know how to interpret his own evidence.

"Eviction is a cause, not just a condition, of poverty," is one of Desmond's most often quoted insights. None of the stories in the book support this contention. All the families he profiles had deep problems prior to their first evictions. Some are drug users or criminals; others are victims of crime; most are unemployed or have insecure low-wage employment without benefits; many have washed out of social programs like public housing and job training.

There are two heartwarming success stories driven by quitting heroin in one case and getting a good job in another. Neither was triggered by finding secure housing.

TRADEOFFS

Desmond never grapples with the fact that housing is different from other forms of social welfare because it involves neighbors. Many of the tenants in his story are people no one is willing to live next to, so they get kicked out of shelters and public housing and turned down by landlords concerned with their effect on neighborhoods.

If Desmond were a serious housing policy analyst, he would understand the tradeoffs at play. High physical standards for occupancy eliminate much of the low-cost housing stock, but lack of standards can mean people live in unhealthful, unpleasant slums. Allowing bad tenants to stay in good places degrades neighborhoods. Concentrating low-income people in public housing projects can lead to conditions as bad as in any urban slum. Making it difficult for landlords to evict non-payers, squatters, and vandals reduces the available housing stock as landlords abandon properties or refuse to rent to poor people, and it doesn't free up units for better tenants.

Desmond's book actually tells an inspiring story of people working hard to solve these problems, usually with their own time and money. The solutions are never perfect, but lots of people are trying, with patience and skill, to keep everyone housed as best they can.

The book repeats the claim at several points that "the majority of poor renting families in America spend over half of their income on housing, and at least one in four dedicates over 70 percent," which is another misreading of the evidence. Those numbers come from the American Housing Survey, which yields very low-quality information about family income.

Desmond should have consulted the Bureau of Labor Statistics Consumer Expenditure Survey, which uses much higher-quality economic data about households and actually covers the population Desmond is writing about.

From those surveys, as of 2021, the most recent year available, we find that the poorest 10% of the population spends an average of $12,416 per year on housing—including not just rent or mortgage payments but utilities, insurance, taxes, late fees, and other charges. That is 180% of their average pre-tax income—$6,916—but only 41% of their average annual total expenditures—$30,433—mildly higher than the overall population average of 34%.

How do families spend more than four times their pre-tax income? It's not by taking on debt or dipping into savings. On average, these same families added $5,570 to net assets. Low-income households get more money back from the government than they pay in taxes, and they receive subsidies and in-kind assistance that are not measured in most income numbers, including the American Housing Survey numbers. They also earn cash income in the underground economy.

There are certainly people forced to devote the majority of their financial resources to housing, and that's a problem worth caring about. But they account for a fraction of a percent of the US population, much less than what Desmond claims.

EVICTION

Halting all evictions, which some policymakers have called for since the publication of *Evicted*, would have catastrophic consequences. It would chase away honest landlords and embolden abusive ones, who will simply change the locks, cut off utilities, refuse essential repairs, or threaten their tenants with violence. As discussed in Chapter 4, there are seven forced moves for every legal eviction. Legal evictions come with due process, legal protections, and involvement of social services; forced moves do not.

Desmond misinterprets his own evidence and favors moral grandstanding over serious policy analysis. His stories actually point to the conclusion that the biggest cause of poverty is crime. If poor neighborhoods were safe, if middle-class people didn't fear crime associated with housing projects, if poor people weren't routinely cheated and abused, poverty would be reduced to a simple problem of lack of money and could be eliminated for far less cost than current social spending.

Desmond's analysis never goes deeper than his facile assertion that "poverty persists because some wish and will it to." "Abolishing poverty," as he sees it, means looking inside ourselves and finding the will to act. His books have had such a wide reach, I fear that this simplistic nonsense will cause policymakers to forget the hard-won lessons of the 1960s in favor of policies that leave the American poor worse off than they already are.

I HAVEN'T FORGOTTEN YOU

By this point in the book, I've criticized a large number of researchers, gatekeepers, and journalists. I don't know the extent to which I have convinced you, and the extent to which you think I'm the one in the wrong. Fair enough, I'm writing *Wrong Number* in the hopes it will encourage and empower you to think for yourself, not for you to adopt my position on any of the issues in the research papers. In most cases, I have no strong opinions on those issues.

In the next chapter, I'm going to ask you to turn inward and see if you may be acting on the basis of Wrong Numbers yourself.

CHAPTER TWENTY-FOUR
PHILIP TETLOCK

P sychologist Philip Tetlock did a 20-year study in which 284 experts in many different fields were asked to make 28,000 predictions. The result, which has been corroborated many times by other researchers, is that the experts' answers were either near or worse than chance (and much worse than a simple computer algorithm), but that the experts expressed high confidence in their guesses. Moreover, their performance in their fields of expertise was no better than their performance in other fields, although their confidence was much higher. Perhaps worst of all, the more famous the forecaster, the worse the results.

MODERN FINANCIAL RISK MANAGEMENT

Around the time Tetlock was beginning his study, I was working with an ad hoc group of Wall Street traders on what would become modern financial risk management. Some of us met in the Odeon bar in Manhattan's Tribeca neighborhood after a class Nassim Taleb (who was not yet famous for writing *Fooled by Randomness*, *The Black Swan*, and other bestsellers) taught at New York University.

WHAT'S IN A NAME?

We chose the name "risk management" carefully. It's hard to talk about risk in English without expressing an opinion about it. The meanings of "bold" and "reckless" differ mainly in the speaker's viewpoint. "Risk" is often considered a synonym of "danger," when it can equally well refer to opportunity.

We viewed risk as an essential driver of finance and progress in general, the equivalent of energy to an engineer. Like energy, you need risk to do useful work, but it can shock you, burn you, or blow you up if handled badly. We wanted to manage risk—select the right type and amount—not to minimize danger or merely to measure uncertainty. This nearly always meant getting people to take more risk, not less, but big right risks rather than small wrong risks.

One of the most important tools, and the task that occupies much of the effort of professional risk managers, is rigorous tracking of risk decisions and outcomes. And one of the most consistent and obvious findings is nearly everyone—including the most successful traders, bettors, and other risk takers—bets more when they're wrong than when they're right.

I have some pop psychology/sociology explanations for this. Disclaimer: while I claim expertise in statistics, betting, and risk management, my pop explanations are no better than any random click-bait you see on the web, or deep wisdom offered up in after-midnight dormroom marijuana-enhanced bull sessions. I don't advance them as serious scientific hypotheses, just ways to help remember puzzling results. The loudest voices are what drive the biggest bets, and they are nearly always overconfident and often wrong. This is true both in an institution, in which lucky fools advance faster than shrewd calculators and appearing overconfident is rewarded, and within individuals, where strong mental components like fear and greed can shut down more reliable bases for decisions.

THE MEDIAN QUIET VOICE

A key risk management maxim is to seek out the median quiet voice. Ignore the loud chest beaters in an organization, or the strong mental forces of fear and greed. Carefully poll the quieter voices to find the median. If 10% of people are loudly insisting 90% confidence, start by ignoring them. If 40% of the rest are confident of one thing, but 60% have the opposite opinion but are less sure, go with the bigger group, not the more confident one. Don't try to average opinions.

Similarly, when making personal decisions, tune out your loud emotions and strong feelings to listen to your quieter sides—calculation, hunches, memories of wise people and advice you know, your better nature, etc.—and try to decide which decision has more supporters among them.

Of course, this is not meant to be a rigid rule, as many voices are correlated and some are more authoritative and reasoned than others. But it's a useful perspective to approach decisions under disagreement.

Anyway, I somehow heard about Phil's work and started discussing issues and collaborating with him. He hired my daughter as a researcher. One of his most impressive achievements was when the Intelligence Advanced Projects Research Activity (IAPRA) arranged a competition on questions submitted by real military, political, and intelligence policymakers. Phil's team was not only pitted against other academic forecasters, but against professional intelligence analysts who specialized in narrow areas and had access to classified information. Phil's amateur generalists predicting as a hobby, later dubbed "superforecasters," blew away the competition in accuracy, despite having no specialized expertise and only public information.

KELLY

As a brief aside, people I know who make successful quantitative decisions about risk in all aspects of their lives focus on median. Back in the 1950s, physicist John Kelly came up with a median rule that Ed Thorp called "Fortune's Formula." It's usually presented in dumbed-down form that misses the essential point.

The full discussion is too long and tangential to present here. I've written full accounts in other books and articles, as have other people. Kelly showed that if you maximize the median outcome—what you will get with average luck—in all risk decisions, you maximize your median lifetime outcome. Since you'll make millions of risk decisions in your life, like flipping millions of coins, you'll very likely end up close to your median outcome.

Now there are some qualifications and important technical details to this, so don't try it at home without some more research. My point here is the medians are actually useful for real decisions. Academic alternatives like maximizing the mean or mean utility are not. You can measure medians reliably with limited data; this is not true of means and no one has any clue about utility. For Kelly, all risk is the same regardless of what the outcome is measured in; with means and utility, you can only compare risks measured in the same units. For that reason, Kelly risk aggregates over your entire life in all domains, so you can count on the law of large numbers to steer you near your median; that benefit is lost if you use mean utility. Finally, maximizing the mean utility of each decision does not maximize mean lifetime utility or anything else meaningful. It almost always leads to strategies with microscopic probabilities of astronomical returns—returns too large to be realized in the physical universe.

WHAT YOU PROBABLY GET WRONG

One particular observation that was made early in the development of modern financial risk management is that risk takers bet more when they were wrong than when they were right. We first noticed this among successful Wall Street traders, and later verified it among a wide variety of risk takers.

This led to another risk management rule of thumb—you're better off making the same size bet all the time, rather than betting more when you think you have a larger edge. Of course, like the "median quiet voice," this is a useful first assumption rather than a strict rule. In fact, there are often good reasons to vary bet sizes, including when you can estimate your edge with some precision. Also, risk managers have found ways to coach risk takers to make good rather than perverse sizing decisions.

I suspect perverse bet sizing is related to the tendency to rely on loud voices and average opinions. The biggest bets come from the loudest voices shouting together and substantial minorities of people with strong opinions in the same direction—and this is the least reliable evidence for decisions. A quiet consensus of a small-but-definite edge is a much better indicator, but tends to support cautious betting.

I have another pop explanation, this one from evolutionary behavior. Suppose you are in the old west and there are rumors of gold strikes. A guy brings some nuggets into town and tells people he found them about 40 miles northwest of town. But you have some small indication that he's lying; perhaps you saw him two weeks ago 40 miles southeast of town, or you recognize the horse he rode in on as belonging to a livery stable to the southeast.

This is pretty weak evidence to go dashing off to the southeast while everyone else in town is heading northwest, but there's an undeniable frisson to the observation. It's similar to the feeling when watching a thriller when the person the heroine trusts makes some tiny slip, such as remarking he can't understand who would have shot the victim, when only the killer and the heroine know how the victim was killed.

Human behavior may have evolved in circumstances in which strong evidence was usually well known, with limited payoff for exploitation, but faint hunches were often private with large payoffs. But whether or not that mental tendency helped your ancestors survive and reproduce, it's a handicap in situations where payoffs are known.

BINARY BETTING

Anyway, I worked with Phil to design an experiment to demonstrate the bet sizing phenomenon. I published it as "Rationality and Risk Intelligence in Binary Betting," with co-authors Raph Di Guisto and Nick Maughan. The paper contains considerable technical detail, which I will omit here. You're welcome to look up the paper if you're curious.

Raph, Nick, and I got data on 1.6 million "binary bets" placed by 21,000 bettors from a major betting site that wishes to remain anonymous. The total stake was $600 million, an average bet size of $375. We had considerable demographic information on the bettors, enough to be confident these were meaningful stakes to most of them.

Bettors could select simple propositions about a large selection of major liquid financial variables such as stock market indices or foreign currency prices, with terms from five minutes to several days. For example, as I write this, it costs US$1.17 to buy one euro. A bettor might select a bet that the price would be above $1.17 in one day, this would have near even odds. Or she might take a longshot and bet that it would go above $1.18 in the next five minutes, or make a short odds bet on euro remaining above $1.15 for the next hour. She could bet any amount up to some fairly high limits—limits that depended on the customer, the underlying variable, and the odds.

There were two important features of this data set that made it useful for our study. First, unlike most retail betting sites, this provider did not cut off or limit winners. We had strong inside information on this point, and could also verify it from the data. Interestingly, the reason the company could afford this was that although a significant minority of bettors were able to win at rates that should have given them a profit, nearly all of them were net losers due to perverse bet sizing—betting more when they were wrong than when they were right. More on that later.

The other feature is, we could use financial markets to get accurate estimates of the standard deviation of each bet. For example, suppose someone paid $500 to win $1,000 if it cost more than US$1.17 to buy one euro in one day. We might use standard high-frequency trading financial models to estimate the probability of the customer winning. If it's 50%, the bet is fair, no edge to bookmaker or customer, and the standard deviation of the outcome is $500.00. If the probability is only 45%, the customer has a negative edge of $50, and the standard deviation is $497.49. If the probability is 55%, the customer has a positive edge of $50, and the standard deviation is $497.49.

While it's hard to be sure of the precise probability, and therefore the expected value of the bet, probability doesn't have much effect on the standard deviation. This allows us to confidently identify customers who made consistently good bets, more than could plausibly be explained by random chance.

THE RESULTS

Some 2,349 of the bettors made at least 100 bets. If they were betting with zero edge, we would expect 0.07 to have results more than four standard deviations above zero, in fact 11 did. We would expect 3.2 to have results more than three standard deviations above zero, in fact 23 did. And note that someone betting randomly would have a negative edge due to the built-in spread. So, these bettors not only overcame the vigorish but demonstrated ability to make consistent profits.

The table below shows the results for these 23 bettors. The t-value is how many standard deviations their bet success rate was above zero. Profit is their actual cash profits from the betting. Normalized profit is how much they would have made had they sized all bets at their average bet size.

Number of bets	t-value	Profit	Average bet size	Normalized profit	Profit / Normalized profit
4,108	7.7	95,895	210	104,225	0.9
2,664	7.6	9,170	220	86,244	0.1
1,751	5.8	229,252	681	164,718	1.4
1,196	5.2	132,057	706	127,397	1.0
7,685	5.1	93,894	216	95,881	1.0
152	4.8	2,761	427	25,002	0.1
1,879	4.4	55,138	589	112,415	0.5
1,400	4.4	14,708	89	14,518	1.0
489	4.2	4,556	62	5,838	0.8
204	4.0	239,278	2,278	130,489	1.8
267	4.0	15,969	225	14,536	1.1
354	3.8	−1,784	924	65,858	−0.0

Number of bets	t-value	Profit	Average bet size	Normalized profit	Profit / Normalized profit
113	3.8	3,583	144	5,742	0.6
781	3.7	10,594	903	94,600	0.1
235	3.6	19,401	375	20,907	0.9
275	3.6	10,809	113	6,644	1.6
195	3.5	8,328	160	7,849	1.1
303	3.4	9,032	158	9,240	1.0
1,124	3.3	8,658	76	8,454	1.0
329	3.3	19,938	851	50,615	0.4
983	3.2	34,060	309	31,424	1.1
127	3.2	4,860	143	5,170	0.9
11,997	3.0	−169,263	849	280,949	−0.6

Only three of the 23 bettors improved their profit significantly by varying bet sizes. Another six made small improvements. But 14 of the 23 lost money from varying bet sizes, including three who lost almost all their profits, and two who converted profit to loss. The most spectacular example is the last row in the table—a bettor who would have been the biggest winner with $280,949 profits with constant bet sizing, who managed to lose $169,263. Only nine bettors among the entire 21,000 lost more money and all nine of them had significant negative prediction ability—they lost money due to making bad bets, not due to sizing them perversely.

Collectively, our 23 most accurate predictors lost 42% of their potential profits by varying bet sizes.

A more surprising finding is when we look at all bettors, the vast majority of whom demonstrate no skill in picking winning bets. A skilled bettor acts perversely by betting more when she has less chance of winning, but how do we explain a random bettor betting more when he loses?

He must have some information about his chances of winning, but he uses it to bet more when he's wrong, rather than to either select the winning side or bet more when he's right.

The next table puts all bets into buckets based on their fraction of the same bettor's average bet size (the buckets are logarithmic). For example, 51,001 bets were less than 10% of the average bet size for that bettor, and lost 2.67% as a group. At the other extreme, 4,620 bets were more than 10 times the size of the average bet for that bettor, and those lost 7.53%. The table shows that smaller than average bets lose between 1.79% and 2.67%, while larger than average bets lose 4.98–8.95%. Average size bets are in between with a 3.20% average loss.

Midpoint of size bucket	Number of bets	Average bet size	Average profit (loss)	Standardized profit (loss)
<10%	51,001	$67	−$1.64	−2.67%
14%	53,961	$111	−$2.61	−2.41%
22%	108,684	$135	−$2.00	−1.81%
37%	194,702	$172	−$2.49	−2.02%
61%	295,240	$222	−$3.69	−1.79%
100%	280,591	$344	−$6.32	−3.20%
165%	138,709	$702	−$25.20	−4.98%
272%	61,012	$1,350	−$76.09	−6.78%
448%	23,222	$2,426	−$165.70	−7.79%
739%	8,383	$4,288	−$312.96	−8.95%
>1,000%	4,620	$17,134	−$862.00	−7.53%

There's a lot more in the paper. We did some deeper statistical analysis and also looked at how bettors learn (they do get better on average with number of past bets, but only because losing bettors drop out while winners continue).

MOVIES AND MARRIAGE

In any event, my message to you is to track some of your own risk decisions to see whether you're betting more when you're wrong than when you're right. I'll bet you are.

What's your track record on low-stakes risk decisions, like which movie to stream or whether to call in sick at work to attend Opening Day of the baseball season? How about on high-stakes decisions like getting married (or not, or divorced), cheating on your taxes, choosing a career, or driving home from a bar with a 0.20 blood alcohol level?

I admit this is unfair. We get a lot of experience with the routine, everyday risk decisions, so we can learn to make them well. Some of the biggest ones are made only rarely. Moreover, we don't always get to choose the stakes.

Where successful risk takers I know differ from most people is seeking out lots of risks for which they can get experience, and do have talent and inclination. Advantage gambling in a casino, poker, sports betting, financial trading, and investing can build up profits to cover losses from bigger risks. More important, they build up skills that dramatically improve your ability to use quantitative analysis to make higher-stakes decisions in life.

There are many ways to get the same skills without involving money—taking risks in sports, combat, politics, law, science, love, and other arenas. If you have talent or inclination for these things, or if you value the accomplishments they can bring more than you value money, they can be better choices. But it's harder to track your results, and some of them don't build up assets to see you through downswings. Some of them have worse downsides—even played at low stakes—than merely losing money. So, I always advise students to pick some money ones in addition.

PROHIBITION AND CRIME

Even the most ruthless governments in world history, with the most efficient secret police and least regard for individual rights, have seldom succeeded in prohibiting anything. What they can do is move a legal, regulated business into the illegal, unregulated domain. The next chapter takes a look at a Wrong Number used to support that dubious approach.

CHAPTER TWENTY-FIVE

SEX AND TRAFFIC COPS

Most crimes, like assault and fraud, have a complaining victim—or a body in the case of murder—to initiate a police investigation. In protecting individuals from these crimes, and catching perpetrators, law enforcement officers are serving the public. But crimes without complaining victims, like buying and selling forbidden recreational drugs and/or most forms of gambling, are "victimless" in the sense that no participant is filing complaints.

SECRET POLICE

Of course, victimless crimes in this sense can still do harm, and proponents of enforcing them often claim things like "society is the victim," or perhaps "public morality is harmed." But this misunderstands the term "victimless." Without a complaining victim, law enforcement must resort to unpleasant secret police tactics like paid or coerced informers, sting operations, no-knock warrants with stun grenades, mass surveillance, and entrapment.

Another problem is these efforts lead to law enforcement corruption and make large numbers of good citizens into criminals. It's pretty hard to frame someone for bank robbery, but easy to claim they were carrying heroin or offered sex for money. Prohibitions enrich criminals and often lead to extraordinary violence. Moreover, they generally have small success in reducing the prohibited activity, at least when weighed against the ruined lives and cost in money and civil rights. And since you can't regulate something after you make it illegal, citizens are exposed to fraudulent, dangerous, and defective products; minors find it easier to get illegal products than legal regulated ones; and people are beaten, robbed, or worse in connection with the activity and have no recourse to the police.

PROHIBITION AND TRAFFICKING

One of the most influential social science papers of the 21st century argued that when countries legalize prostitution between consenting adults, it causes more people to be coerced into sex work.

The study, published in 2013 in the journal *World Development*, has been used to stop legalization initiatives around the world and to justify harsh new laws that turn customers of voluntary sex work into criminals, often in the name of stopping human trafficking.

Unfortunately, the authors of the study used a flawed economic model and abysmal data to reach their conclusion. When crucial information was missing, they guessed and filled it in (see "imputation" in Chapter 6). Then, when the analysis didn't yield what seemed to be the authors' desired finding, they threw out contrary data. There is no evidence that legalizing prostitution increases human trafficking.

Despite its obvious flaws, the paper has been widely influential, cited not only in the press but by advocates and lawmakers writing policy.

The Canadian government referenced the paper when crafting a 2014 law criminalizing the purchase of sexual services, and it influenced a similar law passed in France. An open letter signed by 800 feminist activists pointed to the study as evidence that legalization had failed to reduce "the harms that surround prostitution."

The *Nevada Independent* cited the paper as one of "[n]umerous studies … show[ing] that prostitution and sex trafficking are inextricably linked." It has also been referenced in policy debates all over the United States, as various localities have debated decriminalizing sex work.

THE STUDY

So, how do you demonstrate that allowing consenting adults to exchange money for sex causes more people to be driven into sexual slavery?

The authors classified countries based on 4,950 accounts of human trafficking from 1996 to 2003, tabulated in a data set put together by the United Nations Office on Drugs and Crime (UNODC).

The UNODC report was compiled from official government reports, news and opinion articles, and materials produced by activist groups. These sources aren't consistently trustworthy, and yet the study authors weighted them equally and didn't bother taking into account the number of reported victims in each incident. Almost half the accounts were missing crucial data, and the United Nations only included English-language sources.

Another problem with the data is that it included human trafficking unrelated to sex, like people forced to clean houses and prepare food. The data set is also limited by only counting people trafficked across international borders, ignoring domestic exploitation.

The authors conceded that, given all of these problems, their data "needs to be interpreted cautiously." But they plowed ahead anyway, asserting that their index was still "meaningful."

After tabulating the human trafficking incidents by destination country, the authors looked at whether or not sex work was legal in each place. A problem is that most countries allow some types of sex work but not others, and the laws often vary in different parts of the same country. Some places changed laws significantly during the study period. Enforcement also varies widely, from non-existent to very strict. The binary classification into legal or illegal that the authors used misses more information than it reveals.

And yet, the data set they compiled showed no statistically significant link between legalized sex work and trafficking—until the authors eliminated 34 countries from their analysis.

What was their rationale for deleting data? The authors claimed that some of the countries were so poor that their citizens wouldn't have enough money to pay for sex work. That is unlikely to be true, and in any case, wasn't a good reason to exclude data, since the study already controlled for per-capita income.

If the authors really believed this, they shouldn't have omitted the fact that they suppressed 23% of their data. The abstract should have read: "Legalization increases trafficking in rich countries" and claimed that only 116 countries were included in the analysis, not 150.

After boiling the list down to 116 countries, they re-ran the analysis, but there was another problem. The authors had made so many adjustments and imputed so much data that the results were statistically unreliable. But they ran with them anyway.

END DEMOCRACY NOW!

It turned out that the study's strongest finding was that human trafficking destinations happen to be countries with democratic governments, not where sex work is legal. Why didn't they make that the banner claim of their study? Can you imagine any journalists or policymakers citing such a finding to argue that we need more dictatorships?

So, the authors ran with the sixth strongest effect they found, suggesting, falsely, that legalizing prostitution caused more human trafficking. That's the finding that would sell.

But logically, we expect legalizing sex work to reduce human trafficking. Criminalization discourages voluntary but not coerced sex work, causing trafficking to increase to fill the vacuum left by departing voluntary workers.

When sex work is a crime, formerly legal providers face the trauma and stigma of jail, along with the cost of fines and bribes. They also lose the ability to complain to authorities about rape, robbery, and other abuse in connection with their work.

The situation is entirely different for traffickers. They were violating the law all along, so they face no additional costs, and the trauma is borne by their enslaved workers. Therefore, we expect criminalization to mean more coerced and less voluntary sex work.

There's no good reason for the government to interfere with competent adults choosing to exchange money for sexual services. But even people who think the government exists to force their moral choices on unwilling others should not support the criminalization of sex work.

If the goal is to reduce trafficking, put more resources into enforcing anti-coercion laws. If the goal is to discourage paid sex work, decriminalization, which means removing criminal penalties but allowing fines, sin taxes, and other penalties, accomplishes the goal with far less undeserved suffering and official corruption. It also allows sex workers to access police protection against rape, robbery, and assault in connection with their work.

Sex work criminalization leads to trafficking for the same reason alcohol prohibition in the United States created bootleggers. Bootleggers had the same policy goal as temperance activists, who opposed drinking on moral grounds. That's the origin of the term in economics: "bootleggers and Baptists." Criminalization brings together people who dislike an activity and criminal providers who want to discourage competition.

It's unfortunate that such a poorly executed study with a conclusion that defies economic common sense received so much attention from advocates and policymakers. Its perverse finding has likely only led to an increase in human trafficking, while making willing, adult sex workers and their customers considerably worse off.

FACT VERSUS FICTION

Most of *Wrong Number* is devoted to fictional numbers presented as fact. Let's reverse that for a chapter and try to deduce fact about a fictional number.

CHAPTER TWENTY-SIX

WHAT IS THE INTEREST RATE IN HELL?

I read a lot, and I have a lot of opinions, and I enjoy expressing them. So naturally I have been a professional book reviewer since the 1970s, mostly for *Publishers Weekly*.

BEST AMERICAN NOVEL

These short reviews, presented without byline, used to be extremely influential. They were usually the first reviews available and because the author's name was not disclosed, tended to be more about the book and less about the reviewer. They were reasonably neutral and came from a known, trusted source. Before the Internet gave instant access to all reviews, professional and amateur, and books were mostly bought on-line rather than by recommendation of a bookseller, *Publishers Weekly* reviews mattered—or at least publishers and authors thought they did.

As a result, I was an early member of the National Book Critics Circle (NBCC), the organization of professional book reviewers. As a result of that, in 2006, PBS asked me to vote on some questions for their documentary *The American Novel*. It was not precisely a vote—a group of us met in New York to send our consensus answers to the NBCC, which would pass them along to PBS.

I got in trouble early with our selection of the best line from an American novel. Our final selection was "Lolita, light of my life, fire of my loins. My sin, my soul." I said the author, Vladimir Nabokov, was a Russian and *Lolita* was a Russian novel, even if Nabokov had taken American citizenship and set his story in the United States. The line was not well known among Americans, and fit into no larger American tradition. It was pure literary embellishment.

I suggested "When you call me that—smile," from Owen Wister's *The Virginian*. That's a line every American knows, and everyone, American or not, understands and recognizes as American. There's no embellishment, it's a hard-working, plain-spoken line essential to the plot. It's part of a great, and purely American, tradition of western novels.

An English professor at the table asked, "Isn't that a poker saying?" The line is spoken during a poker game in the novel, but I suspect he had never heard of the book and remembered variants of the line from western movies, such as "Smile when you call me that, mister." To me, one of the indications of a great line is it is copied and evolves.

Only two of my suggestions got respect. I nominated Patricia Highsmith's Tom Ripley as the best series character in American novels—although I had to remind half the group that Patricia Highsmith was an American. The other suggestion that got traction was Jim Thompson for best noir novelist.

"WILLA CATHER STEEPED IN ROTGUT—AND ARMED WITH A .45"

Jim Thompson is conventionally described as the best pure writer among mid-20th-century pulp fiction authors. This is misleading. As biographer Robert Polito points out, Thompson is the only writer of any significance to ply his trade in the true crime pulps rather than detective fiction or other genres. True crime appealed to both sexes in poor and rural markets, not upwardly mobile urban males. It was illustrated by grainy black-and-white crime-scene photographs, often faked, rather than colorful cover drawings of semi-clad women lit by muzzle flash. Because the stories were true, partly and sometimes anyway, daring writers could go well beyond the limits imposed by fiction publishers.

Thompson is beloved of American literature professors because he is an important avantgarde writer whose books sold to a wide popular readership. Readers bought the direct-to-paperback novels from drugstore racks by inspection or word of mouth, not reviews. Unlike noir authors such as Dashiell Hammett, Raymond Chandler, Cornell Woolrich, and James M. Cain, Thompson did not accept and expand the conventions of the genre. He subverted them. You think you're reading a crime novel, but the story falls to pieces.

The Criminal, for example, begins with the rape/murder of a 15-year-old, then forgets about the crime as the story is told through overlapping and conflicting serial accounts by a dozen characters in a dozen different personal hells, with the action directed by a faceless God who speaks only on the telephone. It ends with the death of a beloved wife and mother from breast cancer; the only thing in the whole miserable thread that God is sorry about.

Thompson experimented with other techniques usually confined to unreadable critical darlings: random word generators, characters reappearing with their names spelled backward to reverse actions, impossible chronologies, split characters, wild surrealism, and plot developments observed through psychotics, drunks, and dead people.

Nevertheless, his true crime accounts, short stories, novels, and screenplays (including for Stanley Kubrick's masterpieces *The Killing* and *Paths of Glory*) were widely popular and influential. Many of his novels were made into movies, although usually with substantial changes.

ROTGUT, A .45 AND ... CALCULUS?

Pulp fiction may not seem a natural place to find sophisticated quantitative and financial reasoning, but Jim Thompson's work contains many gems of both. His novels include detailed and accurate discussions of mathematics, accounting, and finance that are stylistically and thematically set off from the gritty stories.

The Grifters is the story of Roy Dillon, a short-con operator who maintains a front as a salesman. Severely abused as a child by a mother who was 14 when he was born, and was severely abused herself, Roy has learned to make everyone like him by repressing himself to the point he cannot enjoy anything.

His profitable existence is threatened by Percival Kaggs, Roy's opposite: completely unlikable, tormented by ulcers, yet sourly happy. Kaggs wants to make Roy the sales manager, preventing him from hanging around bars and pool halls all day without suspicion, working short cons.

Roy doesn't want to attract attention by turning down a promotion, so he sets out to use his people skills in reverse, to make Kaggs dislike him and withdraw the promotion. But despite all his efforts, Roy, the guy who doesn't like anybody, ends up friends with Kaggs, the guy nobody likes.

The turning point is when Roy starts leafing through the salesmen's files. For six hours and four pages (but omitted entirely from the movie version), the story shifts from intense introspective accounts of deeply searing personal encounters to dialog like the following.

R: "But where are the sales slips?"
K: "Accounting gets a copy, inventory gets a copy, and of course the customer gets one at time of purchase."
R: "Why does inventory need a copy? The stuff is checked off at the time it leaves the shop isn't it? Or at least it could be. You've got some duplicate effort if it isn't. Where you need a copy is here in the salesman's file."
K: "But—"

For the first time in his life, Roy has made a friend and is happy. What did it? Working on the functional specification for a sales tracking system.

Roy resolves to pursue this path to a happy, honest existence, but two extremely predatory females will have something to say about it first.

Lots of fictional criminals dream of going straight, but you rarely find one interested in designing accounting systems. More to the point, few pulp authors devote four pages of detailed, accurate dialog about the system.

Thompson's *Now and On Earth* is the semi-autobiographical story of a masochistic alcoholic with writer's block and a highly dysfunctional, psychotically intense family. Jimmie takes a job in the inventory department of an aircraft manufacturer.

Among accounts of the unrelenting torture of his life, he spends long passages explaining how he is reorganizing his work. In one passage he discards the inventory sheets for a card-based system:

> I'm simply taking the parts off the release books and putting them on the cards, the cards to be filed in chronological order. This does away with any chance of duplications. It makes it possible to locate a part and the data on it in a second instead of fifteen minutes. And there is only one posting to make, instead of from one to thirty as used to be the case.
>
> There are two columns per card: one for stockroom inventory, one for the assemblies. Debits and credits are reflected within the balances, not set out by themselves, so the number of parts needed to complete 750 ships can be obtained instantly by adding the two balances—less any "X" items—and subtracting the total from that amount. "X" items are spare or extra parts.
>
> The thing has one serious flaw, or will when I have it finished. We issue parts and make shortage reports by positions. My cards are filed in chronological order. This will mean that to locate all the cards in one position I will have to search through the file of several thousand cards. I'll have to get around that some way. I've been playing with several ideas.

This system saves him from poverty and persecution, and seems to offer the solution to his problems, but he cannot give up his painful attempts to write.

THE GETAWAY

The Getaway begins with a clockwork bank robbery. The skillful precision of the crime contrasts with the chaotic misadventures of Doc and Carol as they flee with the loot, dogged by mutual suspicion, multiple double-crosses, and bad luck.

This conventional plot takes an unexpected mythic turn in San Diego. The pair are killed by proxy and entombed, after which they rot and pay a ferryman to take them across the water, in the course of which they are tested. The destination is a place that "appears on no maps," from which "no one with a good reputation for truth and veracity has ever returned."

This criminal sanctuary is run by El Rey, a courteous man with "ageless old eyes," who may be God or the Devil. Almost everything is perfect. "Disease is almost unknown." "Accommodations are strictly first-class" and reasonably priced. "A four-bathroom villa, which might cost several thousand a month in some French Riviera resort, will rent for no more than a few hundred." "The largest per capita police force in the world" is polite and unobtrusive, but ensures (with two exceptions) a zero crime rate.

There is only one problem, which changes this symbolic place from Heaven to Hell:

> *Which brings us to the subject of El Rey's bank. The bank makes no loans, of course. Who would it make them to? So the only available revenue is interest, paid by the depositor rather than to him.*
>
> *On balances of $100,000 or more, the rate is 6 per cent; but on lesser sums it rises sharply, reaching a murderous 25 per cent on amounts of $50,000—When one's monthly withdrawals fall under an arbitrary total—the approximate amount it should cost him to live at the prevailing first class scale—he becomes subject to certain "inactive account" charges …*
>
> *No one is compelled to deposit his money in El Rey's bank. But the police will assume no responsibility if it is stolen—as it is very likely to be. There is good reason to believe that the police themselves do the stealing from non-depositors.*

THE MATH

Doc and Carol steal $340,000 but with losses and expenses along the way, arrive in Mexico with about $300,000, about $3.4 million in 2025 dollars. Figuring $12,000 a year expenses, about $136,000 in 2025 dollars, that would last 25 years without the bank charges. But with prices much lower—$2,500/month in 2025 dollars to rent a four-bathroom villa on the beach—and quality of goods and services higher than in other places, and no income, sales, or property taxes, excellent public services, and no inflation, El Rey seems to be offering a pretty good deal.

If you're not interested in the math, you can skip the rest of this section. If $W(t)$ is your wealth at time t, r is the interest rate (negative 6%), and C is your annual expenditure ($12,000), then $W(t) = \left[\left(W(0) - \frac{C}{r}\right)e^{rt} + \frac{C}{r}\right]$ and your money runs out at $t = \frac{-1}{r}\ln\left(1 - \frac{W(0)r}{C}\right)$. With $W(0) = \$300,000$, $C = \$12,000$, and $r = -0.06$, this comes to 15.3 years. The money would last the same amount of time if El Rey charged nothing on bank accounts and some combination of income, value-added, and sales taxes that added to 39%. So far, so good.

But in 8.5 years, Doc and Carol's bank balance will fall to $100,000 and the interest rate will become increasingly negative. Thompson does not give the exact schedule of rate changes, but at a negative 25% interest rate, $100,000 would last only 4.5 more years. The money would last a total of 13 years from arrival. Still, most governments take more and deliver less. Unfortunately for Doc, Carol, and the other residents of El Rey's realm, the problem begins long before the money runs out.

WHAT THEN?

What happens when the money runs out is the climatic horror of the novel. The two movie versions cut all the mythic and financial stuff and ended with conventional shootouts and Doc and Carol living happily ever after. The movie *From Dusk to Dawn* is a loose adaptation that does preserve the genre shift, although not the math.

Doc and Carol's real problem is that the bank has no one to loan money to; there is no productive economic activity going on in El Rey's domain. With only a 4% real rate of interest their money would last forever—and 4% is the conventional figure for the fraction of assets a retiree can spend for her portfolio to retain constant purchasing power in the long run.

At any interest rate less than 4%, the survival time depends on the logarithm of initial wealth. To double survival time, you have to show up in El Rey's kingdom with 3.5 times as much money—$1.05 million for Doc and Carol. Thompson is illustrating the economic futility of taking things if you must then flee to an economically unproductive place, however perfect in all other respects.

Although these mathematical considerations are not explained, they are woven into a brilliantly symmetrical story in which money is removed from one bank and put back into another by characters who descend from Earth to Hell by getting exactly what they want. The economic rationale for El Rey's system is flawless and the impact on his immigrants is remorselessly logical.

IS THERE REALLY CALCULUS IN A CRIME THRILLER?

With many authors you would dismiss the above as over-analysis. But Thompson never wastes words on external description; his stories are told almost completely through the distorted impressions of his characters. You rarely learn what the weather is, what people look like, what they wear, or other factual details. Passages like the one about the bank stand out sharply (his publisher urged him to get rid of "the financial stuff").

A classic Thompson character acts like a dim-witted rustic, whose conversation seems excruciatingly banal, but upon close reading is erudite and literally true. On the rare occasions that Thompson assumes the narrator's voice, he does exactly the same thing. His novels are filled with clichéd dialog and situations that are slightly off-kilter. Think about them for a minute (often with the aid of a reference book) and the meaning inverts.

With few exceptions, such as the forgettable *Recoil*, Thompson's characters end badly. They get what they want, but they cannot keep it. They fail through bad math, bad accounting, or bad investments. They have plenty of love and toughness and skill, but none of this helps unless they can balance their books (and they never can).

POLITICS AND LIFE

Not only is the viewpoint out of place among tough criminals and psychotics, it seems to conflict with Thompson's politics: an active member of the Communist Party in the 1930s, his books generally depict the rich or powerful as heartless and corrupt, and show graphically the hardship of racism, intolerance, repression, and social injustice.

One clue may be found in his family history: his father lost the only two comfortable situations he ever had through faulty bookkeeping (possibly embezzlement) and the declining commodity prices and poor investment opportunities that characterized the 1920s and 1930s.

But why seize on economics? Both Thompson and his father lost far more through alcoholism, drug abuse, and personal irresponsibility than money problems. Each was suffocated in the presence of his family and lost without it: that dilemma transcends economics. Medical, sexual, moral, and emotional difficulties loom larger in their personal lives than poverty.

An important clue is given in a dreamlike monologue that gives the title to *Now and On Earth*. It is addressed to Jesus Christ and Karl Marx, and attacks both their promises of Heaven for being too remote. Thompson clearly believed in literal Hell on Earth, like his midwestern Baptist grandmother who was a strong negative influence on him, and also like doctrinaire communists. But he knew there was no literal Heaven, now and on Earth.

Could there be a literal Heaven on Earth someday? No Thompson character ever achieves it, but the possibility seems to be there. You must be very tough and skillful, but also honest and kind. You need strong, true, deep love, familial and sexual. But most of all you need to clean up your desk. Everything you need is there, but you have to be able to find it. Hell is the frustration of looking and looking.

HOW DO CIGARETTES HARM YOU, LET ME COUNT THE WAYS

The smoke destroys alveoli, paralyzes cilia, and damages DNA of lung cells. Nicotine and other chemicals thicken and narrow blood vessels, encouraging plague buildup and atherosclerosis, and blocking blood to the heart and oxygen to the brain. Cigarettes lead to cancer, redirect the immune system to fight the body instead of disease, delay healing, and promote many specific conditions. Freebasing nicotine would seem to avoid at least some of these harms. So why is it so unpopular among public health authorities?

CHAPTER TWENTY-SEVEN

THE 5% SOLUTION

In February 2022, the *World Journal of Oncology* (WJO) published an article by a team of 13 researchers claiming that vapers are about as likely to get cancer as people who smoke traditional cigarettes. WJO is not a top medical journal like *The Lancet*, but it's among the top 10%.

JUMPING THE GUN

Citing this article, Stanton Glantz, a tobacco control activist and retired professor of medicine at the University of California, San Francisco, claimed that not only are there "some carcinogens in e-cigarette aerosol" but "now there is also direct evidence that people who use e-cigarettes are at increased risk of some cancers."

And then the WJO's editors retracted the study because "concerns have been raised regarding the article's methodology, source data processing including statistical analysis, and reliability of conclusions."

The study is indeed riddled with errors. For example, the paper claimed "Cancer respondents had a lower prevalence of e-cigarette use than traditional smoking (2.3% vs. 16.8%)." Actually, what the study showed was that 2.3% of e-cigarette users had cancer, compared to 16.8% of traditional smokers. Neither statistic on its own is meaningful, but this is the kind of sloppiness that got the paper retracted. Despite the retraction, it continues to be cited and show up in AI answers, and Stanton Glantz has not updated his web page touting it.

I won't spend much time on this study since it was retracted, and also because it made most of the same errors at the marijuana-causes-heart-problems study. It relied on telephone surveys asking people "Have you ever been told that you had cancer or malignancy?" which we know generates unreliable data. It asked about current smoking, but lifetime vaping. It studied people who survived cancer, not people who got cancer. It used logistic regression inappropriately to torture the data. It ignored the strongest finding—using cocaine, heroin, or methamphetamine cut your cancer risk by 54% (being an alcoholic wasn't as good, but it did cut cancer risk by 6%)—and puzzling findings like earning between $65,000 and $99,000 cut your cancer risk by 66% compared to earning between $25,000 and $64,999 or $100,000 or over; or that being White raised your cancer risk by 433% compared to selecting "Other" for race. It reported a sample size of 154,856, but only 180 observations were vapers with cancer, which is far too few for the analysis.

It did make one new error. Nearly all the vapers in the study were former cigarette smokers, about half of whom had switched from smoking to vaping after being diagnosed with cancer. Only 7 of the 180 were diagnosed with cancer after they started vaping, and 5 of those had also smoked cigarettes before diagnosis. For a good comparison, you need matched samples of people who vaped but never smoked, and people who smoked by never vaped, and in both cases, who got cancer after vaping or smoking.

SURGEON GENERAL'S WARNING

Proving that traditional cigarettes cause cancer, which they do, required two types of data: observational studies and experimental studies. First, people noticed that cancer patients were more likely to be smokers than non-cancer patients, and then careful experimentation teased out some of the mechanisms by which smoking led to cancer.

Observational studies, even without data issues, can show only an association, not causation. Although most vaping studies claim only an association, journalists, activists, and public officials are quick to assert causation. Experimental studies can show causation but can't measure the practical extent of an issue or possible offsetting factors.

One experimental study of vaping that drew press attention was published in the *Journal of Nuclear Medicine* under the title "Molecular Imaging of Pulmonary Inflammation in Electronic and Combustible Cigarette Users: A Pilot Study."

One problem with this particular paper is that it studied only 15 people: five vapers, five users of traditional cigarettes, and five people who don't smoke at all. However carefully you select groups of five subjects, they can't represent a broad enough cross-section of users to draw any solid conclusions. That would require hundreds of participants. This experiment also relied on screening volunteers and made no attempt at randomness or sampling the range of the population, meaning that each of the three groups of five subjects differed from each other in important ways.

The paper didn't show that vaping causes lung damage—in fact, the researchers didn't check for that. Instead, it looked at "biomarkers," or chemicals thought to be associated with lung damage. By that measure, they found no difference between the five vapers and the control group of five people who had never vaped or smoked.

The study did find that uptake of a chemical thought to react to a biomarker for lung damage was higher in the five vapers than in the control group. But the five cigarette smokers included in the study had a lower uptake of that chemical than the controls, which makes the conclusion suspect since we know traditional cigarettes cause lung damage. Most likely, this correlation can be attributed to random chance. And this was a pilot study, meaning it was aimed not at generating firm conclusions but at testing procedures and determining which hypotheses could be tested in a subsequent study.

The authors mentioned more than 30 statistical tests at the 5% level of significance, and they may have conducted more. A 5% significance level means there is a 5% chance of getting a positive result by random chance even if there is no association at all in your data. With 30 tests, you should expect 1.5 positive results even if vaping is unrelated to lung health. The authors got two positive results out of 30, which is hardly strong evidence of anything. And the two results are among the least direct in terms of linking vaping to lung damage. The more direct tests of biomarkers failed to find any differences among the groups.

MOTHER'S MILK: THE GATEWAY DRUG TO EVERYTHING

A classic prohibitionist argument is that while a controversial activity may not be harmful in itself, it leads to bad things. In the case of vaping, several studies suggest that young vapers are something like seven times as likely to smoke traditional cigarettes in the future than similar young people who don't vape.

An oft-cited paper in this area, "E-Cigarettes and Future Cigarette Use," is typical of the genre. Out of 298 Southern California 17-year-old high school students who didn't vape, only 11% were smoking cigarettes a year later. Among those who were vaping at 17, 40% had taken up old-fashioned cigarettes at 18.

The paper did a lot of additional analysis, but this is the basic statistic driving the conclusion. To the authors' credit, they were careful to label this as an "association" between vaping and future smoking, rather than claiming that vaping caused future smoking. Yet when this paper was cited by regulatory authorities, they interpreted it as causal evidence and therefore as a justification to restrict vaping.

There are reasons to be skeptical about this kind of research. Not everyone is honest when they fill out a survey, especially young people asked about activities that are frowned upon. And only 14% of the students interviewed at age 17 participated in the follow-up survey a year later. The missing students might be systematically different from the ones recorded in the study.

It's also plausible that teenagers who vape differ from teenagers who don't in ways that independently affect their likelihood of smoking. Perhaps the type of kid who vapes at 17 is more likely to smoke at 18. In that case, restricting vaping among 17-year-olds probably won't reduce smoking at age 18. In fact, some 17-year-old vapers will switch to traditional cigarettes or turn to underground purveyors of e-cigarettes, which would pose a much more serious health risk. There is plenty of evidence that many smokers use vaping to reduce or quit smoking. In fact, adolescent smoking has continued to fall as adolescent vaping has increased.

PSYCHOLOGY OF VAPING

Another anti-vaping argument is that it has negative mental or social health consequences. Studies like "Electronic Cigarette Use and Mental Health: A Canadian Population-Based Study" suffer from the same issues as studies linking vaping to future smoking. It's easy to show that vapers have more psychological and social issues than non-vapers, but that's only an association. An obvious alternative explanation is that troubled kids are more likely to vape—either as a form of self-medication, or because they have less regard for adult opinion and rules, or perhaps because they are less supervised or have less to lose by acting in a deviant way.

Even if we did have good observational studies suggesting that vaping is reliably associated with future smoking, or that vaping is associated with mental and social problems, we would need experimental studies to support causal claims. Most real experiments are unethical, since participants would have to be randomly assigned to vape or avoid vaping, which is why researchers look for natural experiments.

THE NATURAL

A good example of a natural experiment is "Intended and Unintended Effects of E-Cigarette Taxes on Youth Tobacco Use." The authors used data on youth smoking and vaping rates in 10 states and two large counties that enacted e-cigarette taxes between 2010 and mid-2019. They found that taxes were associated with a reduction in vaping among young people. But they were also associated with an increase in young people smoking traditional cigarettes. That's good evidence that vaping and smoking are substitutes. If vaping led to smoking, a decrease in vaping would lead to a decrease in smoking.

Several other natural-experiment studies reinforce the idea that vaping and smoking are substitutes, although the rate of substitution seems to vary in different populations. While we still have a lot to learn in this area, the evidence to date suggests that discouraging vaping will lead to increased smoking and very likely worse public health.

This research suggests that the 15–20% e-cigarette tax, which was part of the original Build Back Better Act (though was eventually taken out), probably would have reduced youth vaping by about 3% and increased youth smoking by about 2%. Given the evidence that vaping is far less hazardous than smoking, more teens smoking instead of vaping doesn't represent an improvement in public health. None of this research shows that vaping is safe, and it doesn't rule out the possibility of negative health effects that haven't yet been found. But in public policy, the most important question is: "Instead of what?"

In real life, there are no solutions, only tradeoffs. There's overwhelming evidence that if the alternative to vaping is cigarette smoking, vaping represents a huge improvement for public health. Government officials generally fail to reason in these terms. They tax, ban, and regulate as if their policies exist in a vacuum, citing statistically dubious studies to support their preconceived policies.

FOOTBALL OR, IN AMERICAN ENGLISH, SOCCER

We've played with some numbers in baseball and American football. In the next chapter, we introduce a new kind of Wrong Number in another sport: one that accurately reflects reality, but a wrong reality.

CHAPTER TWENTY-EIGHT

FOOTBALL FIXES

In most sports, bettors look for fixes by analyzing betting patterns and calculating the relative interests of the two sides. Match fixing is common enough that it is a serious concern for bookmakers and bettors—not to mention people concerned with the sport. Soccer betting (I will use the American term throughout) has a useful feature for direct fix detection. The data used in this chapter were uploaded by Elad Silvas to Kaggle.

SOCCER BETTING 101

Soccer odds are usually quoted as the payout for £1 bet on the event: home team win, away team win, or tie. For example, the most common payout line is 2.50/2.65/3.00 for home team win/away team win/tie result. A £1 bet on the home team pays £2.50 if the home team wins, meaning you have a £1.50 profit. A winning bet on the visitor pays £2.65, and if you bet on a tie, and there is a tie, you get paid £3.00.

If a bookmaker can manage a perfectly balanced book, she will take in $\dfrac{£10,000}{2.50} = £4,000$ on the home team, $\dfrac{£10,000}{2.65} = £3,774$ on the away team, and $\dfrac{£10,000}{3.00}$ = £3,333 on a tie. Her revenue is £4,000 + £3,774 + £3,333 = £11,107, and she pays out £10,000 whatever happens. Payouts are typically set to deliver a 9–12% return to the bookmaker on perfectly balanced books. In this example, the bookmaker's edge is $\dfrac{£11,107 - £10,000}{£11,107}$ = 0.0997, or 9.97%. Of course, bookmakers cannot get perfect balance and sometimes even have large enough imbalances that they lose money on unwelcome results.

For each bet, we can compute the probability that makes the bet a breakeven proposition by taking the inverse, $\dfrac{1}{2.50}$ = 0.4, so the home team bettor needs a 40% chance of the home team winning for a breakeven bet, with no edge to either the bettor or the bookmaker. Betting on the visitor requires a 37.74% chance of that event, and betting on a tie requires 33.33%. The sum of those probabilities is 111.07%—the 11.07% extra is the bookmaker's advantage. It is impossible for all three bettors to have breakeven bets.

If we assume the bookmaker sets odds to make all three bets have the same 9.97% edge, we get standardized implied probabilities of 36% for a home team win, 34% for a visiting team win, and 30% for a tie.

THE BELL CURVE STRIKES AGAIN

There is a tight relation in most matches between the odds offered on the favorite and the odds offered on a tie. The reason is easy to see. For most matches there is a most likely outcome, say the favorite winning by one goal. Outcomes one goal away from this—a tie or a favorite two-goal win—will generally have somewhat less probability. Outcomes two goals away will have even less probability, and so on. The lower the payout on the favorite, meaning the higher its standardized implied probability of winning, the farther away the tie outcome is from the most likely outcome, and the less likely a tie is.

For example, a common offering is 1.38/7.50/4.00. The standardized implied probabilities are 65% for the home team, 12% for the away team, and 23% for a tie. Compared to the 2.50/2.65/3.00 example, the chance for the home team to win has increased from 36% to 65%, while the chance for a tie has declined from 33% to 23%. The chance for the visitor has dropped from 34% to 12%.

Call the standardized implied probabilities F for the favorite, U for the underdog, and T for a tie. The relation $T = 0.34 - 0.15F$ (or equivalently, $U = 0.66 - 0.85F$) captures most matches within about 2%—that is, if F is 40%, T will generally be between 26% and 30%. For 2.50/2.65/3.00, F = 36% so $0.34 - 0.15F = 29\%$, and T was 30%. For 1.38/7.50/4.00, F was 65%, $0.34 - 0.15F = 24\%$, and T was 23%.

Now, there are legitimate reasons why bookmaker offerings differ from this relation. For example, suppose there is an event—whether a star player is available to play, whether it rains—that would change the game significantly. These can lead to goal differential distributions that are not bell-shaped—perhaps ones with two modes. Or there are sometimes strategic reasons why both teams might be satisfied with a tie, or both teams might want to avoid a tie. But these kinds of situations are rare, and generally move the standardized implied probability on the tie outcome only 1% or 2% from its usual value.

FIXES CHANGE EVERYTHING

What happens if there is probability p that the match is fixed to deliver a win for the underdog? This takes a little algebra and you can skip the rest of this and the next two paragraphs if you like. F and T are the values if the match were not fixed. The observed value for the standardized implied probability of the favorite, F^*, should be $(1 - p)F$ and the observed tie value, T^*, should be $(1 - p)T = (1 - p)(0.34 - 0.15F)$. Substituting $F^*/(1 - p)$ for F gives $T^* = (1 - p)0.34 - 0.15F^*$, which implies $p = 1 - (0.15F^* + T^*)/0.34$.

If the match is fixed in favor of the favorite, the equations are $F^* = p + (1 - p)F$ and $T^* = (1 - p)T = (1 - p)(0.34 - 0.15F)$. Now we substitute $(F^* - p)/(1 - p)$ for F to get $T^* = (1 - p)0.34 - 0.15(F^* - p)$, so $p = (0.34 - 0.15F^* - T^*)/0.19$. This is less common, however.

There's one more case, where the match is fixed to favor the original underdog, which becomes the favorite as a result. Now we have $F^* = p + (1 - p)$ $U = p + (1 - p)(1 - F - 0.34 + 0.15F) = p + (1 - p)(0.66 - 0.85F)$ and we get $T^* = (1 - p)0.34 - 0.15(0.66 - 0.85F^*)$ and $p = (0.10 + 0.13F^* - T^*)/0.34$.

Obviously, this is a highly simplified model, but it does suggest we can diagnose match fixes by tie payoffs that diverge from the usual relation with favorite odds. As mentioned above, there can be other explanations for these divergences, so we'll have to test our hypotheses. And note that our model assumes that bookmakers continue to take bets on matches they suspect may be fixed; they merely adjust the payouts offered to reflect their degree of suspicion.

Before getting to the test, let's apply the formulae to ordinary match returns. In the most common offering of 2.50/2.65/3.00, with observed standardized implied probabilities of $F^* = 36\%$, $U^* = 34\%$, and $T^* = 30\%$. Putting these values in the formula for p gives −4% for a matched fixed in favor of the favorite, and negative values for fixes for the underdog or underdog that became a favorite. Small negative values like this do not suggest bookmakers suspect a fix. In the fourth-most-common set of returns, 2.50/2.50/3.00 ($F^* = 65\%$, $U^* = 12\%$, $T^* = 23\%$) we get a +2% probability, which also seems close enough to zero to ignore.

Next consider the line 9.50/1.20/5.75, which occurred 24 times in the data, with normalized standardized probabilities of 9%, 75%, and 16%. With $F = 75\%$, we expect T of $0.34 - 0.15 \times 0.75 = 23\%$ versus 16%

observed, and U of 2% versus 9% observed. Clearly this offering does not conform to the usual pattern.

Applying our formula for p above, we get 20% that the match is fixed for the underdog (the home team in this case), 36% that it's fixed for the favorite (the visitor), and 11% that it was fixed for the true underdog (the visiting team, which became the favorite due to the fix). Now, these are not probabilities to add, at most one of them can be true. The best explanation of the data is a 36% chance that a fix is in to make the visiting team—which is a favorite even without a fix—certain of winning.

This implies that without the fix, the home team would have a 14% chance of winning, the visitor 61%, and 25% chance of a tie result.

TESTING THE MATCH-FIXING EXPLANATION

One implication of the match-fixing hypothesis is that the high estimated p values should be in leagues with well-known match-fixing scandals. Some 1.0% of all matches in the data (0.9% from opening lines, 1.0% from closing lines) have estimated p above 25%, but in 347 of the 546 leagues there are zero examples. The top 20 leagues in p > 25% matches account for 48% of all such games, and 20 leagues have over 20% of their matches with p > 25%. Leagues in the two (overlapping) groups of 20 have all been named in major scandals. To be fair, since estimated p values are based on bookmaker assessments of the chance of match fixing, this could be circular; perhaps the well-publicized scandals have led to bookies treating matches from these leagues as likely fixes.

The "Number of matches" columns in the table below show matches by estimated p at both the opening and closing lines. Three-quarters of matches have either zero or negative estimated p (74% at the opening line,

76% at the closing line), suggesting no suspicion of a fix. But one-quarter have a tie payout that is too high relative to the payout on the favorite, which could result from suspicion of a fix, or something else.

Fix probability	Number of matches		Fix bet return		Anti-fix bet return		Tie bet return	
	Open	Close	Open	Close	Open	Close	Open	Close
None	24,665	25,309	−10%				−11%	−11%
<5%	4,565	4,175	5%	−8%	−23%	−12%	−12%	−13%
5–10%	2,039	1,852	7%	1%	−20%	−12%	−18%	−26%
10–15%	965	884	11%	−10%	−31%	−20%	−14%	−21%
15–20%	576	576	6%	−12%	−28%	−15%	−26%	−21%
20–25%	358	336	−27%	−33%	−14%	−33%	−42%	−29%
25–30%	173	193	−32%	−26%	−43%	−49%	15%	−16%
30–35%	83	88	−49%	−38%	−54%	−49%	−34%	−63%
35–40%	32	43	−33%	−32%	−68%	−74%	−50%	16%
>40%	4	4	−75%	−24%	−49%	−75%	400%	−100%

One feature consistent with the fix explanation is there are more small suspicions at the open (estimated p greater than zero but less than 25%) which have a tendency to resolve either into zero p or p > 25% by the close. It's not a strong tendency. That suggests retail bookmakers do not devote great resources to investigating or preventing fixes, but that some evidence nonetheless does accumulate.

This approach cannot distinguish between a possible hard fix—one in which enough players and officials are committed to a result that it is almost certain, even at the cost of being obvious to investigators—and a certain soft fix—one in which some players may not try hard or officials will favor one side, but not to the point of embarrassment. The estimated p represents the probability that the fix result will occur, which depends on both the intention and the success of the fixers.

For the three-quarters of matches with tie payout in line with favorite payout, the average return to retail bettors is −10% for home or away bets and −11% for tie bets. Since these matches have zero estimated p, there is no fix or anti-fix betting.

If the payout structure suggests the suspicion of a fix, however, things change dramatically. At the close, a fix bet means to bet on the team whose payout has declined since the open line. At the open you have to determine the fix bet based on which fix explanation (fix for the favorite, fix for the underdog, or fix for an underdog that thereby became the favorite) has the highest p. An anti-fix bet is a bet against the possible fix.

BETTING THE FIX AND ANTI-FIX

The data suggest that betting the fix at the open when estimated p is under 25% produces a positive average return to the bettor. So, if you look for matches with high tie payouts adjusted for the favorite payout, identify the probable fix team—it looks as if you can make money.

In virtually all other situations—higher fix probabilities, anti-fix bets, tie bets, and betting at the close—high fix probabilities result in large negative returns for bettors. The higher the estimated p, the worse for bettors—even bettors who bet on the fix at the open. This is further evidence for the fix explanation—when a fix is suspected, bookmakers shorten payouts on all bets, making them unprofitable for all bettors.

The simple story is, when bookmakers suspect a fix, they pull back on payouts to protect themselves, leading to lines that imply inconsistent outcome probabilities. So why positive return to bettors who pick the suspected fix team at the opening line when estimated p is under 20%?

I think the answer here is that these represent 24% of all matches and bookmakers are unwilling to sacrifice profit by offering unattractive lines to bettors. The main risk management strategy of retail bookmakers is to cut off winning bettors and to refuse suspicious bets from new customers. But if the bookmaker refuses fix bets at the opening line from all but proven losing customers, it will end up with an unbalanced book.

Allowing proven losing customers to have some positive expected return bets reduces bookmaker risk without really costing the bookmaker anything. The bookmaker revenue is limited by how much customers are willing to lose. Bookmakers have no interest in taking the money too quickly, as that kills existing customers and hurts word-of-mouth referrals. Retail bookmakers prefer all customers to lose slowly and steadily. Giving proven losing customers a positive edge in some bets costs little, since the bookmaker will eventually get everything those customers are willing to lose. And proven losing customers are as likely to make anti-fix bets as fix bets.

An advantage gambler cannot exploit these opportunities, except via deception. That means buying accounts from proven losers and running them with positive edge bets until they are closed. This is an expensive and risky strategy.

While this is just a casual look at the data, it does suggest that soccer match fixing is common and has been absorbed into the bookmaking business as a minor irritant rather than a major issue to be rooted out and destroyed. Bettors who want an honest wager and accept that the bookmakers have an edge should avoid matches where the tie payoffs look too large. Bettors looking to beat the bookie should add some match-fixing estimates to their toolbox.

PRIVATE EQUITY AND PUBLIC INEQUITY

In the late 1970s a new villain emerged in US finance. It was identified by various terms like leveraged buyouts, corporate raiders, junk bonds, "barbarians at the gate," vulture capitalism, slash-and-burn management, and locust looting, but few people could give precise definitions of those terms. In the 21st century it acquired the more neutral name of private equity—aren't privacy and equity both good things? But it still carries a taint in the public mind of greedy Wall Street sneaks cheating everyone while wrecking the world. In the next chapter we'll see what happens when the vinegar of private equity mixes with the baking soda of healthcare.

CHAPTER TWENTY-NINE

PRIVATE ROOMS AND PRIVATE EQUITY

"Serious Medical Errors Rose After Private Equity Firms Bought Hospitals" was the headline of a *New York Times* article looking at the findings of "a major study of the effects of such acquisitions on patient care in recent years," published in the December issue of *Journal of the American Medical Association* (JAMA). The paper was also written up in *USA Today*, *MarketWatch*, *Common Dreams*, and *The Harvard Gazette*.

THE ART OF THE DEAL

"This is a big deal," Ashish Jha, dean of the Brown University School of Public Health, told *New York Times* reporters Reed Abelson and Margot Sanger-Katz. "It's the first piece of data that I think pretty strongly suggests that there is a quality problem when private equity takes over."

Abelson, Sanger-Katz, and their fellow reporters misrepresented the findings of the study, which suffers from its own "quality problems."

Even its premise is fuzzy. The authors never say what they mean by "private equity," which has no formal definition. Half of the hospitals in the study were already privately owned, for-profit hospitals before they were acquired. The authors suggest that what they call "private equity" is characterized by excessive leverage and short horizons, but present no data on either factor. *New York Times* readers may interpret the phrase private equity to mean "evil Wall Street greedheads," in which case it seems logical that patient care would deteriorate.

Even the paper's lead author started with that assumption. "We were not surprised there was a signal," Massachusetts General Hospital's Sneha Kannan told *The New York Times*, "I will say we were surprised at how strong it was."

It's clear Kannan and the journalists covering the story had in mind an investment firm that buys up all the stock in a publicly traded company, loads up on debt, slashes costs—often meaning layoffs and wage cuts—fixes problems, cuts corners, and sells the company back to the public a few years later at a higher price because it now appears to be more profitable, better managed, and faster growing. This is a caricature at best. Some aspects are true of some private equity deals, but none of the hospital acquisitions in the study resembled this stereotype.

A more careful study would have either defined private equity carefully, or studied aspects like leverage, horizon, type of investor, and type of hospital individually. Instead, the authors relied mainly on what the investor was called in media accounts and marketing materials.

ALWAYS LOOK ON THE DIM SIDE

Bias was built into the study design. Research that looks only at "adverse" events and outcomes is designed to dig up dirt and will tend to come up with meaningless conclusions. Serious investigators study all events and outcomes—good and bad—in search of accurate, balanced conclusions.

The study's strongest finding shows that lives were saved in hospitals acquired by private equity—the opposite of what Kannan expected to find. Patient mortality, the most important measure, dropped a statistically significant 9% in the study group, which represents nearly 500 lives saved.

The paper could have been headlined "Patient Mortality Fell After Private Equity Firms Bought Hospitals," except JAMA might not have published it, *The New York Times* certainly wouldn't have bothered to write it up, and *Common Dreams* couldn't have run with the headline "We Deserve Medicare for All, but What We Get Is Medicare for Wall Street."

So, the study authors fell all over themselves to explain this finding away. They theorized, without any evidence, that private equity hospitals might routinely transfer out patients who are near death. That's certainly possible, and a legitimate reason for skepticism that private equity acquisition saved patient lives. But that same speculation applies equally to the negative findings that are trumpeted both in the study and in news write-ups. Whether the findings are positive or negative for private equity acquisitions, they are questionable due to defects in the study that make all its findings unreliable.

Another one of the 17 measures the study authors looked at was length of stay. They found that at the private equity hospitals, the duration of stay was a statistically significant 3.4% shorter, which was another finding the authors were quick to downplay.

AVOIDING FALLS

Falls are the most common adverse events in hospitals, and the study found that they were more likely to occur in hospitals acquired by private equity. According to *The New York Times*, the "researchers reported … a 27 percent increase in falls by patients while staying in the hospital."

This isn't what the study says. The rate of falls stayed the same at hospitals after they were acquired by private equity, at 0.068%. In the control group hospitals, falls declined from 0.083% to 0.069%.

In other words, the situation improved 17% (don't ask how that morphed to 27%) in the control group but didn't get worse or better in hospitals acquired by private equity. The authors assumed that there was an industry-wide drop in hospital falls and that this positive trend didn't take place at the private equity hospitals.

What this finding actually suggests is that the control hospitals were badly chosen and run worse (at least when it comes to preventing patient falls) than the acquired hospitals, both before and after private equity acquisition. That falls could change by 17% without any cause (the control hospitals were not purchased by anyone) makes nonsense of claiming statistical significance for much smaller changes in other factors.

Let's even assume that there was an industry-wide decline in falls and that private equity hospitals didn't see the improvement that would have taken place had their greedy new owners not been allowed to acquire them. If that improvement had taken place, there would have been 20 fewer falls in the study group. Doesn't that matter less than the 500 deaths prevented—the statistic that the authors chose to downplay?

STATISTICAL SIGNIFICANCE

The New York Times article mentions that bed sores increased at the private equity hospitals, even though that wasn't a statistically significant finding, meaning that there weren't enough data included in the study to make that assertion. The study authors acknowledged that this finding wasn't significant, but *The New York Times* journalists chose to report it anyway.

The study authors did claim that another one of their adverse findings was statistically significant: bloodstream infections allegedly increased in private equity hospitals from about 65 to 99 cases. This is indeed serious, as such infections can easily be fatal. However, the finding had marginal statistical significance, meaning it was unlikely, but not completely implausible, to have arisen by random chance if private equity acquisition did not affect the rate of bloodstream infections. If the only hypothesis that the authors had tested was whether private equity acquisition increased bloodstream infections, then the finding would meet standard criteria for statistical significance.

If you run a fishing expedition for adverse events and outcomes, you are very likely to find some findings that occur by random chance. The authors were aware of this and adjusted the claimed significance of this result as if they had tested eight hypotheses. But the paper reported 17 measures, and the authors may have tested more. If we adjust for 17 hypotheses, the bloodstream infection result loses its statistical significance.

The rigorous way to do studies is to pre-register hypotheses to ensure that the authors can't go fishing in a large amount of data to pick out a few conclusions that they like, which happen to appear statistically significant by random chance. The authors did not report pre-registration.

So, what can we conclude from this study? *The New York Times* reporters seem to have gone on a second fishing expedition, this one for a scholar willing to conclude from the study's findings that we need more government regulation, or perhaps a ban on private equity hospital acquisitions. To their credit, none of the experts they quoted fully delivered, forcing the reporters to blandly conclude that the study "leaves some important questions unanswered for policymakers." It sure does; all the questions that were unanswered before the study.

"This should make us lean forward and pay attention," was the best Yale economist Zack Cooper was willing to give Abelson and Sanger-Katz, adding that it shouldn't lead us to "introduce wholesale policies yet." Rice economist Vivian Ho told the *Times* that she "was eager to see more evidence."

Setting out to find "more evidence" of a conclusion that researchers already believe to be true, instead of going where the data point, is what leads to such sloppy and meaningless research in the first place.

PURE WRONG NUMBER

Next we'll look at the least consequential Wrong Number in the book, but the purest example. The entire story is about a number and how to get it wrong.

CHAPTER THIRTY

THE REASON THAT THEY DON'T TEACH AT SCHOOLS LIKE WHARTON

A good rule of thumb is people complaining about everyone else usually illustrate their own guilt. A recent case in point is a tweet (this was in January 2022, before Elon Musk bought the company and changed the word to "posts" or "xs") by Wharton professor Nina Strohminger that went viral and generated a lot of news coverage.

> *I asked Wharton students what they thought the average American worker makes per year and 25% of them thought it was over six figures. One of them thought it was $800k. Really not sure what to make of this (The real number is $45k).*

REALLY, A BUSINESS SCHOOL PROFESSOR?

It's disappointing that a business school professor would ask such an ambiguous question. "Average" is usually taken as "arithmetic mean," but asking about "the average American" suggests a median. Does "worker" mean we should include only wage income, or is it asking about total income? And does "worker" include part-time and unpaid work, or only full-time employed prime-age adults in the regular labor force?

None of those interpretations give numbers very close to what Strohminger claims is the "real number" of $45,000. If I had to pick the most natural interpretation of the question, I would use the median earnings of full-time workers aged 16 or over (from the Bureau of Labor Statistics, $51,882 for 2021—the most recent available at the time of the tweet) and perhaps answer "about $65,000" to cover typical benefit packages.

Now, of course, it's possible that students answering $100,000 were deluded, as Strohminger and most commentators seem to assume. It's easy to explain surprising observations by "everyone but me is stupid," but it rarely leads to learning. So $100,000 might have been a guess at the mean household income in the United States ($121,800 in 2020, depressed by COVID). Asking students who gave high answers how they interpreted the question would seem to be more productive than trashing Wharton students on Twitter for not reading the professor's mind.

I grant that $800,000 is hard to understand, but not for the reason I suspect most people think. It's common knowledge that there are many people with incomes in the billions. Even if you know the median worker's salary is around $65,000, it's not statistically implausible that the mean worker earns far more—even $800,000. You can't estimate extreme values by looking at typical observations.

The problem with $800,000 is anyone who knows US national income is in the neighborhood of $20 trillion should figure that it could only support around 25 million workers earning $800,000, and there have to be more than 25 million workers among a population of well over 300 million. My guess is the person answering $800,000 wasn't taking the question seriously, or didn't have even ballpark ideas about US national income and population, or accidentally added a zero, or didn't bother to do the math.

THE REAL ISSUE

While I don't think this experiment tells us anything about Wharton students' knowledge of economic conditions, it does relate to two points I stress in my own classes. First is that most students who do not support themselves, in my experience, have no idea how much their own family earns, nor how the money is allocated to taxes, rent, food, and other expenses. Those who do know are embarrassed to discuss it, whether the numbers are high, median, or low. Students are far more open about their sex lives, drug use, and health problems than their family finances, and far more knowledgeable as well.

This presents problems when I'm advising students on career choices. How can a student choose between an offer of $60,000/year in San Francisco and $65,000 in Minneapolis (multiply by five for Wharton MBAs) without some idea of what kind of living standard those pre-tax salaries will support? How can a student know if she needs a top professional salary to live in comfortable style, or if she can be happy on what public-interest jobs pay? How can college-educated citizens opine on economic policy without knowing how to relate money to living standards?

The other issue is our education system puts too much emphasis on looking things up versus thinking. Tests generally reward students either for parroting the approved "real" answers, as Strohminger prefers, or expressing some internal subjective truth. You can't make profitable trades based on things anyone can look up, and your internal subjective truth is useless. You're not likely to change the world or make breakthroughs this way in non-financial fields either. Things you look up are often wrong (hence this book), and nearly always rely on assumptions and definitions you don't know. Thinking for yourself, and then gathering reliable data you do understand, produces much more robust and useful knowledge.

FERMI PROBLEMS

The great physicist Enrico Fermi was famous for asking his students "Fermi problems." A classic example is, "How many piano tuners are there in Chicago?" A first reaction is often, "I have no idea," but some reflection shows that you do in fact have some ability to hazard a plausible range. You can reason from the population of Chicago, the fraction of homes with pianos, the frequency pianos are tuned, the number of pianos one tuner can service. You can think about whether you know or have ever met a piano tuner. You can recall if you've ever seen piano tuning businesses, or if Home Depot has an aisle for piano-tuning supplies.

Once you start thinking, it's addictive. You realize you need some definitions—only full-time professional tuners, or should you include part-timers and people who tune as part of other duties? Is it tuners who live in Chicago, or those who tune there? Chicago city limits or metropolitan area? How about harpsichords and clavichords? Do electric keyboards need to be tuned? These kinds of questions can lead to specific research much more reliable than simply entering "number piano tuners Chicago" in Google. (The proprietary trading firm Jane Street invented a game with Fermi-type questions, Estimathon, that I like to use in the classroom.)

There aren't many trade theses that depend on the number of piano tuners in Chicago, nor is it a key metric in any other field I can think of.

But practice in putting plausible estimation ranges on things using what you actually know or can determine accurately, and reasoning rather than parroting or introspecting, should be a big part of education if we want graduates who think.

My guess is most of the answers Strohminger got were reasonable interpretations of her ambiguous question—it's not that Wharton students need better information, they need more thoughtful professors, ones who learn from their students rather than making fun of them on Twitter. But I am not surprised she also got some wildly incorrect answers based on any interpretation—like $800,000. I suspect she would get some equally or more absurd answers if she asked her students to estimate mean global temperature, the amount of water used in a typical shower, or what average grocery store profit margins are. Even elite schools like Wharton typically don't teach their students to reason from what they observe versus looking things up or expressing what they feel.

HOME STRETCH

You're nearly set to graduate from my Wrong Number academy. One more chapter and you're qualified to go out into the world to find and defeat your own Wrong Numbers.

CHAPTER THIRTY-ONE
CONCLUDING THOUGHTS

By this point, you should know a lot about Wrong Numbers. I hope I've convinced you that you cannot trust the most respected institutions, the most prestigious journals, the most credentialed experts, and the most aggressive journalists to filter out obvious nonsense if it's clothed as a number. I further hope that you've learned some red flags to watch for when a number is reported. On the other hand, I hope you retain faith that quantitative analysis is useful when done honestly and properly, and that it's not too complicated for ordinary people to understand.

As a farewell present, I'm going to toss out a comparison that may seem a bit wild. For most of human history, argument was by authority. Truth came from God, oracles, prophets, ancient ancestors, or common wisdom.

Around 500 years ago, a movement that came to be called The Enlightenment attempted to replace authority with reason and empirical evidence. Numbers, including Wrong Numbers, have the form of Enlightenment argument.

The trouble with arguing from authority is not just that the authority might be wrong. "Thou shalt not kill," for example, is a good principle. But if you try to apply reason to it, it gets complicated. You'd need considerable expertise in ancient texts to have any idea of what early Canaanite script was on the tablets Moses got on Mount Sinai, and what meaning its words had at the time. Moreover, the commandment has been embedded in many different sophisticated moral traditions, with different answers to practical questions like self-defense, capital punishment, war, euthanasia, and abortion. On top of that, there are many other moral dictates that seem to argue in favor of killing.

The complex underpinnings of the four simple words discourage ordinary people from applying the principles directly. Instead, they defer to anointed experts, who are clever enough to select and interpret principles to justify anything. It's not just religious authority, the same thing applies to political maxims like "No taxation without representation" and legal principles like "Ignorance of the law is no excuse." These things all seem simple and clear until you start to think about them. You will find them unreliable allies if you try to use them in an argument with established experts like priests, politicians, and judges.

Now, let's go back to Chapter 1 and think about the claim that curbside busses have seven times the fatal accident rate of traditional carriers. As we know, the claim was not true, but suppose it were. Like "thou shalt not kill," and the other maxims, it sounds like something an ordinary person can understand. If you take a curbside bus from New York to Boston, you have seven times the risk of being killed in a traffic accident than if you took a Greyhound instead.

But in fact, the statement meant something entirely different. It claimed that if a curbside bus company bought a bus, it was seven times as likely to be involved in a fatal accident over its life than if Greyhound had bought the bus. Moreover, nearly all the fatalities were not bus passengers but pedestrians. And most of the accidents were not the fault of the bus; in fact, a good number were multi-vehicle accidents in which the bus had no connection to the fatality.

It's not clear why anyone would care about this number if it were true. It likely means the curbside companies operate disproportionately in crowded cities with lots of pedestrians, or perhaps that they use their busses for more miles. Only if curbside busses killed more people in bus-at-fault accidents per passenger mile on comparable routes would there be reason to tighten their regulation.

But let's assume not only that the Wrong Number was correct, but that it meant what it seemed to mean. Why would anyone care about the relative risk of dying on a bus ride from New York to Boston? It's the absolute risk that matters. Intercity bus travel is extremely safe for bus riders. You have considerably more chance of dying of a heart attack or being murdered in an average five hours than dying as a passenger on a five-hour intercity bus ride from a bus-at-fault accident. In fact, you have more chance of dying from crossing a street than from the bus accident. So even if curbside busses are seven times as dangerous, if you have to cross more than seven extra streets to get to and from the bus terminal, you'd be better off going curbside. And if shutting down the low-cost, convenient bus carriers resulted in more people traveling in cars, it would lead to many more deaths.

Wrong Numbers, like appeals to authority, are not intended for ordinary people to understand or to help them make decisions. They are intended to get ordinary people to accept the wishes of the expert. Rather than claiming support from God or ancient wisdom, they claim support from science. And many people who have learned to be skeptical of traditional wisdom retain uncritical belief in anything that claims to be scientific.

REFERENCES

CHAPTER 1

Aaron Brown, "National Transportation Safety Board Report on Bus Safety Is Deeply Flawed" (Minyanville, July 30, 2012) http://www.minyanville.com/business-news/politics-and-regulation/articles/Transportation-Safety-financial-regulation-safety-statistics/7/30/2012/id/42805?page=1

Jim Epstein, "Government Assault on the Chinatown Bus Industry Fueled by Bogus Federal Study" (Reason, May 7, 2013) https://reason.com/2013/05/07/government-assault-on-chinatown-bus-indu/?nab=1

Michael M. Grynbaum, "High Fatality Rate Found for Low-Cost Buses" (The New York Times, October 31, 2011) https://www.nytimes.com/2011/11/01/nyregion/transportation-safety-board-releases-report-on-low-cost-bus-safety.html?_r=3&ref=nyregion&

Bart Jansen, "Bus Regulators Hasten Shutdowns to Prevent Crashes" (USA Today, October 22, 2011) https://www.usatoday.com/story/news/nation/2012/10/22/bus-crashes/1649975/

National Transportation Safety Board, "Report on Curbside Motorcoach Safety" (NTSB/SR-11/01 PB2011-917002, October 12, 2011) https://www.ntsb.gov/safety/safety-studies/Documents/SR1101.pdf

New York Daily News, "Bus Busts Soar as State Continues to Press Roadside Safety Checks in Wake of Deadly Crashes" (October 27, 2011) https://www.nydailynews.com/2011/10/27/bus-busts-soar-as-state-continues-to-press-roadside-safety-checks-in-wake-of-deadly-crashes/

REFERENCES

Jim O'Grady, "Fed Study Says Small Curbside Bus Companies Have More Accidents" (WNYC, October 31, 2011) https://www.wnyc.org/story/286739-fed-study-says-small-curbside-bus-companies-have-more-accidents/

Jeff Plungis, "Chinatown Buses' Death Rate Said Seven Times That of Others" (Businessweek, October 31, 2011) https://www.bloomberg.com/news/articles/2011-10-31/chinatown-buses-death-rate-said-seven-times-that-of-competitors

Reuters, "Curbside Buses Much Less Safe than Regular Coaches: NTSB" (October 31, 2011) https://www.reuters.com/article/2011/10/31/us-buses-safety-idUSTRE79U72320111031/

Charles Schumer and Nydia Velazquez, "Letter to Deborah Hersman, Chair of the National Transportation Safety Board" (March 14, 2011) https://reason.com/wp-content/uploads/assets/db/13674376667822.pdf

John Schwarz, "What If the Magic School Bus Came from Chinatown?" (College Humor, June 25, 2013) https://www.bubbleblabber.com/2013/06/watch-what-if-the-magic-school-bus-came-from-chinatown/

Alexa Vaughn, "Safety Report Warns of 'Curbside' Buses" (Los Angeles Times, October 31, 2011) https://www.latimes.com/world/la-xpm-2011-oct-31-la-na-bus-safety-20111101-story.html

CHAPTER 2

Aria Bendix, "USAID Cuts Could Lead to 14 Million Deaths Over the Next Five Years, Researchers Say" (NBC, June 30, 2025) https://www.nbcnews.com/health/health-news/usaid-cuts-lead-14-million-deaths-five-years-researchers-say-rcna216095

Daniella Medeiros Cavalcanti, Lucas de Oliveira Ferreira de Sales, Andrea Ferreira da Silva, Elisa Landin Basterra, Daiana Pena, Caterina Monti, Gonzalo Barreix, Natanael J. Silva, Paula Vaz, Francisco Saute, Gonzalo Fanjul, Quique Bassat, Denise Naniche, James Macinko, and Davide Rasella, "Evaluating the Impact of Two Decades of USAID Interventions and Projecting the Effects of Defunding on Mortality up to 2030: A Retrospective Impact Evaluation and Forecasting Analysis" (The Lancet, 406(10500), 283–294, July 19, 2025) https://www.thelancet.com/journals/lancet/article/PIIS0140-6736(25)01186-9/fulltext

Ellen Knickmeyer and Monika Pronczuk, "The US Says 'Little to Show' for Six-Decade Aid Agency. Supporters Point to Millions of Lives Saved" (AP, July 1, 2025) https://apnews.com/article/usaid-trump-obama-cuts-famine-19e628eb360833f94bb64cd2479d7cb6

Jonathan Lambert, "Study: 14 Million Lives Could Be Lost Due to Trump Aid Cuts" (NPR, July 1, 2025) https://www.npr.org/sections/goats-and-soda/2025/07/01/nx-s1-5452513/trump-usaid-foreign-aid-deaths

Stuart Lau, "Trump Global Aid Cuts Risk 14 Million Deaths in Five Years, Report Says" (BBC, July 1, 2025) https://www.bbc.com/news/articles/cx2jjpm7zv8o

Ken Paxton, Brent Webster, and Lawrence Joseph, "State of Texas v. Commonwealth of Pennsylvania, State of Georgia, State of Michigan and State of Wisconsin" (Supreme Court filing, Motion for leave to file bill of complaint, 2020) https://www.texasattorneygeneral.gov/sites/default/files/images/admin/2020/Press/SCOTUSFiling.pdf

Marco Rubio, "Marco Rubio Strongly Pushes Back on USAID Cuts' Impact Across World" (Good Morning America, July 1, 2025) https://www.youtube.com/watch?v=Ov3WKdcc4as

The Lancet, "Editorial Policies" https://www.thelancet.com/editorial-policies

United Nations Department of Economic and Social Affairs Population Division, "World Population Prospects 2024" https://population.un.org/wpp/downloads?folder=Standard%20Projections&group=Most%20used

US House of Representatives, "Hearing on USAID and Justice Department Grants" (July 16, 2025) https://www.youtube.com/watch?v=90DaRQplzg8

CHAPTER 3

Allana Akhtar, "The Typical Full-Time Salary in America Would Be $102,000 If Wages Had Kept Up with Growth—But the Economy Has Failed 90% of Workers" (Business Insider, September 19, 2020) https://www.businessinsider.com/median-us-worker-salaries-could-have-been-102000-without-inequality-2020-9

Carter Price and Kathryn Edwards, "Trends in Income from 1975 to 2018" (Rand Corporation, September 14, 2020) https://www.rand.org/pubs/working_papers/WRA516-1.html

REFERENCES

CHAPTER 4

Duke University Nicholas Institute for Energy, Environment & Sustainability, "Moratoria on Utility Shutoffs and Evictions Reduced COVID-19 Infection Rates, Duke Analysis Finds" (Duke University, January 26, 2021) https://nicholasinstitute.duke.edu/articles/moratoria-utility-shutoffs-and-evictions-reduced-covid-19-infection-rates-duke-analysis

Kay Jowers, Christopher Timmins, Nrupen Bhavsar, Qihui Hu, and Julia Marshall, "Housing Precarity & the COVID-19 Pandemic: Impacts of Utility Disconnection and Eviction Moratoria on Infections and Deaths Across US Counties" (National Bureau of Economic Research, Working Paper 28394, DOI: 10.3386/w28394, January 2021) https://www.nber.org/papers/w28394

Thad Moore, "SC Landlords Sue Tenants Over and Over, Using Threat of Eviction to Collect Rent" (The Post and Courier, October 3, 2020) https://www.postandcourier.com/business/real_estate/sc-landlords-sue-tenants-over-and-over-using-threat-of-eviction-to-collect-rent/article_01eac40e-fcdf-11ea-acac-a3853e2459b3.html

Notice by the Centers for Disease Control and Prevention, "Temporary Halt in Residential Evictions to Prevent the Further Spread of COVID-19" (CDC, March 31, 2021) https://www.federalregister.gov/documents/2021/03/31/2021-06718/temporary-halt-in-residential-evictions-to-prevent-the-further-spread-of-covid-19

CHAPTER 5

Abra Jeffers, Stanton Glantz, Amy Byers, and Salomeh Keyhani, "Association of Cannabis Use with Cardiovascular Outcomes Among US Adults" (Journal of the American Heart Association, 13(5), e030178, February 28, 2024) DOI: 10.1161/JAHA.123.030178

Craig Reinarman, "The Social Construction of Drug Scares" (Chapter 15 in *Constructions of Deviance: Social Power, Context, Interaction*, Patricia A. Adler and Peter Adler, eds. Wadsworth, 1994) https://selfteachingresources.pbworks.com/f/The+Social+Construction+of+Drug+Scares+(Reinarman).pdf

Benjamin Ryan, "Frequent Marijuana Use May Raise Risk of Heart Attack, Study Suggests" (The New York Times, February 28, 2024) https://www.nytimes.com/2024/02/28/health/marijuana-heart-attack-stroke.html

Marty Makary, *Blind Spots: When Medicine Gets It Wrong, and What It Means for Our Health* (Bloomsbury Publishing, September 17, 2024)

Linda Searing, "Daily Marijuana Users 25 Percent More Likely to Have a Heart Attack" (The Washington Post, March 11, 2024) https://www.washingtonpost.com/wellness/2024/03/12/marijuana-heart-attack-stroke-risk/

CHAPTER 6

Hannah Frishberg, "Death Rates Surged for This Housing Demographic During COVID-19: Study" (New York Post, February 21, 2024) https://nypost.com/2024/02/21/real-estate/death-rates-surged-for-renters-facing-eviction-during-covid/

Claudine Gay, "The Effect of Black Congressional Representation on Political Participation" (American Political Science Review, 95(3), 589–602, September 2001) https://scholar.harvard.edu/files/cgay/files/Gay_APSR_Sep_01.pdf

Nick Graetz, Peter Hepburn, Carl Gershenson, Sonya R. Porter, Danielle H. Sandler, Emily Lemmerman, and Matthew Desmond, "Examining Excess Mortality Associated with the COVID-19 Pandemic for Renters Threatened with Eviction" (Journal of the American Medical Association, 331(7), 592–600, February 20, 2024) DOI: 10.1001/jama.2023.27005

Almas Heshmati and Mike Tsionas, "RETRACTED: Green Innovations and Patents in OECD Countries" (Journal of Cleaner Production, 418, 138092, September 15, 2023) https://www.sciencedirect.com/science/article/pii/S0959652623022503

Deidre McPhillips, "Mortality Surged for Renters Facing Eviction During the Pandemic, Study Finds" (CNN, February 20, 2024) https://www.cnn.com/2024/02/20/health/eviction-mortality-risk-covid/index.html

Retraction Watch, "No Data? No Problem! Undisclosed Tinkering in Excel Behind Economics Paper" (February 5, 2024) https://retractionwatch.com/2024/02/05/no-data-no-problem-undisclosed-tinkering-in-excel-behind-economics-paper/

Retraction Watch, "Exclusive: Elsevier to Retract Paper by Economist Who Failed to Disclose Data Tinkering" (February 22, 2024) https://retractionwatch.com/2024/02/22/exclusive-elsevier-to-retract-paper-by-economist-who-failed-to-disclose-data-tinkering/

Tilly Robinson and Neil H. Shah, "Harvard President Claudine Gay to Submit 3 Additional Corrections, Corporation Says Improper Citations Fall Short of

REFERENCES

Research Misconduct" (The Harvard Crimson, December 21, 2023) https://www.thecrimson.com/article/2023/12/21/gay-plagiarism-dissertation-corrections/

Kara Rudolph, Elizabeth Stuart, Jon Vernick, and Daniel Webster, "Association Between Connecticut's Permit-to-Purchase Handgun Law and Homicides" (Home American Journal of Public Health, 105(8), e49–e54, August 2015) https://ajph.aphapublications.org/doi/full/10.2105/AJPH.2015.302703

Gary Smith, "How (Not) to Deal with Missing Data: An Economist's Take on a Controversial Study" (Retraction Watch, February 21, 2024) https://retractionwatch.com/2024/02/21/how-not-to-deal-with-missing-data-an-economists-take-on-a-controversial-study/

CHAPTER 7

Nick Brown and James Heathers, "The GRIM Test: A Simple Technique Detects Numerous Anomalies in the Reporting of Results in Psychology" (Social Psychological and Personality Science, 8(4), 363–369, 2017) DOI: 10.1177/1948550616673876

John Carlisle, Nathan Pace, Jane Cracknell, Ann Møller, Tom Pedersen, and Mathew Zacharias "What Should the Cochrane Collaboration Do About Research That Is, or Might Be, Fraudulent?" (Cochrane Database Systematic Reviews, 2013(5), ED000060, May 31, 2013) DOI: 10.1002/14651858.ED000060

Gregory Eckhartt and Graeme Ruxton, "Investigating and Preventing Scientific Misconduct Using Benford's Law" (Research Integrity Peer Review, 8(1), April 11, 2023) DOI: 10.1186/s41073-022-00126-w

Peter Kranke, Christian Apfel, and Norbert Roewer, "Reported Data on Granisetron and Postoperative Nausea and Vomiting by Fujii et al. Are Incredibly Nice!" (Anesthesia & Analgesia, 90(4), 1004–1006, April 2000) DOI: 10.1213/00000539-200004000-00053

Michèle Nuijten and Joshua Polanin, "'statcheck': Automatically Detect Statistical Reporting Inconsistencies to Increase Reproducibility of Meta-Analyses" (Research Synthesis Methods, 11(5), 574–579, April 27, 2020) DOI: 10.1002/jrsm.1408

Kara Rudolph, Elizabeth Stuart, Jon Vernick, and Daniel Webster, "Association Between Connecticut's Permit-to-Purchase Handgun Law and Homicides" (Home American Journal of Public Health, 105(8), e49–e54, August 2015) https://ajph.aphapublications.org/doi/full/10.2105/AJPH.2015.302703

Rosanna Smart, Andrew Morral, James Murphy, Rupa Jose, Amanda Charbonneau, and Sierra Smucker, "The Science of Gun Policy" (Rand Corporation, July 16, 2024) https://www.rand.org/pubs/research_reports/RRA243-9.html

CHAPTER 8

Amy Bohnert, Marcia Valenstein, Matthew Bair, Dara Ganoczy, John McCarthy, Mark Ilgen, and Frederic Blow, "Association Between Opioid Prescribing Patterns and Opioid Overdose-Related Deaths" (Journal of the American Medical Association, 305(13), 1315–1321, 2011) DOI: 10.1001/jama.2011.370

Chris Christie, Charlie Baker, Roy Cooper, Patrick Kennedy, Bertha Madras, and Pam Bondi, "The President's Commission on Combating Drug Addiction and the Opioid Crisis" (2017) https://trumpwhitehouse.archives.gov/sites/whitehouse.gov/files/images/Final_Report_Draft_11-15-2017.pdf

Kate Dunn, Kathleen Saunders, Carolyn Rutter, Caleb Banta-Green, Joseph Merrill, Mark Sullivan, Constance Weisner, Michael Silverberg, Cynthia Campbell, Bruce Psaty, and Michael Von Korff, "Opioid Prescriptions for Chronic Pain and Overdose: A Cohort Study" (Annals of Internal Medicine, 152(2), 85–92, January 19, 2010) DOI: 10.7326/0003-4819-152-2-201001190-00006

CHAPTER 9

Ernest Abel and Michael Kruger, "Smile Intensity in Photographs Predicts Longevity" (Psychological Science, 21(4), 542–544, April 2010) DOI: 10.1177/0956797610363775

José Azar, Emiliano Huet-Vaughn, Ioana Marinescu, Bledi Taska, and Till von Wachter, "Minimum Wage Employment Effects and Labor Market Concentration" (National Bureau of Economic Research, Working Paper 26101, DOI: 10.3386/w26101, July 2019)

Scott Cassidy, Ralitza Dimova, Benjamin Giguère, Jeffrey Spence, and David Stanley, "Failing Grade: 89% of Introduction-to-Psychology Textbooks That Define or Explain Statistical Significance Do So Incorrectly" (Advances in Methods and Practices in Psychological Science, 2(3), 233–239, 2019) DOI: 10.1177/2515245919858072

REFERENCES

Diederik Stapel (translated by Nicholas Brown), *Faking Science: A True Story of Academic Fraud* https://errorstatistics.com/wp-content/uploads/2014/12/fakingscience-20141214.pdf

Lauren Whiteside, Joan Russo, Jin Wang, Megan Ranney, Victoria Neam, and Douglas Zatzick, "Predictors of Sustained Prescription Opioid Use After Admission for Trauma in Adolescents" (Journal of Adolescent Health, 58(1), 92–97, January 2016) DOI: 10.1016/j.jadohealth.2015.08.011

CHAPTER 10

Clive Cussler, *Raise the Titanic* (Viking Press, January 1, 1976) ISBN-13: 978-0670589333

Francesca Gino, *Rebel Talent: Why It Pays to Break the Rules at Work and in Life* (Dey Street Books, May 1, 2018) ISBN-13: 978-0062694638

John Hampson, "Photochemical War on the Atmosphere" (Nature, 250, 189–191, 1974) DOI: 10.1038/250189a0

Stephen Schneider, *Science as a Contact Sport: Inside the Battle to Save Earth's Climate* (National Geographic Society, January 1, 2009) ASIN: B002YX0F4M

Sarah Stock, Jade Carruthers, Clara Calvert, Ting Shi, Colin Simpson, Eleftheria Vasileiou, Aziz Sheikh, Rachael Wood, Cheryl Denny, Jack Donaghy, Anna Goulding, Lisa Hopcroft, Leanne Hopkins, Terry McLaughlin, Jiafeng Pan, Bob Taylor, Srinivasa Katikireddi, Josie Murray, Chris Robertson, Utkarsh Agrawal, Colin McCowan, and Bonny Auyeung, "SARS-CoV-2 Infection and COVID-19 Vaccination Rates in Pregnant Women in Scotland" (Nature Medicine, 28, 504–512, 2022). DOI: 10.1038/s41591-021-01666-2

Brent Taylor, E. Miller, C. P. Farrington, M. C. Petropoulos, I. Favot-Mayaud, J. Li, and P. A. Waight, "Autism and Measles, Mumps, and Rubella Vaccine: No Epidemiological Evidence for a Causal Association" (The Lancet, 353(9169), 2026–2029, June 12, 1999) DOI: 10.1016/s0140-6736(99)01239-8. PMID: 10376617

The Lancet, "Paolo Macchiarini is Not Guilty of Scientific Misconduct" (The Lancet, 386(9997), 932, September 5, 2015) DOI: 10.1016/S0140-6736(15)00118-X

Andrew J. Wakefield, "MMR Vaccination and Autism" (The Lancet, 354(9182), 949–950, September 11, 1999) https://www.thelancet.com/journals/lancet/article/piis0140673605756968/fulltext

CHAPTER 11

Zeina Jamaluddine, Hanan Abukmail, Sarah Aly, Oona Campbell, and Francesco Checchi, "Traumatic Injury Mortality in the Gaza Strip from Oct 7, 2023, to June 30, 2024: A Capture–Recapture Analysis" (The Lancet, 405(10477), 469–477, February 8, 2025) https://www.thelancet.com/journals/lancet/article/PIIS0140-6736(24)02678-3/fulltext

CHAPTER 12

Steve Forbes, "The Case of Greta Thunberg's Deleted Tweet—What Alarmists Need to Hear" (Forbes, July 14, 2023) https://www.forbes.com/sites/steveforbes/2023/07/14/the-case-of-greta-thunbergs-deleted-tweet---what-alarmists-need-to-hear/

Intergovernmental Panel on Climate Change, "Global Warming of 1.5°C" https://www.ipcc.ch/site/assets/uploads/sites/2/2018/07/SR15_SPM_version_stand_alone_LR.pdf

John Kerry, "John Kerry Says Earth Has 9 Years to Avert the Worst Consequences of Climate Crisis: 'There's No Faking It on This One'" (CBS Mornings, February 19, 2021) https://www.cbsnews.com/news/climate-change-9-years-john-kerry/

Jeffrey Kluger, "Why We Keep Ignoring Even the Most Dire Climate Change Warnings" (Time, October 8, 2018) https://time.com/5418690/why-ignore-climate-change-warnings-un-report/?xid=tcoshare#:~:text=Why%20We%20Keep%20Ignoring%20Even%20the%20Most%20Dire%20Climate%20Change%20Warnings

Dan Merica and Gregory Krieg, "Democratic Candidates Unveil Sweeping Climate Proposals Ahead of CNN Town Hall" (CNN, September 4, 2019) https://www.cnn.com/2019/09/04/politics/democratic-candidates-climate-crisis-plan

Dan Zak, "'Everything Is Not Going to Be Okay': How to Live with Constant Reminders That the Earth Is in Trouble" (The Washington Post, January 24, 2019) https://www.washingtonpost.com/lifestyle/style/everything-is-not-going-to-be-okay-how-to-live-with-constant-reminders-that-the-earth-is-in-trouble/2019/01/24/9dd9d6e6-1e53-11e9-8b59-0a28f2191131_story.html

REFERENCES

CHAPTER 13

Torsten Bell, "The Science Behind Winning a Nobel Prize? Being a Man from a Wealthy Family" (The Guardian, December 7, 2024) https://www.theguardian.com/commentisfree/2024/dec/07/the-science-behind-winning-nobel-prize-being-man-from-wealthy-family-torsten-bell

Paul Novosad, Sam Asher, Catriona Farquharson, and Eni Iljazi, "Access to Opportunity in the Sciences: Evidence from the Nobel Laureates" (Centre for Economic Policy Research, DP19551, October 2, 2024) https://cepr.org/publications/dp19551

Kate Shaw, "The Nobel Prizes Highlight What Is Wrong with Recognition in Science" (Physics World, December 9, 2024) https://physicsworld.com/a/the-nobel-prizes-highlight-what-is-wrong-with-recognition-in-science/

CHAPTER 15

Gottfried Achenwall, *Statsverfassung der heutigen vornehmsten Europaischen Reiche und Volker* (1749) https://www.google.com/books/edition/Statsverfassung_der_heutigen_vornehmsten/YJ5BAAAAcAAJ?hl=en

Victoria Bisset, "Barbiecore? Bed rotting? Greedflation? Dictionary.com Adds New 2024 Words" (The Washington Post, February 13, 2024) https://www.washingtonpost.com/style/2024/02/13/dictionary-com-new-words-2024/

Groundwork Collaborative, "ICYMI: 'Greedflation' Added to Dictionary.com" (February 15, 2024) https://groundworkcollaborative.org/news/icymi-greedflation-added-to-dictionary-com/?t

Kim Lyons, "New Report from Sen. Bob Casey Outlines Impact of 'Greedflation'" (Pennsylvania Capital-Star, November 8, 2023) 12: 21 pmhttps://penncapital-star.com/economy/new-report-from-sen-bob-casey-outlines-impact-of-greedflation/ [The report itself is no longer available on-line].

Liz Pancotti and Lindsay Owens, "Inflation Revelation: How Outsized Corporate Profits Drive Rising Costs" (Groundwork Collaborative, January 17, 2024) https://groundworkcollaborative.org/wp-content/uploads/2024/01/24.01.17-GWC-Corporate-Profits-Report.pdf

U.S. Department of Energy Economic Regulatory Administration Office of Regulations and Emergency Planning, *Standby Gasoline Rationing Plan* (DOE/RG-0029 Standby Rationing Plan 80-1 June 1980) https://rosap.ntl.bts.gov/view/dot/15008

CHAPTER 16

Katherine Baicker, Sarah Taubman, Heidi Allen, Mira Bernstein, Jonathan Gruber, Joseph Newhouse, Eric Schneider, Bill Wright, Alan Zaslavsky, and Amy N. Finkelstein, "The Oregon Experiment—Effects of Medicaid on Clinical Outcomes" (New England Journal of Medicine, 368(18), 1713–1722, May 2, 2013) DOI: 10.1056/NEJMsa1212321

Sarah Kliff and Margot Sanger-Katz, "As Congress Debates Cutting Medicaid, a Major Study Shows It Saves Lives" (The New York Times, May 16, 2025) https://www.nytimes.com/2025/05/16/health/medicaid-cuts-congress.html

Peter G. Peterson Foundation, "How Do States Pay for Medicaid?" (April 16, 2025) https://www.pgpf.org/article/budget-explainer-how-do-states-pay-for-medicaid/?utm_source=chatgpt.com

Avik Roy, "Oregon Study: Medicaid 'Had No Significant Effect' on Health Outcomes vs. Being Uninsured" (Forbes, May 2, 2013) https://manhattan.institute/article/oregon-study-medicaid-had-no-significant-effect-on-health-outcomes-vs-being-uninsured

Natasha Sarin, "This Senator's Comment on Medicaid Cuts Was Brutal but Accurate" (The Washington Post, June 9, 2025) https://www.washingtonpost.com/opinions/2025/06/09/medicaid-budget-bill-deaths-trump/

Alana Semuels, "Medicaid Expansions Saved Tens of Thousands of Lives, Study Finds" (Time, May 7, 2025) https://time.com/7283419/medicaid-expansion-saves-lives-study/

Kaitlin Sullivan, "Proposed Medicaid Cuts Could Lead to Thousands of Deaths, Study Finds" (NBC News, June 16, 2025) https://www.nbcnews.com/health/health-care/proposed-medicaid-cuts-lead-thousands-deaths-study-finds-rcna213265

UChicago News, "New Research Shows Medicaid Expansion Reduced Mortality in Low-Income Adults" (May 30, 2025) https://news.uchicago.edu/story/new-research-shows-medicaid-expansion-reduced-mortality-low-income-adults

Leslie Walker, "New Studies Show What's at Stake If Medicaid Is Scaled Back" (NPR, May 20, 2025) https://www.npr.org/sections/shots-health-news/2025/05/20/g-s1-67813/medicaid-cuts-congress-republicans-reconciliation-bill

Angela Wyse and Bruce D. Meyer, "Saved by Medicaid: New Evidence on Health Insurance and Mortality from the Universe of Low-Income Adults" (National Bureau of Economic Research, Working Paper 33719, May 2025) DOI 10.3386/w33719

REFERENCES

CHAPTER 17

Brian Dawson, "'It Was Really a Love Story.' How an N.R.A. Ally Became a Gun Safety Advocate" (The New York Times, June 22, 2022) https://www.nytimes.com/2022/06/22/opinion/gun-safety-research.html

Arthur Kellermann, Frederick Rivara, Norman Rushforth, Joyce Banton, Donald Reay, Jerry Francisco, Ana Locci, Janice Prodzinski, Bela Hackman, and Grant Somes, "Gun Ownership as a Risk Factor for Homicide in the Home" (New England Journal of Medicine, 329(15), 1084–1091, October 7, 1993) https://www.nejm.org/doi/full/10.1056/NEJM199310073291506

CHAPTER 18

Joseph Cesario, "Why We Withdrew the Police Shooting Study" (Wall Street Journal, July 14, 2020) https://www.wsj.com/articles/why-we-withdrew-the-police-shooting-study-11594756799?gaa_at=eafs&gaa_n=AWEtsqcI_3x0h1HUdRRhR-CyKPCSMsjRwLJm3OEs4fsk3WAB0hdnvV3DwHWCnQeNE3-U%3D&gaa_ts=68f55e17&gaa_sig=pfEltVMo--DowZHHegG68vL7CzcIGDKl2BhxjGUTD-5qDFtWRowqFVyRm2k7k7hkkUoznJ-Be6YzNrCh7oj-6uw%3D%3D

David Johnson, Trevor Tress, Nicole Burkel, and Joseph Cesario, "RETRACTED: Officer Characteristics and Racial Disparities in Fatal Officer-Involved Shootings" (Proceedings of the National Academy of Sciences, 116(32), 15877–15882, July 22, 2019) DOI: 10.1073/pnas.1903856116

Heather Mac Donald, "Additional Testimony to the Committee on the Judiciary of the United States House of Representatives Oversight Hearing on Policing Practices" (September 19, 2019) https://www.congress.gov/116/meeting/house/109952/documents/HHRG-116-JU00-20190919-SD035.pdf

CHAPTER 20

Jason Bittel, "Climate Change Is Amazing—If You're a Rat" (National Geographic, January 31, 2025) https://www.nationalgeographic.com/animals/article/cities-urban-rat-populations-warmer-climate

CBS News, "Rat Populations Spiking in Cities Due to Warming Temperatures, Study Finds" (February 7, 2025) https://www.cbsnews.com/video/rat-populations-spiking-in-cities-due-to-warming-temperatures-study-finds/

Marieke de Cock, Helen Esser, Wim van der Poel, Hein Sprong, and Miriam Maas, "Higher Rat Abundance in Greener Urban Areas" (Urban Ecosystems, 27, 1389–1401, March 1, 2024) https://link.springer.com/article/10.1007/s11252-024-01513-5

Jordi Pascual, Sandra Franco, Rubén Bueno-Marí, Víctor Peracho, and Tomás Montalvo, "Demography and Ecology of Norway Rats, Rattus norvegicus, in the Sewer System of Barcelona (Catalonia, Spain)" (Journal of Pest Science, 93, 711–722, December 18, 2019)

Jonathan Richardson, Elizabeth McCoy, Nicholas Parlavecchio, Ryan Szykowny, Eli Beech-Brown, Jan Buijs, Jacqueline Buckley, Robert Corrigan, Federico Costa, Ray DeLaney, Rachel Denny, Leah Helms, Wade Lee, Maureen Murray, Claudia Riegel, Fabio Souza, John Ulrich, Adena Why, and Yasushi Kiyokawa, "Increasing Rat Numbers in Cities Are Linked to Climate Warming, Urbanization, and Human Population" (Science Advances, 11(5), eads6782, January 31, 2025) DOI: 10.1126/sciadv.ads6782

CHAPTER 21

Mark Boslough, "A Critical Review of Steven Koonin's 'Unsettled'" (Yale Climate Connections, May 25, 2021) https://yaleclimateconnections.org/2021/05/a-critical-review-of-steven-koonins-unsettled/

Andrew King, Daniel Swain, Ilissa Ocko, Justin Schoof, Kerry Emanuel, Kevin Walsh, Mark Richardson, Mark Zelinka, and Mat Collins, "PragerU Video on Climate Change Repeats a Range of Misleading Claims by Steven Koonin" (Climate Feedback, November 29, 2021) https://climatefeedback.org/evaluation/prageru-video-on-climate-change-repeats-a-range-of-misleading-claims-by-steven-koonin/

Steven E. Koonin, *Unsettled: What Climate Science Tells Us, What It Doesn't, and Why It Matters* (BenBella Books, April 27, 2021) ISBN-13: 978-1950665792

Steven E. Koonin, "Is There Really a Climate Emergency?" (PragerU, 2021) https://www.youtube.com/watch?v=P19ywkobLX8

Steven E. Koonin, "Greenland's Melting Ice Is No Cause for Climate-Change Panic" (Wall Street Journal, February 17, 2022) https://www.wsj.com/opinion/greenland-melting-ice-panic-sheets-global-warming-variance-seal-level-rise-climate-change-carbon-fossil-fuel-11645131739

Naomi Oreskes, Michael E. Mann, Gernot Wagner, Don Wuebbles, Andrew Dessler, Andrea Dutton, Geoffrey Supran, Matthew Huber, Thomas Lovejoy, Ilissa Ocko, Peter C. Frumhoff, and Joel Clement, "That 'Obama Scientist' Climate Skeptic You've Been Hearing About …" (Scientific American, June 1, 2021) https://www.scientificamerican.com/article/that-obama-scientist-climate-skeptic-youve-been-hearing-about/

Doyle Rice, "Global Warming Is Making Hurricanes Stronger, Study Says" (USA Today, May 18, 2020) https://www.usatoday.com/story/news/nation/2020/05/18/global-warming-making-hurricanes-stronger-study-suggests/5216028002/

Eric Rignot, Jason Briner, Lauren Simkins, and Marco Tedesco, "Wall Street Journal Op-Ed by Steven Koonin Publishes Misleading Claims About How Climate Change Influences Greenland Ice Melt" (Climate Feedback, February 24, 2022) https://climatefeedback.org/evaluation/wall-street-journal-steven-koonin-publishes-misleading-claims-climate-change-influences-greenland-ice-melt/

Bob Ward, "Book Review: Unsettled: What Climate Science Tells Us, What It Doesn't, and Why It Matters by Steve Koonin" (LSE Blog, August 15, 2021) https://blogs.lse.ac.uk/usappblog/2021/08/15/book-review-unsettled-what-climate-science-tells-us-what-it-doesnt-and-why-it-matters-by-steve-koonin/

Gary Yohe, "A New Book Manages to Get Climate Science Badly Wrong" (Scientific American, May 13, 2021) https://www.scientificamerican.com/article/a-new-book-manages-to-get-climate-science-badly-wrong/

Gary Yohe, "Appropriately Accounting for Risk: Why Steven Koonin and George Will Are Unsettling" (Union of Concerned Scientists, August 17, 2021) https://blog.ucs.org/science-blogger/accurately-and-appropriately-accounting-for-risk-why-steven-koonin-and-george-will-are-unsettling/

CHAPTER 22

Dame Vivian Hunt, Dennis Layton, and Sara Prince, "Why Diversity Matters" (McKinsey, January 1, 2015) https://www.mckinsey.com/capabilities/people-and-organizational-performance/our-insights/why-diversity-matters

Rocío Lorenzo, Nicole Voigt, Karin Schetelig, Annika Zawadzki, Isabelle Welpe, and Prisca Brosi, "The Mix That Matters" (BCG, April 26, 2017) https://www.bcg.com/publications/2017/people-organization-leadership-talent-innovation-through-diversity-mix-that-matters

Securities and Exchange Commission (Release No. 34-92590; File Nos. SR-NASDAQ-2020-081; SR-NASDAQ-2020-082, August 6, 2021) https://www.sec.gov/files/rules/sro/nasdaq/2021/34-92590.pdf

Andrew Ross Sorkin, "The Missing Piece in the Push for Boardroom Diversity" (The New York Times, September 7, 2021) https://www.nytimes.com/2021/09/07/business/dealbook/board-diversity-private-companies.html

Tatiana Walk-Morris, "DEI Is a Lightning Rod for Controversy—But the Practice Isn't Dead" (BBC, March 5, 2024) https://www.bbc.com/worklife/article/20240304-us-corporate-diversity-equity-and-inclusion-programme-controversy

CHAPTER 23

Matthew Desmond, *Poverty, by America* (Crown, March 21, 2023) ISBN-13: 978-0593239919

Matthew Desmond and Nathan Wilmers, "Do the Poor Pay More for Housing? Exploitation, Profit, and Risk in Rental Markets" (American Journal of Sociology, 124(4), 1090–1124, January 2019) https://www.journals.uchicago.edu/doi/full/10.1086/701697#d2833442e1

CHAPTER 24

Raph Di Guisto, Nick Maughan, and Aaron Brown, "Rationality and Risk Intelligence in Binary Betting" (AQR Insights, May 21, 2013) https://www.aqr.com/Insights/Research/Working-Paper/Rationality-and-Risk-Intelligence-in-Binary-Betting

Philip E. Tetlock, *Expert Political Judgment: How Good Is It? How Can We Know?* (Princeton University Press, July 25, 2005) ISBN-13: 978-0691123028

CHAPTER 25

Rebecca Bender, Taina Bien-Aimé, Katie Feifer, Rachel Foster, Marian Hatcher, Lauren Hersh, Alexi Ashe Meyers, Anne K. Ream, Shea Rhodes, and Rebecca Zipkin, "Equality Not Exploitation: An Overview of the Global Sex Trade and Trafficking Crisis, and the Case for the Equality Model" (World Without Exploitation, November 2019) https://www.equalitymodelus.org/wp-content/uploads/2020/02/Equality-Not-Exploitation-white-paper-November-2019.pdf#:~:text=1,both%20countries%20has%20been%20an

Seo-Young Cho, Axel Dreher, and Eric Neumayer, "Does Legalized Prostitution Increase Human Trafficking?" (World Development, 41, 67–82, January 2013) https://doi.org/10.1016/j.worlddev.2012.05.023

Department of Justice Canada, "Bill C-36, An Act to Amend the Criminal Code in Response to the Supreme Court of Canada Decision in Attorney General of Canada v. Bedford and to Make Consequential Amendments to Other Acts (Protection of Communities and Exploited Persons Act)" (December 1, 2014) https://www.justice.gc.ca/eng/rp-pr/other-autre/protect/p2.html

Jason Guinasso, "If Nevadans Are Serious About Ending Sex Trafficking, They Must Abolish Legal Prostitution" (The Nevada Independent, September 16, 2022) https://thenevadaindependent.com/article/if-nevadans-are-serious-about-ending-sex-trafficking-they-must-abolish-legal-prostitution

Meghan Murphy, "Open Letter in Support of Adopting the Nordic Model in Canada Garners Over 800 Signatures" (Feminist Current, April 23, 2014) https://www.feministcurrent.com/2014/04/23/open-letter-in-support-of-adopting-the-nordic-model-in-canada-garners-over-800-signatures/

Ronald Weitzer, "Legalizing Prostitution: Does It Increase or Decrease Sex Trafficking?" (Global Policy Journal, July 21, 2021) https://www.globalpolicyjournal.com/blog/21/07/2021/legalizing-prostitution-does-it-increase-or-decrease-sex-trafficking

CHAPTER 27

Rahi Abouk, Charles J. Courtemanche, Dhaval M. Dave, Bo Feng, Abigail S. Friedman, Johanna Catherine Maclean, Michael F. Pesko, Joseph J. Sabia, and Samuel Safford, "Intended and Unintended Effects of E-Cigarette Taxes on

Youth Tobacco Use" (National Bureau of Economic Research, Working Paper 29216) http://www.nber.org/papers/w29216

Jessica Barrington-Trimis, Robert Urman, Kiros Berhane, Jennifer Unger, Tess Boley Cruz, Mary Ann Pentz, Jonathan Samet, Adam Leventhal, and Rob McConnell, "E-Cigarettes and Future Cigarette Use" (Pediatrics, July 13, 2016) DOI: 10.1542/peds.2016-0379

Anusha Chidharla, Kriti Agarwal, Salwa Abdelwahed, Renu Bhandari, Abhishek Singh, Rizwan Rabbani, Kajal Patel, Priyanka Singh, Deep Mehta, Pritika Manaktala, Shreejith Pillai, Sachin Gupta, and Thoyaja Koritala, "RETRACTED: Cancer Prevalence in E-Cigarette Users: A Retrospective Cross-Sectional NHANES Study" (World Journal of Oncology, 13(1), 20–26, 2022) https://reason.com/wp-content/uploads/2023/01/1438-9260-6-PB.pdf

Stanton Glantz, "First Epidemiological Evidence Linking E-Cigs to Cancer in People" (Blog Post, July 25, 2022) https://profglantz.com/2022/07/25/first-epidemiological-evidence-linking-e-cigs-to-cancer-in-people/

Tram Pham, Jeanne V. A. Williams, Asmita Bhattarai, Ashley K. Dores, Leah J. Isherwood, and Scott B. Patten, "Electronic Cigarette Use and Mental Health: A Canadian Population-Based Study" (Journal of Affective Disorders, 260(Jan), 646–652, 2020). https://doi.org/10.1016/j.jad.2019.09.026

Brad Rodu and Nantaporn Plurphanswat, "Cross-Sectional E-Cigarette Studies Are Unreliable Without Timing of Exposure and Disease Diagnosis" (Internal and Emergency Medicine, October 17, 2022) https://reason.com/wp-content/uploads/2022/12/Rodu-Plurphanswat-CrossSec-Studies-IAEM-2022.pdf

Reagan R. Wetherill, Robert K. Doot, Anthony J. Young, Hsiaoju Lee, Erin K. Schubert, Corinde E. Wiers, Frank T. Leone, Robert H. Mach, Henry R. Kranzler, and Jacob G. Dubroff, "Molecular Imaging of Pulmonary Inflammation in Users of Electronic and Combustible Cigarettes: A Pilot Study" (Journal of Nuclear Medicine, 64(5), 797–802, 2023) https://doi.org/10.2967/jnumed.122.264529

CHAPTER 28

Elad Silvas, Kaggle Dataset https://www.kaggle.com/datasets/eladsil/soccer-games-odds

CHAPTER 29

Reed Abelson and Margot Sanger-Katz, "Serious Medical Errors Rose After Private Equity Firms Bought Hospitals" (The New York Times, December 26, 2023) https://www.nytimes.com/2023/12/26/upshot/hospitals-medical-errors.html

Brett Arends, "Injuries and Infections of Medicare Patients Spike in Hospitals Owned by Private Equity, Research Says" (MarketWatch, January 3, 2024) https://www.marketwatch.com/story/private-equity-hospitals-put-medicare-patients-at-risk-new-research-says-dbf56319

HMS Communications, "Care Riskier for Patients at Private Equity Hospitals" (The Harvard Gazette, January 2, 2024) https://news.harvard.edu/gazette/story/2024/01/healthcare-riskier-for-patients-at-private-equity-hospitals/

Sneha Kannan, Joseph Dov Bruch, and Zirui Song, "Changes in Hospital Adverse Events and Patient Outcomes Associated with Private Equity Acquisition" (Journal of the American Medical Association, 330(24), 2365–2375, 2023) DOI: 10.1001/jama.2023.23147

Les Leopold, "We Deserve Medicare for All, but What We Get Is Medicare for Wall Street" (Common Dreams, January 3, 2024) https://www.commondreams.org/opinion/medicare-for-all-wall-street

Karen Weintraub, "You're More Likely to Catch an Infection or Fall at These Hospitals" (USA Today, December 26, 2023) https://www.usatoday.com/story/news/health/2023/12/26/infections-falls-more-common-these-hospitals/72001617007/

CHAPTER 30

Amiah Taylor, "A Wharton Business School Professor Says Her Students Think the Average American Makes Six Figures, and One Thought $800,000 Was an Average Salary" (Fortune, January 21, 2022) https://fortune.com/2022/01/21/business-school-professor-average-us-salary/

ABOUT THE AUTHOR

I am a lifelong numbers guy, making my living by quantitative betting in poker, financial trading, sports betting, and advantage casino gambling. I have also worked on hundreds of scientific projects as a data analyst, programmer, and statistician. I've served as a methodology peer reviewer for major journals and taught quantitative subjects at major universities. All of this has given me great respect for numbers, and a deep enmity toward Wrong Numbers.

I was born in Seattle and spent most of my adult life in New York City. I now divide my time between Manhattan, Coronado Island, and Las Cruces. I have a wife of 38 years, Deborah Pastor, and two grown children, Jacob and Aviva.

INDEX

Note: Page numbers in *italics* refer to figures.

A
academic crime, 259
academic research
   binary factor models, 207–208
   correlation *vs.* causation, 203
   effective sports-betting factors, 211–212
   logistic regressions, 214–215
   low-quality data, 200–201
   maintenance and validation, 213–215
   model design, 208–210
   publication, 202–203
   quality, critique of, 200–201
   statistical significance problems, 202
   system track record, 205–207
accounting fraud, 115
Achenwall, Gottfried, 219
ad hominem attacks, 278
advantage gamblers, 195–199
   vs. academics knowledge, 196–198
   NFL betting study, 198–199
Affordable Care Act, 234, 235
agriculture, fuel supplies for, 224–225
Air Force, 189
Ally, N.R.A., 241
American Community Survey, 49
American Housing Survey, 44
American Journal of Public Health, 77
American Novel, The, 326
American Political Science Review, 70
Anatomy of Kinship (Harrison), 291
anesthesiology, 87–88
Annals of Internal Medicine, 108
anthropogenic warming, 176, 179
anti-Black disparities across shootings, 258
anti-fix bets, 351
anti-Hispanic disparities across shootings, 258
Asimov, Isaac, 27–29, 291
assault weapons, 100–101

B
Babbage engine, 152–154
Baseball Register, 120
Bayes, Betty, 193–194
Bayesian, 123, 156, 193–194, 237
Beiner, Bob, 199
Benford's Law, 89–91
bet sizing phenomenon, 312–313
Big-Box *vs.* Mom-and-Pop counties, 126–128
binary factor models, 207–208
Black, Fischer, 221–222
Black–Scholes option pricing model, 221
Black workers
   education levels of, 251–253
   sex discrimination, 253–255
Blind Spots (Makary), 54
bookmakers, 209–210, 352
bootleggers, 323–324
Boslough, Mark, 280
Boston Consulting Group (BCG), 295
Build Back Better Act, 342
Bureau of Economic Analysis (BEA), 222
Bureau of Labor Statistics Consumer Expenditure Survey, 304
Business Insider, 33–35

C
cancer surgeon general's warning, 339–340
Carlisle, John, 87–89
Casey, Bob, 231–232

INDEX

Centers for Disease Control and Prevention (CDC), 42, 45–46, 77, 94, 108–109, 241
Chinatown bus, 1–2
Cicchetti's logic, 31–32
cigarette smoking, 99, 335
climate catastrophe, 173–174
climate change, 149–150
    Biden, Joe, 173–174
    to linking rat populations, 271–273
    linking rats and global warming, 275
    New York City, 175–176
    short-term vs. long-term policies, 177–178
    temperature and rat populations, data comparison, 273–274
    2030–2052 climate crisis, 174–179
Climate Feedback, 283–284
Cohort Study, 108–109
Common Dreams, 357
confidence intervals, 155
    Canada vs. Gaza deaths, 159–160
    capture–recapture analysis, 163–167
    combining estimates, 167–169
    confidence game, 155–157
    estimation, 169–170
    Gaza deaths analyses, 160–162
    Hamas death claims, 158–159
    layers of reliability, 162–163
    misdirection, 171–172
    mortality in Palestine, 157–158
conspiracy theory, 6
Consumer Financial Protection Bureau (CFPB), 43
Consumer Price Index, 230–231
coronary heart disease, 54, 55, 60
corporate performance
    BCG definition of, 296
    McKinsey definition of, 293–294
corporate profits, 232
corruption, 6–7
COVID-19 pandemic, 41
    abandon hope, 42–43
    census of, 44–45
    Centers for Disease Control and Prevention (CDC), 45–46
    data transparency problems, 48–50
    Duke's academic frauds, 50–51
    Duke University researchers, 43–44
    eviction data problem, 47–48
    eviction moratorium, 46–47
    pregnant women vaccines, 144–148
    public health discovery, 51–52

credible interval, 156–157
crime(s)
    sex work as, 323
    thriller, calculus in, 333–334
Criminal, The, 327
criminalization, 324
crowding, 42
curbside buses, 2–5

D
DARPAnet, 228
data
    fiction studies, 69–70
    imputation, 73–75
    killer filings, 75–77
    synthetic Connecticut, 77–79
    voter participation, ecology of, 70–72
    wins-above-average (WAA), 80–81
    wins-above-replacement (WAR), 79–81
deal, art of, 355–356
Desmond, Matthew, 299
Dickey, Jay, 241
diversity
    BCG study, 295–296
    in corporate boards, 287–288
    and corporate performance measurement, 293–294
    H&H juries about, 290–291
    jury project by Harrison White, 291–293
    McKinsey choosing perverse measure of, 289–290
    p-value analysis, 294–295
    question about, 296–298
dose–response, 215
double-blind controlled study, 193–194
drug overdoses, 106–107

E
Eadington, Bill, 195, 199
e-cigarette, 338
    tax, 342
ecological fallacy, 71, 72
Enlightenment, The, 367
equal-opportunity misrepresentation, 235–236
equity risk premium puzzle, 223
ethnic diversity, 295
Evicted: Poverty and Profit in the American City (Desmond), 303, 305
eviction moratoriums, 42–46
exploratory data analysis in baseball, 263–270
Exploring General Equilibrium (Fischer), 224

392

F

FBI data, 94
FBI Uniform Crime Reporting (UCR), 96–97
Federal Reserve Economic Data (FRED), 228
Fermi problems, 364–365
fiction studies, 69–70
financial analogy, 29–30
financial markets, 210–211
Fortune's Formula, 310
Foundation series (Asimov), 291–292
4H club, 245
Freedom of Information Act, 5
From Dusk to Dawn (movie), 332
fuel supplies for agriculture, 224–225
full-time, full-year, prime-age (FTFYPA), 34, 36–37
Fung Wah, 1–3

G

Gay, Claudine, 70–71
Getaway, The
  crime with chaotic misadventures, 330–332
  money runs out climatic horror, 332–333
Gino, Francesca, 133–136
Glantz, Stanton, 337
global mortality, 24–26
global warming, 174, 176–177, 275
Gordon model, 223
greed, measuring, 229–230
greedflation 229–232
"Green Innovations and Patents in OECD Countries," 73, 75
Grifters, The, 328
GRIM test, 85–86
  violation, 117
gross domestic product (GDP), 222
Groundwork Collaborative, 229–230
gun control, 92–94
  cautious of public health, 249–250
  CDC from using federal funds, prohibiting, 241–242
  data sources, 102
  effectiveness, 95–97
  explosive study, 243–244
  eye of beholder, 242–243
  gun control, 103
  hypotheses test, 102
  incomplete and unreliable, studies of 98
  as issue of crime, violence, rights, and policy effects, 247–248
  legislation, 92, 94, 96–99
  research problems, 103

  scare tactics on, 248–249
  selection, 244–247
  sensible justification, 102
  study of, 81
gun ownership, 245–246
gun violence, 99–100

H

Hamas Ministry of Health, 165
Hamas survey, 164, 166–167
Hampson, John, 149
heart disease, 54–56
Herfindahl–Hirschman (H&H) index, 289
honesty
  and balancing usefulness, 136–137
  vs. dishonesty, 133–135
  fudging data, 135–136

I

incompetence, 6–7
Intelligence Advanced Projects Research Activity (IAPRA), 309

J

Jim Crow laws, 71
Journal of Adolescent Health, 124
Journal of Predicting Tomorrow's Stock Market Direction (JPTSMD), 118–119
Journal of the American Heart Association, 53–54, 58
Journal of the American Medical Association (JAMA), 75, 88, 107, 355, 357

K

Kelly, John, 310
Keynesian economics, 226
Killing, The (Kubrick), 328
kinky demand curve theory, 227
Koonin, Steven, 277–284
Kubrick, Stanley, 328

L

Lancet, The, 14–20, 142, 157, 159, 337
law enforcement corruption, 320
life, politics and, 334–335
Lolita (Nabokov), 326
low-power tests, 122

M

Macchiarini, Paolo, 142–143
Macinko, James, 20

INDEX

marijuana, 53–54, 124–126
  annual telephone surveys, 57–59
  heart disease, 54–56
  impact cardiovascular health, 60
  linear model, 65–66
  logistic regression, 60–62
  multivariable logistic regression, 63–66
  panel studies, 54–56
  survey data excluded, 68
  treatment variable, 66–68
"marijuana causes heart trouble" paper, 123
mass shootings, 100–101
match fixing
  explanation, testing, 349–352
  probability, 347–349
  soccer betting, 345–346
McKinsey & Company
  definition of corporate performance, 293–294
  tetralogy, 288
measles, mumps, and rubella (MMR) vaccine, 139–142
Medicaid expansion
  equal-opportunity misrepresentation, 235–236
  good studies leading to bad reporting, 239–240
  during Obama administration, 235
  Oregon trail, 238–239
  turning attention to, 237–238
  uncertainty, 236–237
Mendel, Gregor, 135–136, 150–151
Meyer, Bruce D., 234
middle-school science-fair projects, 20–22
modern financial risk management, 307–308
Mosteller, Frederick, 261
multinomial regression, 256–257
Murray, Charles, 300

N

Nabokov, Vladimir, 326
NASA-GISS Land-Ocean Temperature Index, 174, 175
National Book Critics Circle (NBCC), 326
National Bureau of Economic Research (NBER), 50–51, 234, 235
National Football League (NFL), 199
  betting study, 198–199
  sports betting system, 199–200
National Institute on Drug Abuse, 109
National Rifle Association (NRA), 242
National Standby Gas Rationing Plan, 226
National Standby Gas Rationing Project, 224
National Transportation Safety Board (NTSB), 2–8
Nature Medicine, 145, 149
Nevada Independent, 321
New England Journal of Medicine, The (NEJM), 88, 235
New York Times, The (newspaper), 3, 54, 356
Nobel Prize, 181
  academic paper errors, 186–187
  bandwagon, 181–182
  ecological fallacy, 185–186
  redirection, 184–185
  scientific achievement, genetics and culture, 183–184
  scientist father advantage, 182–184
  socioeconomic status, 186
Now and On Earth (Thompson), 329, 335
nuclear winter, 149–151
null hypotheses, 201–202

O

One Big Beautiful Bill Act, 235
opioid abuse, 124–126
opioid crisis, 106–107
opioid deaths, 110–111
Opioid Prescriptions for Chronic Pain and Overdose: A Cohort Study, 108–109
Oregon trail, 238–239
overfit models, 208

P

pain, 105
  Cohort Study, 108–109
  "deaths of despair," 105–107
  studies, 109–111
  Veterans Health Administration (VHA) study, 107–108
Palestine, 157–158
pari-mutuel betting, 215
Paths of Glory (Kubrick), 328
Pauling, Linus, 186
Pleasures of Statistics, The (Mosteller), 262
politics and life, 334–335
Post and Courier, The (newspaper), 43
Poverty, by America—a New York Times (Desmond), 299
power, 121–124
"Predictors of Sustained Prescription Opioid Use After Admission for Trauma in Adolescents," 124

private equity
  hospitals acquired by, 357–358
  investigators study, 356–357
  statistical significance, 358–360
Proceedings of the National Academy of Sciences, 255
Producer Price Index, 230
profits, prices and, 231–232
pro forma calculation, 236–237
prohibitions and trafficking, 320–321
Psychological Science, 120
public inequity, 353
Publishers Weekly, 325
pulp fiction, 328–330
p-values, 32
  confidence intervals, 119–120
  fact, 115–116
  hypothesis, 119–120
  Journal of Predicting Tomorrow's Stock Market Direction (JPTSMD), 118–119
  misleading of, 128–129
  new drug, 192–193
  null hypothesis, 117–118
  probability, 117–118
P-values, Prior Probability, and Power (four Ps), 116–119

Q
quantitative analysis, 367
Quine, Willard Van Orman, 221–222

R
racism
  anti-Black or anti-Hispanic disparities, 258–260
  in fatal police shootings, 255–258
Raise the Titanic! (Cussler), 152
RAND Corporation, 34–36
  gun control, 92–93
  stock, 93–95
Rationality and Risk Intelligence in Binary Betting (Philip), 312
Reason (magazine), 50
  video team, 8–9
Reno conference, 195–196
replication crisis, 116
researchers *vs.* journals, 129–131
Retraction Watch, 74, 87
risk management
  binary betting, 312–313
  finding median, 309–310
  Kelly about, 310–311
  modern financial, 307–308
  results, 313–316
  risk decisions, 317
  rule of thumb, 311–312
  strategy of retail bookmakers, 352
Roy, Avik, 239
Royal Air Force (RAF), 58–59
Rubio, Marco, 15

S
S&P500 stock market index, 223
Sagan, Carl, 149–150
Sarin, Natasha, 233
science, 150–151
  vs. business, 114–115
Science as a Contact Sport (Schneider), 150
secret police, 319
sex discrimination, 253
sex work criminalization, 323
"Smile Intensity in Photographs Predicts Longevity," 120–121
smoking, 99–100
  natural experiment studies on, 342–343
sports betting, 199
  demonstration, 203–204
  diverse and competitive marketplace, 217–218
  mob system, 216–217
  National Football League (NFL), 199–200
  organization monopoly (1980s), 217
  organized crime (1960s and 1970s), 215
  smart money, 217
stagflation, 226
Statcheck, 86
statistical lives saved, concept of, 234
statistical significance, 191–193
statistics, faces of, 219–220
Strohminger, Nina, 361

T
Taleb, Nassim, 308
Taylor, Brent, 140
Tetlock, Philip, 307
Thompson, Jim, 327–328
tie bets, 351
tokenism, 290
tradeoffs, 303–305
trafficking
  finding, 322–323
  prohibition and, 320–321
  study, 321–322
Trump, Donald, 15, 74
Tukey, John, 261

INDEX

21st-century muckraking
  capitalist exploitation, 300–301
  critique of greed, 302–303
  eviction, 305–306
  investigative journalists, 299–300
  tradeoffs, 303–305
  welfare for rich, 301–302
2017 President's Commission on Combating Drug Addiction and the Opioid Crisis, 109–110
Type-II error, 281–282

U

uncertainty, 236–237
UN Intergovernmental Panel on Climate Change (IPCC), 173, 174
  global warming uncertainty, 178–179
United Nations Office on Drugs and Crime (UNODC), 321
United States Agency for International Development (USAID), 13
  Asimov, Isaac, 27–29
  categories, 24–25
  causation *vs.* correlation, 30–31
  Cicchetti's logic, 31–32
  confounding variables, 22–23
  deaths, 16–17
  establishment, 15
  exclusions, 26–27
  expert reviewers and journalists, 19
  financial analogy, 29–30
  lifesavers, 14
  lives-saved claim, 33–34
  misuse of statistics, 31
  perspective, 20
  polio vaccine, 16
  programs elimination, 15–16
  saved lives, 15–17
  UN global mortality, 16–18, *16*
  unit of analysis, 23
university press officer (UPO), 129–131
Unsettled: What Climate Science Tells Us, What It Doesn't, and Why It Matters (Koonin)
  criticism on, 280–281
  error types, 281–282
  illustrating Greenland, 283
  rehashing US heatwaves, 284–285
  review of, 278
  Yohe review about, 278–280
Urey, Harold, 186

U.S. Census, 75–77
US national income per capita, 35–36, 363

V

vaccines, 137–139
  COVID-19, 144–148
  herd immunity, 137
  MMR, 139–142
  personal benefits, 138–139
  public health, 138–139
  social benefits, 138
  worst publication, 142–144
vaping
  psychology of, 341–342
  smoking and, 342–343
Veterans Health Administration (VHA) study, 107–108
victimless crimes, 319
Virginian, The (Wister), 326

W

Wakefield, Andrew, 139–142
Wharton schools
  business school professor in, 362–363
  Fermi problems, 364–365
  issue of education system in, 363–364
  rule of thumb, 361
White, Harrison, 291
White workers
  education levels of, 251–253
  sex discrimination, 253–255
windfall profit tax, 229
wins-above-average (WAA), 80–81
wins-above-replacement (WAR), 79–81
Wister, Owen, 326
worker pay
  claims of, 34–35
  full-time, full-year, prime-age (FTFYPA), 34, 36–37
  income of, 33–34
  money limits, reality of, 35–39
  US national income per capita, 35–36
World Journal of Oncology (WJO), 337
World Wide Tours accident, 2–3
Wrong Numbers
  briefing of, 9–11
  ordinary people and, 368–369
Wyse, Angela, 234

Y

Yohe, Gary, 278
Yonath, Ada, 185